T0267032

First published 2022

The History Press
97 St George's Place, Cheltenham,
Gloucestershire, GL50 3QB
www.thehistorypress.co.uk

British Library Cataloguing in Publication Data.
A catalogue record for this book is available from the British Library.

ISBN 978 0 7509 9682 2

Typesetting and origination by The History Press
Printed and bound in Great Britain by TJ Books Limited, Padstow, Cornwall.

MIX
Paper from
responsible sources
FSC® C013056

Trees for L♥fe

CONTENTS

FOREWORD BY MAGGIE APPLETON MBE

Alison Hill's work on Pauline Gower MBE is a welcome addition to our appreciation and understanding of this true pioneer of flight. Alison highlights beautifully the inspiration that Pauline Gower and other leading female aviators provided for those around them and those who followed. Just as importantly, she has brought their passion for flight to the fore.

The valuable contribution of the women of the Air Transport Auxiliary has had a welcome spotlight shone upon it in recent years. However, Pauline's place in its history is less widely known. Without her indefatigable determination, laced with charm and diplomacy, the women's section may never have been born. Certainly this pioneering operation is unlikely to have achieved the success that it did. Hers is an important personal story that was waiting to be shared more widely.

This work will be a fascinating read not only for those interested in aviation, but also for the general history lover. Moreover, it marks Pauline Gower's quiet but resolute place in the panoply of women who have pushed forward the rights of women to be treated – and paid – equally.

Readers will also find some valuable lessons in leadership. Pauline's political savviness and her warmth and humour shine through the pages of this work, as do all the characteristics that mark her out as a shining standard-bearer and trailblazer.

Maggie Appleton MBE
CEO, The Royal Air Force Museum

'For me, aviation is top-ranking among all the careers open to women. More than that, I would say that every woman should learn to fly. Psychologically, it is the best antidote to the manifold neuroses which beset modern women.'

Pauline Gower

INTRODUCTION

I first encountered Pauline Gower and the 'Spitfire Women' in Hampton Court Emporium, a meandering antique shop full of the dust of generations and glimmers of past lives. Unaware, like many others as I discovered, that women flew Spitfires during the Second World War, let alone Tiger Moths, Hurricanes, Wellingtons and many more types, I purchased the pristine copy of *Spitfire Women of World War II* that had caught my attention (Giles Whittell, 2007). The book provided a lively overview and sparked a major flight of research, which in turn led to a new poetry collection, *Sisters in Spitfires*, to commemorate the women pilots of the Air Transport Auxiliary (ATA) – their lives, flights and achievements, during and after the war.

I was lucky enough to have had the chance to talk to Molly Rose during the research; a telephone conversation clearly remembered – as clearly as she recalled her first Spitfire decades after flying it – and to meet fellow pilots Joy Lofthouse and Mary Ellis at White Waltham, the spiritual home of the ATA. Mary had celebrated her 100th birthday earlier that year, and as she signed her poem in the collection – 'I AM the Pilot' – she looked up as a classic car whizzed by and the thrill of remembered speed danced in her eyes. In May 2018 I was flown over to Sandown Airfield on the Isle of Wight to visit Mary and learn more about her 'charmed life' and her memories of Pauline Gower. Just four months later, I wrote a new poem for her memorial service in Cowes, when her wartime flying record was commemorated with a Spitfire flypast and a church packed to the rafters. It was an honour to read

'Spitfire Salute' from the ornate eagle pulpit at the end of the service. Mary admired Pauline and recognised the significance of her legacy.

This new biography explores the life of a strong and resolute woman of humour, wisdom and incredible bravery in the air; who encouraged other women to fly; who achieved equal pay for equal work in the ATA; and who proved herself a resourceful and diplomatic leader throughout the war. Pauline's sense of humour, often self-effacing, shines through her own autobiography, *Women with Wings*, as I hope it does here. A copy of her photograph in the National Portrait Gallery, taken in 1937, hung over my desk as I wrote and her calm gaze, clear strength of character and general good cheer accompanied me along the flight path. It would have been thrilling to have been one of her passengers of the air circus years, or to have met her for a cup of tea or something stronger. She was an inspiration to many.

In his 40s, her son Michael Fahie researched Pauline's life in detail to discover more about his mother from those who had known her best. His tribute, *A Harvest of Memories: The Life of Pauline Gower MBE*, was published in 1995, and there are only a handful of copies left in print. Michael sent me bound copies of letters that formed his research from August 1992 to May 1994, intriguing documents in themselves. We were both relieved when the packages made their way safely from Australia to London in 2021, with minimal lockdown delays. What struck me, as I read the rich correspondence between long-lost family members and friends, and from fellow ATA pilots, sadly no longer with us, was the enthusiasm, respect and warmth with which they all remembered Pauline; and the way in which each of them, from around the world, gave Michael new insights into the mother he and his twin brother never knew. Each letter formed a piece of a jigsaw that enabled him to gain a fuller picture of his mother's extraordinary life. Extracts from those letters, from pilots, friends and family, are woven throughout as testament to Pauline's character and her pioneering achievements for women in aviation.

This book aims to remind future generations of Pauline's remarkable life and legacy, and to highlight her many amazing firsts and achievements in aviation and during the Second World War, in a life lived very much to the full. I am grateful to The History Press for helping to keep her life story and legacy alive to new generations.

I was always drawn to Pauline. Her composure, intelligent gaze and ready sense of humour flickering at the corners of her mouth. She was born into wealth and a life of advantages, but she used it to fuel her own passion and to encourage other women to seek the skies and to go further, to fulfil their potential. She learnt a great deal from her father's long political career, but she had her own way of achieving goals. Timing was everything and her natural diplomacy was evident in the progress she made so quickly, at a time when women were not even allowed inside RAF planes, let alone ferrying them from factory to frontline bases throughout the war. Pauline's influence is there in her clear gaze, her forthright pose, her no-nonsense attitude to most things. *If you don't try, you won't succeed.* Something surely that the nuns at her Sacred Heart School in Tunbridge Wells would have instilled; some gently, some with a firmer approach. Pauline's practical and direct nature was to play a crucial part in her wartime role, as it did in the lives and careers of the 164 pilots she recruited as commandant of the Women's Section of the ATA.

Pauline Gower's legacy, and indeed that of her high-achieving partner Dorothy Spicer, lives on in those women still breaking boundaries, following their ambitions of learning to fly or to become engineers – pushing past barriers that still exist. *And why not?* Pauline would have asked with a characteristic twinkle and arch of an eyebrow. This book also highlights some contemporary women pilots, particularly members of the British Women Pilots' Association, and some of their success stories are outlined in Chapter 9. Many have achieved personal goals, aviation highs and commercial success. Pauline would have been proud of them all – she firmly believed that every woman should learn to fly.

KEY DATES

22 JULY 1910 – Pauline Mary de Peauly Gower is born in Tunbridge Wells, Kent, the second daughter of parents Robert and Dorothy Gower.

1922 – Starts at Beechwood Sacred Heart Convent School in Tunbridge Wells.

16 JULY 1926 – Makes her first Holy Communion and is received into the Catholic faith.

19 JULY 1927 – A serious mastoid operation, for which Pauline was anointed beforehand, results in double pleural pneumonia and near death. She was left with weakened lungs as a result and could not take part in active exercise again.

1928 – Pauline leaves Beechwood but maintains close links with the school for many years.

SEPTEMBER 1930 – Gains her 'A' licence at the Phillips & Powis School of Flying in Reading.

1931 – Trains for her 'B' licence at Stag Lane Aerodrome in north London, where she meets engineer Dorothy Spicer and record-breaking pilot Amy Johnson.

Given a plane by her father for her 21st birthday and sets up in business with Dorothy, initially running an air-taxi service in Kent.

MAY 1932 – Joins the Crimson Fleet Air Circus summer tour.

1933 – Pauline and Dorothy tour the country with the British Hospitals' Air Pageant, visiting 200 towns.

1934 – Publishes a collection of poetry, *Piffling Poems for Pilots*, alongside later short stories for *Chatterbox* and *Girl's Own Paper*.

1935 – Appointed as a council member for the Women's Engineering Society.

1936 – Pauline is the first woman to be awarded the Air Ministry's Second-Class Navigator's Licence.

1 NOVEMBER 1936 – Dorothy Gower, Pauline's mother, takes her own life. This has a profound and lasting effect on Pauline.

1938 – Publishes *Women with Wings*, her lively account of pre-war flying and memorable air circus summers with Dorothy Spicer. Amy Johnson, their close friend, writes the foreword.

1939 – Pauline is appointed a commissioner of the Civil Air Guard, a scheme to train a reserve of British pilots.

1 JANUARY 1940 – Pauline is authorised to form the women's section of the ATA and recruits the First Eight pilots, to much press attention.

SUMMER 1941 – Fifty women pilots are now on board and a second all-women's ferry pool is established at Hamble, near Southampton. Pauline moves permanently to White Waltham, the ATA headquarters.

NEW YEAR'S HONOURS 1942 – Pauline receives an MBE for her work as Commander of the Women's Section, the first ATA member to receive such an award.

13 FEBRUARY 1942 – King George VI and Queen Elizabeth visit White Waltham.

SPRING 1942 – The first group of American women pilots, recruited by Jacqueline Cochran, travel to Liverpool to be met by Pauline and welcomed into the ATA.

MAY 1943 – Pauline is appointed to the board of the British Overseas Airways Corporation (BOAC), the first woman to hold such a position in the United Kingdom. She serves until January 1946.

2 JUNE 1945 – Pauline marries Wing Commander William Fahie at Brompton Oratory, London, with many ATA women pilots present. They move to a house in Chelsea.

SEPTEMBER 1945 – The ATA is wound down and an air pageant is staged at White Waltham. On 30 November, First Officer Audrey Sale-Barker lowers the ATA flag and the pilots disperse.

1946 – Pauline becomes pregnant but suffers from poor health throughout her pregnancy.

2 MARCH 1947 – Twins Paul and Michael are born safely but Pauline dies three hours later from heart failure. A tragic loss to family and friends, and the many women pilots she led throughout the war.

1950 – Pauline was posthumously given the Harmon Trophy Award, a green patina bronze sculpture of an aviator holding a biplane overhead with an eagle emerging from a stone.

PROLOGUE

FLYING ON AHEAD

I took several wrong turnings, as she had done many times in the sky, decades previously. Alone in her plane, who was to know? Studying her map before take-off, watching out for landmarks familiar and strange, following rivers and railway lines, occasionally putting down in the wrong airfield. Never daunted for long, flying on again, finding the right destination with a triumphant smile. A flourish of a successful landing. Her patient engineer accepted these diversions but sighed at the length of some of her *Piffling Poems for Pilots*. They often had time on their hands, waiting around in empty fields for paying passengers. But by then they had broken several records between them, for women in aviation in the 1930s, and had set up the first all-women joy-riding business. Days were long and arduous, but with their three-seater Spartan *Helen of Troy* the sky was theirs, all day, every day. Never mind the occasional mishap – landing in a swamp in a brand-new plane, with two passengers thrown into the murky waters, or having a serious near-miss on another forced landing, resulting in a cracked head and several weeks in hospital for the pilot, and some careful aircraft reconstruction for the engineer. Resilience was key.

They set up home in a caravan near their plane, saw off night prowlers – real and imagined – cooked, ate and worked side by side, thousands of flights, routes and destinations over six summers. They formed a unique and successful partnership, paving the way for women pilots and engineers in their pioneering trail. Air circus life was tough – a new town every day, another crowd to entertain with stunts, flights and more – but youth was on their side. For the most part, life was fun and full of airborne adventure. It was the life they had chosen, a job they carried out with dedication. Making a living from aviation had always been their plan.

After consulting my digital map and discarding a layer on that warm May afternoon in 2021, I found my own destination. Six years previously, on my first research trip to Pauline Gower's home town of Tunbridge Wells in Kent, I had caught a bus to the wrong graveyard. A Victorian picture postcard church and bluebell-carpeted grounds, with helpful volunteers tending graves who pointed out Jane Austen's brother and other local figures of note. I twice met a man walking his dog as I circled the stones; the second time he grinned and asked if I was choosing my spot. The visit led to a poem, 'The Wrong Graveyard', but not to the right grave. Timing was everything, as Pauline herself knew.

This time I was in the right place and almost by instinct made my way through the long grass towards the Gower memorial. An auspicious moment, as a light plane circled overhead – the only sound on the springtime air. Here lay Sir Robert Gower and his wife Lady Dorothy Gower and their younger daughter who had her own inscription, as befitted her rank and status. After several days exploring Tunbridge Wells, up and down hill, from school to library to graveyard, this was the source of the research journey, coming full circle.

Standing in front of her grave, I thought about Pauline's many achievements and accolades, her pioneering aviation career, her talent with the written word, her loyalty to friends and family, and her strong and successful leadership of the women pilots of the ATA during the Second World War. I'd seen some of the many trees that she'd climbed as a pupil at Beechwood Sacred Heart School, reaching for the sky from a young age. I'd wandered along streets and discovered tree-lined squares that she may have explored a hundred years previously. I'd watched clouds race across a wide Kent sky and imagined her girlhood fascination with climbing up into the enticing endless blue. I'd caught her smile and ready humour, which leapt from many of her photographs as a young woman, and the character that shone through in her stories and aviation articles – her spirit of adventure and genuine enthusiasm in encouraging other women to fly.

I laid some wildflowers on Pauline Gower's grave, for all the family, and watched as the plane circled overhead.

Maid of the Mist

Maid of the Mist, through cloud and haze
Climbing up into the blue,
Carefree I spend the happy days
Alone in the sky with you.

Maid of the Mist, your engine sings
So tuneful and sweet a song,
The silver glistens on your wings
As swiftly you speed along.

Maid of the Mist, the sky is clear
As far as the eye can see –
Up we soar, for heaven is near,
Beckoning to you and me.

Pauline Gower, *Piffling Poems for Pilots*

I

CLIMBING EVERY TREE, REACHING FOR THE SKY

Women are not born with wings, neither are men for that matter. Wings are won by hard work, just as proficiency is won in any profession.

Pauline Gower

Sir Robert Gower MP compiled fifty large scrapbooks during his lifetime, later donated to Tunbridge Wells Library in Kent. He pasted in everything in the press from 1918 to 1945 relating to his long-standing political career, his animal welfare concerns as chairman of the Royal Society for the Prevention of Cruelty to Animals (RSPCA), and his younger daughter Pauline's pioneering, dare-devil at times, career in aviation. Three concerns close to his heart.

One librarian described him as a 'great hoarder of ephemera', as I soon discovered. Robert Gower also kept dinner menus, invitations, letters, photographs, political banners and the occasional significant serviette. Everything was pasted and ordered neatly by date with hand-numbered pages. Pauline's achievements feature prominently, and the scrapbooks form a rich and valuable archive of her career. Not that Robert was always in favour of her flying, quite the opposite in fact, and his objections may well have caused Pauline to be even more determined to make her way as a joy-riding pilot from the age of 20, and not to rely on an allowance from her father. Headstrong and determined, her early choices clearly reflected her character. Yet her father's inherent pride in her many notable and press-worthy accolades is clearly reflected in the scrapbooks. They are heavy, profession-ally bound books, weighted with memories that mattered. I visited Tunbridge Wells libraries twice to read through them, six years apart; the second time after several lockdowns, during which time the books had been moved between libraries and acquired heavy grey archive boxes, also neatly labelled. Second readings can often yield more.

Pauline Mary de Peauly Gower was born on 22 July 1910 at Sandown Court in Tunbridge Wells, the younger daughter of Robert and Dorothy Gower. Her older sister Dorothy was named after her mother. No son and heir appeared afterwards, which may have disap-pointed their father at times. It was an auspicious year for aviation pioneers: on 23 April, aviation pioneer Claude Grahame-White, who trained at Louis Blériot's flying school, had made the first night flight; Halley's Comet made its closest approach to earth in May; C.S. Rolls made the first roundtrip flight over the English Channel on 2 June; and, on 9 July, Walter Brookins, flying a Wright biplane over Atlantic City, New Jersey, became the first person to fly to an altitude of one mile, in fact reaching 6,175ft (1.169 miles).

In his book *A Harvest of Memories*, Michael Fahie describes his grandfather as 'a vigorous man with a forceful personality' whose influ-ence was strongly felt by all those around him. He was driven by wealth and power to a great extent, neither of which were in his background. Robert was keen to make a name for himself, to further his passions; he did both as a long-standing Member of Parliament who was rarely out of the newspapers. Michael was only 6 when Robert died but remembers him well.

Sir Robert Vaughan Gower KCVO OBE FRGS was not born into an aristocratic family but desired high-society connections. His father, Joshua Robert, was apprenticed as a cobbler but then progressed to become a county court bailiff. Moving into property and climbing the social ladder, he was elected an alderman of the Borough of Royal Tunbridge Wells. The family prospered during his lifetime, and his eldest son seemed determined to follow suit.

Born on 10 November 1880, Robert was the eldest of six children and attended the local church school until the age of 14. He showed a natural intelligence, however, which his father did not want to waste; so he asked a local solicitor, Elvey Robb, to 'make a lawyer of the boy'. Robb immediately spotted his potential and advanced his education to enable him to qualify as a solicitor. Robert also followed his growing interest in politics and his extended education enabled him to enter local government. In 1918, at the age of 38, he became Mayor of Tunbridge Wells and was fully involved in local activities. By 1924 Robert Gower had become Conservative Member of Parliament for Central Hackney and received a knighthood. In the general election of 1929 he was elected MP for Gillingham in Kent, a seat he retained until 1945. He was not considered a natural debater in the House of Commons, being more at ease on parliamentary committees. Robert was also a magistrate and chairman of the Tunbridge Wells Magistrates Court for many years. He was appointed Officer, Order of the British Empire (OBE) in the 1919 New Year's Honours and knighted in the Birthday Honours of the same year. His father had certainly spotted his potential and drive to succeed.

Sir Robert Gower was a prominent figure in the local and national press, wearing his many personal and political hats. All cuttings of note found their way into his fifty scrapbooks. In September 1930, he presided as alderman over a meeting to oppose the town council's proposal – a 'colossal blunder' – for a new town hall and other municipal buildings to the tune of £225,000. At the 750-strong meeting at the local opera house, convened by the Tunbridge Wells Ratepayers' League, he deemed the original council proposal 'an act of criminal folly' and argued that neither the financial position of the country nor the town could justify such a proposition. It was agreed that instead £100,000 would be spent on new municipal buildings for which there was an urgent need.

Interestingly, visiting Tunbridge Wells post-Covid lockdown in 2021, the town hall was sitting partially empty, with council staff working from home and parts of the building available to rent.

Perhaps the most enduring and closest to his heart of all his interests was Robert Gower's involvement as chairman of the RSPCA, which often led him to be called 'the dogs' MP'. For this long-standing commitment he was made Knight Companion of the Royal Victorian Order (KCVO). There were lively press reports of some particularly memorable meetings: 'Uproar at R.S.P.C.A. Meeting. Clash Over Vivisection Question. Angry Women's Shrieks.' This meeting at the Hotel Victoria in London was eventually closed by Robert Gower after two-and-a-quarter hours, with only half of the business finished. It was unclear just how many women were angry, and how many were shrieking! The chairman chose to elect eight new members to the council before he got to the contentious matter of vivisection and blood sports, which likely ramped up the tension in the room. The main clash was between the moderates and those in favour of advanced opposition to blood sports. The meeting's drama quickly escalated. Scottish author Alasdair Alpin MacGregor, a strong opponent of vivisection and cruelty to animals, accused Sir Robert Gower of 'counselling and procuring an assault and battery by divers persons unknown'. The matter was taken to Bow Street Magistrates' Court and had a lengthy hearing. Allegedly, when Robert had given orders for MacGregor to be turned out of the stormy meeting, he was 'ejected with more force' than was necessary. There was no suggestion of Gower being personally involved in the fracas. The Bow Street magistrate dismissed it all:

> At each of the three hearings the proceedings were keenly followed by many fashionable attired Society women, and both for the prosecution and the defence prominent members of the R.S.P.C.A. had been called as witnesses. In dismissing the summons Mr. Graham Campbell declared that the less he said about that unfortunate case the better. Sir Robert was warmly congratulated by a host of friends who were inside and outside the court.

This was not the only case that MacGregor lost. His books were mainly about Scotland, with a typically romanticising nature that was caricatured by novelist Compton Mackenzie. His 1931 book had a short and snappy title: *A Last Voyage to St. Kilda. Being the Observations and Adventures of an Egotistic Private Secretary who was alleged to have been 'warned off' That Island by Admiralty Officials when attempting to emulate Robinson Crusoe at the Time of Its Evacuation.* MacGregor tried to prevent the distribution of a film by Michael Powell, *The Edge of the World*, which he claimed was based on his work, but the injunction came to nothing. Gower had spotted this weakness and used his influence to steer both the RSPCA meeting and the court proceedings, resulting in more press cuttings for his scrapbooks.

As president of the Pit Ponies' Protection Society, another favoured animal cause, Gower campaigned strongly for the abolition of their use in the mines. In 1930, one in every six pit ponies was injured or had to be shot, with the worst cases in Yorkshire where around 7,000 ponies were employed. Those against their use lobbied for reforms in their working conditions and pressed for mechanical haulage to replace them in the pits. The *Daily Herald* of 6 April 1931 reported: 'Sir Robert Gower secured 186,400 signatures to a petition he will present to Parliament for the abolition of ponies in mines.' A month later he'd achieved 190,000 signatures, proof of his doggedness in causes that really mattered to him.

Throughout his prominent career, Robert followed his own interests. Success, or the perception of such, often evokes a mixed response, especially from rivals. One family member said:

> He had a great deal of charm, was extremely clever and had a photographic memory. I suspect that he had few close friends. He was loyal to those he had. He could be ruthless to enemies. These he was not without. There was some local enmity stemming from jealousy of his success.

Robert Gower had a temper, which has been noted, but many also agreed he was kind to those who mattered to him and dedicated to the causes in which he believed. He had interests outside of politics too. Kitty Farrer, one of Pauline's closest friends in the ATA, recalled that Robert was very good to her on her visits to Sandown Court, and encouraged her own interests in china and porcelain: 'He was a keen collector and had a cellar full of the stuff.' A forceful character at times then, with an eye for a delicate tea cup.

Pauline's mother, Dorothy Susie Eleanor, was born on 19 May 1882 in Kensington, London, the only daughter of the Wills family. They were considered of higher social standing than the Gowers, so Robert had moved up in the world. They were married on 29 June 1907 at the historic Holy Rood Church in Southampton. Dorothy had 'a warm, effusive nature and a strong developed sense of humour'. As well as being a gifted musician, Dorothy also enjoyed horse riding; twin passions that she passed on to her younger daughter. They also shared a love of writing; Dorothy published short stories, articles and a longer piece entitled *A Salad of Reflections*. She was prone to depression, and Pauline too suffered from dark periods throughout her life, some of them prolonged. Dorothy Gower is a rather elusive figure in Robert's scrapbooks, there in occasional press cuttings opening a church fete or similar. Or sometimes her absence, with a headache, is noted.

Dorothy and her younger daughter were very close, and she has more prominence in Pauline's own scrapbooks, which were later donated to the RAF Museum in Hendon, north London. In early January 1930, it was reported in the press that Lady Gower was lost overnight, her car nowhere to be found. The family had all suffered from a bout of flu; first Dorothy, then her husband and then Pauline. Between Christmas and New Year, Lady Gower had agreed to present the prizes at the Gillingham Conservative Club whist drive and dance at the town's pavilion. Not long after leaving the family home in Tunbridge Wells, she encountered dense fog and her continued absence led her to being reported missing to the police. The Automobile Association had been actively looking for any stranded motorists that night and had found a shivering Lady Gower near Maidstone at around 11 p.m. She had of course missed the prize-giving event, so drove back to Tunbridge Wells to arrive home around 2 a.m. In a piece entitled 'Lady Gower's "Night Out"', the *Chatham, Rochester and Gillingham Observer* concluded that 'it seems that neither our Member nor his family have had the best of luck this Christmastide'.

Later that week, they had a better night out when Pauline and her mother were guests at the wedding of Captain Richard William Spraggett, Royal Marines, and Miss Mary Lois Cecil Power, eldest daughter of Sir John Power, Bart, MP. It was presumably a political connection through Robert Gower, with the bride acquiring a memorable married name.

Dorothy Gower must have shared some of her husband's interests however, supporting his causes as a loyal society wife. She dutifully opened a dogs' jamboree one summer, its poster asking: 'Is your dog going to Chiswick?' The event was held in 'the beautiful grounds of Chiswick House' and categories included 'dog with the longest tail', 'the most bandy-legged dog' and 'the dog with the longest beg'. The programme was in two parts, presided over by Ringmaster Captain Fergus MacCunn. Luckily, Dorothy did not have to judge all categories!

In April 1930, Lady Gower stood in for her husband at a presentation to the National Association of Navy and Army Pensioners, at the Army and Navy Veterans' Club in Gillingham. Robert Gower had sent written apologies owing to his parliamentary commitments. Coincidentally, it was another foggy day and Dorothy, accompanied by Pauline, arrived late but to a 'rousing reception'. Lady Gower graciously presented an illuminated address to the Honorary Secretary Mr Martin Scamaton for his long-standing 'magnificent work' in connection with the club, while Mrs Scamaton (her Christian name was not recorded) received a China tea service. Duties done, mother and daughter were more than likely treated to tea and cake.

On another occasion, in October 1931, Lady Gower again stood in for her husband. The women's section of Gillingham Conservative Association held a whist drive and dance, attended by both Dorothy and Pauline. Lady Gower apologised for her husband's absence, with a general election likely due soon, but hoped that he could rely on local support of the association and that the majority could be even bigger than last time. Very much a family election campaign!

There is a photo of Pauline's parents from 1931 in *A Harvest of Memories*, from the family album. They are in full country attire in the grounds of Sandown Court, Tunbridge Wells, and holding their pet dogs Kelpie and Wendy. Their younger daughter inherited their love of animals, as she often took her own small dog (also called Wendy) up in her plane. In fact, Wendy was to fly 5,000 miles with Pauline!

Pauline was born two years after her sister Dorothy Vaughan Gower. One photograph shows them aged around 3 and 5, either side of their father, in the gardens of Sandown Court. The sisters are dressed in white, ribbons in their hair, each clutching a posy of flowers and holding their father's hand. Robert Gower has something of the look of T.S. Eliot, the customary parted hair and rather stiff expression. It is difficult to guess the occasion, or if Lady Gower was the photographer. Certainly, this was one for the family album. Thereafter their photographs are of separate women – strong characters in their own different realms. Perhaps they vied for their parents' attention, as siblings do, but Dorothy was there for Pauline after her operation and Pauline was chief bridesmaid at her sister's wedding.

Dorothy also appears in her father's scrapbooks – he includes cuttings of her achievements, as he does for Pauline, although she did not make the papers to the same extent. In April 1931, Dorothy was mentioned in the *Courier* – 'honoured by being appointed a Lady-in-Waiting to H.R.H. the Princess Clotilde, of Belgium. Miss Gower, who recently returned from a tour in Ceylon, is now in attendance on H.R.H.' Robert would have been characteristically proud of the royal connections, bringing fine repute to the family name.

Later that year, Dorothy's engagement to Mr George Hamilton Ferguson, son of the late Mr Henry T. Ferguson and Mrs Ferguson of Bovey Tracey in Devon, was announced, with the wedding due shortly afterwards. Her photograph by Gilbert Bowley, which also appeared in the *Courier*, was rather severe in profile, with a side parting and similar sculpted marcel wave to Pauline's own, but perhaps with not the same twinkle playing around her eyes.

Dorothy's wedding on 8 October was reported with enthusiasm, with mentions of both her father and sister. In the style of the time, the headlines ran 'Sir Robert Gower's Daughter Married' and Dorothy's name appeared lower down the piece. The couple married at the Roman Catholic Church of St James's, Spanish Place, London, as 'the sun shines through the autumn leaves', and with Pauline in attendance as chief bridesmaid. She wore turquoise silk marocain with a matching velvet 'coatee' and a head-dress of pale lemon leaves mixed with blue ('a very new combination of colour'). Hopefully the bride did not mind the papers' focus on her sister as 'the youngest lady aviator to hold the Air Ministry's "B" certificate', but Pauline was the story of the moment. The *Kent Messenger* included a photograph of, 'Sir Robert Gower and Miss Pauline Gower, the noted airwoman, waiting for their car after the ceremony.' Robert has taken off his bowler and Pauline is rather self-consciously holding a small bouquet. Neither look like they have just attended a family wedding, but they may have been caught off guard. They are unmistakably related.

Dorothy and George had three children, keeping traditional Gower family names – their eldest Robert Maule Gower Ferguson, who became a solicitor in his grandfather's footsteps, was born in 1932, followed by Beatrice Margaret Ferguson and Sally Pauline June Ferguson.

Folded into one of the Gower scrapbooks, carefully pressed and preserved, was a celebratory serviette for wedding guests, with delicate blue flower scrolls in each corner, a central illustration of the couple emerging from the church, and the inscription 'All Blessings and Happiness to Them'. Robert clearly wanted to remember the significance of the day. I reflected on the autumn leaves and the wedding party as I folded it back into the book, following the crease marks he had made ninety years ago.

BEECHWOOD SACRED HEART SCHOOL

Pauline Gower's school years were central to her character, fuelling her drive and determination, and establishing her interests and future potential. Her father chose Pauline's school with the 'same degree of determination' he did most things. She very much inherited this characteristic, revealed in her ability to push herself and others to achieve results, despite the challenges and obstacles along the way. She brought her ready smile to most situations, smoothing the path of resistance at just the right moment. Robert Gower's smile does not appear so easily in his many press photographs, the formality of most occasions notwithstanding, except on one occasion when out canvassing and hoping to gain the vote from a group of women. A charming flash that quite changed his otherwise rather stern public persona. Pauline also inherited a strong political awareness and drive from her father, but clearly brought her own skills and sensitivity to issues and circumstances as required.

Robert Gower wanted both his daughters to have a solid education, unusual for the time, and chose Beechwood Sacred Heart School in Tunbridge Wells, not far from Sandown Court. He was not a Catholic but the headmistress at the time, Mother Ashton-Case, was a cousin of Lady Gower's. The convent school was to mould Pauline's character in many ways; Beechwood was 'bred in her bones' it seems, like it was in the many generations of children sent by their families. She attended first as a day girl, then a full-time boarder, despite living locally, and so the school became her whole life, and she made the most of all it had to offer. She did not take a back seat. These were on the whole happy years and, if she had felt constrained within the convent structure and stone walls at times, she found her own ways of quiet rebellion.

Beechwood was part of the innovative Society of the Sacred Heart, founded in 1800 by French post-revolutionary Madeleine Sophie Barat (born 12 December 1779), who had a vision of an influential female religious order, similar to the Jesuits, with a strong focus on teaching. She wanted to bring the nuns out from behind their symbolic grilles and encourage them to travel, teach and inspire. Women in France had almost no legal rights at that time and religious life was under threat. The society was successful – its leader meant business – and it quickly expanded into other parts of Europe, and then to North and South America, New Zealand and Australia. Sophie Barat died in 1865, by which time there was a network of eighty-nine Sacred Heart houses across seventeen countries.

In 1915, in a war-torn world, Madeleine Bodkin brought a small group of nuns to Tunbridge Wells to settle at Beechwood, a former country home. By now the society was established in England with schools in Roehampton, Hammersmith, Brighton and Carlisle. Pauline was only 5, but Robert Gower would have been aware of the debate raging over women's education. Earlier, in 1868, the Taunton Commission had highlighted the lack of adequate private education for girls. Janet Eskine Stuart, leader of the worldwide Sacred Heart movement and long-standing superior at Roehampton, published her book *The Education of Catholic Girls*, which argued that men and women had different roles but that these were equal, and complementary. With such a revolutionary focus on educating girls, it was no wonder that the spirit of Beechwood, founded and rooted in the ideology of the Sacred Heart Sisters, would have such an influence on Pauline's own life and aspirations.

A possible clash of values might have been the Sacred Heart assumption that women should focus on their roles of wife and mother above all else. Pauline was determined to follow her chosen career, once she had a taste for the sky, and may have been ready to fly, literally onwards and upwards, once out of the school gates.

A GLITTERING FIGURE

Many former pupils and peers confirmed that Pauline was a golden Beechwood girl: bright, full of fun and ready for adventure. She was a girl of action, showing early determination and a strong sense of team spirit. A keen hockey player, she was also captain of the netball team, pictured proudly holding trophies in several photographs. At 18, Pauline was part of the Tunbridge Wells Tennis Six, proving that she was indeed an athletic all-rounder.

Musically very talented, she played both violin and five-string banjo and was part of the Sacred Heart Toy Symphony Orchestra. She had inherited her mother's love of music and embraced all else that the school offered in extra-curricular activities. She certainly did not hide in the shadows. School friend Yolande Wheatley, six years her junior and clearly awestruck, offers a glowing memory:

> Successful academically, musical, very good at games, she was popular with her schoolmates and the nuns, not just because of her talents and amusing ways, but because she was even-tempered; I can't reflect her being unfair or unkind to a junior. She could always be relied on to organise treasure hunts in the school grounds, charades or surprise concerts, and her singing Lancashire songs accompanying herself on the ukulele, its ribbons flying as she danced around, is still a jolly memory.

As we shall see later, this innate sense of fun is reflected in Pauline's adventurous partnership with Dorothy Spicer, while her even-tempered nature and kindness are evident in her strong leadership during the ATA years. Beechwood moulded her character, and the school seemed to bring out the best in her. It certainly laid important foundations for the woman she was to become.

Sister Mary Coke was at school with Pauline, and later became provincial archivist at the Society of the Sacred Heart in Roehampton, south-west London, and had access to many school records. She remembers that Pauline's keen and long-lasting interest in music and writing bore fruit at Beechwood and that she was a 'loyal and devoted member of the school entering fully into sporting and musical activities and becoming a prefect (blue ribbon)'.

Beechwood School has always attracted international students – the lure of the country-style house and the nuns' rigorous reputation. One homesick 12-year-old Canadian was grateful to Pauline for taking her under her wing: 'She was such a wonderful person, a blue ribbon and always helped anyone in distress as I felt at the time. She was full of fun too. Her parents used to come to the School on Sundays. She did impress me very much by her kindness.' Fellow pupil Margaret Ritchie, who was two or three years younger, said Pauline was 'in a class well ahead' on all fronts: 'I remember a very active girl, fair, strongly built and very good at games. I would say Pauline was very happy at school, a good "mixer". I was not at all surprised when I learnt that she had her Wings and was doing so well.'

Another schoolgirl memory came from former pupil Elizabeth Bassett. She said they looked up to Pauline as a 'sort of pin-up girl' but they all 'appreciated her generosity, kindness to the younger fry and lack of snobbishness'. Her father was a 'bit of a celebrity' locally with his knighthood and large property. She knew her sister Dorothy too, 'so unlike Pauline in looks and temperament'.

Pauline's potential was already evident at Beechwood, alongside her sense of fun, fairness and adventure. She was a star pupil with a marked absence of 'could do better' – she excelled at all subjects, particularly music and sport.

Yolande Wheatley describes Pauline as: 'A glittering figure … a wonderful personality with such a zest for living and so full of ideas. She managed to carve for herself an outstanding career at a time when it was rare for women to do so, and yet she remained so feminine.'

Was Pauline merely following the fashion of the day, as later she leant coolly against her planes in shirts and trousers, the perfect pilot get-up alongside her partner and engineer Dorothy Spicer? They may have had their sleeves rolled up and smudges of engine oil here and there, but their hair was always neatly curled, standards maintained at all times.

Yolande goes on to say:

> I wish she could be better known in this world of today [writing in June 1993] where women – in this country at any rate – make such an unpleasant fuss of being equal with men. Quite effortlessly she became more than equal to men while remaining gracious and treasuring the domestic roles of women.

Pauline was not a natural cook, leaving that to Dorothy Spicer during their summers together, who luckily enjoyed the challenge of producing a fine meal from limited ingredients, but covered her share of caravan cleaning and food shopping. She did, however, have a natural sense of schoolgirl adventure (see poem from *Sisters in Spitfires* on page 32).

It was this combination of attributes that Pauline would bring to her role in the ATA, formed and nurtured within the walls and grounds of Beechwood. If you are ever passing through Tunbridge Wells, along a busy A-road lined with large Edwardian houses closeted behind gates, you may spot a red plaque. Perhaps you will stop driving or walking to see whose memory it celebrates – the flash of crimson is clearly visible from the road, unlike the school buildings.

BEECHWOOD TODAY

The fabric of the buildings and the sweep of the well-kept lawns are the same, but what about the ethos, the standards, the rigour of the religious education? Would Pauline have recognised her own time there, and would she have felt the same sense of belonging?

I took time to wander around the school grounds on an extended visit to Tunbridge Wells, staying on the historic Pantiles, and felt the spirit of past pupils – imagining Pauline's daredevil joy at climbing the spread of trees still carpeting the grass. I was given two guided tours of the school, as it was about to embark on a significant new stage in its 106-year-old history; leaving behind its Catholic status, a school bought out in the wake of Covid-19 and falling numbers of international students. The frontage looked in need of plaster and fresh paint, and the skip outside was full. Everything was packed away for a move of one part of the school into another, a repurposing of the building that would allow younger pupils to explore the old house and enjoy a new setting. The bell that would have called Pauline and her peers into classrooms and chapel in the 1920s lay silent and upturned on a bench in the high-ceilinged reception room overlooking 23 acres of lawns and woodland. It was an impressive blend of past gentility and the promise of future generations piling into the two large cavernous 'dugouts' at the back of the school – one for each of the older year groups at break time – and racing across the lawns in an eternal game of tag.

My first tour of the school, by the current headteacher, took in the impressive entrance hall, with imposing original fireplace, the chapel in which Pauline's prayer for a friend was framed, and the corridors of black and white photographs revealing the school's long history. Ghostly dormitories from earlier days, shrouded in white, and a fire drill showing how the girls were lowered down from the windows on ropes. Certainly, a far cry from today's more exacting health and safety standards!

I was then taken to the nuns' cemetery, which must remain open to the public as part of the school's resale. Twenty-eight iron crosses marked the nuns who had taught at Beechwood over the decades, flanked by a large wooden crucifix and a bench at one end for quiet reflection. We circled back to the main building, past the nuns' private area, the mysterious 'enclosure', where none of the girls would have dared to venture, a space that they all remembered on return visits, years later. Eternally forbidden.

The same courtyard was about to be ripped apart for new classrooms – it was a space ready for fresh energy. I wondered how many girls had crept past, hoping to catch a glimpse of their teachers at leisure – had Pauline done so? She had climbed all the trees in the grounds and out of most of the dormitory windows – that we know. When I was later shown round by an 'old girl' who loved Beechwood so much she only took one gap year before going back as an RE teacher, I saw the famous dormitory windows. Two storeys up with a balcony that had crumbled over time. I imagined Pauline and her friends planning their descent, choosing their moment. A calculated risk, but one with an element of danger; an early sign of her spirit of adventure.

I was told about the Way of Peace, at one corner of the central Fountains Law (the fountain now silent and invisible) and backing onto the head's garden – a huddle of dark trees with numbered markers for the stations of the cross. Ivy had spread along the paths, and there was a rustle of wind in the trees. The nuns had frowned at the girls for talking in between stations of the cross, apparently; typical of the time. The gardens were full of birdsong then too, now the drone of traffic on the busy A-road is a constant backdrop. Convents and boarding schools offer a sense of belonging but can be restrictive. Stations of the cross can seem like an eternity at 13, long Easter masses heavy with incense. Pupils at Beechwood would have lived and breathed the rhythm of the religious calendar, the candles, processions and confessions, but it may have weighed heavy. Had Pauline felt that restraint at times, despite her love of school life, I wondered, scanning the grounds again. Had she felt a certain relief on departure, a readiness to fly?

A Trail of Oranges

She'd climbed every tree in the grounds
and leapt from every dormitory window,
the scent of oranges, hidden beneath

bloomers, recalling a stolen afternoon
up and over the high school walls
towards a delicious taste of freedom.

Shaking off regulations, bouncing curls
heralding friendship and laughter, a pair
on the cusp of just around the corner.

Strolling through the market, selecting
their fare, the afternoon languished ahead.
Yet the chime of the church clock conjured

nuns' impatience, the sharp tang of incense.
Leaping back over the wall, straight to chapel
Pauline was mortified to feel her elastic give,

half-turning to spot a steady trail of oranges
rolling down the aisle. One came to rest beside
Sister Agatha, who declined to notice.

Alison Hill, *Sisters in Spitfires*

A TURNING POINT

At 17, Pauline had a serious brush with death. During the summer of 1927, she was in and out of the school infirmary with ongoing and prolonged ear infections. Boils and abscesses kept forming in her right ear, a sign that something was seriously wrong. On 18 July her condition escalated, and acute pain and fever led to the discovery of a hidden mastoid infection. Doctors advised an immediate operation, as poison was spreading down her neck and her right lung was already inflamed. We can only imagine Pauline's fear of the unknown. She'd been sheltered, cloistered, despite her tree climbing, and this was a serious, life-threatening illness, especially so at that time.

Writing in the school association report of that year, the reverend mother records:

> As he [the specialist] said the case was very serious and the operation
> a dangerous one, Pauline was anointed, received Holy Viaticum and
> the Enfant de Marie medal. Immediately after the ceremony the

ambulance came to take her away to the home for the operation. A relic of Saint Madeleine Sophie had been put on her and the whole house prayed earnestly and insistently.

We can imagine the hush of the chapel, the flickering of the candles as the young girls prayed into the night, hoping against hope for her recovery. The unspoken left hanging in the gloom. The reverend mother continued in detail: 'That night was very bad as it was found that Pauline was suffering from double pleural pneumonia as well as the effects of the operation, which had been a very extensive one, the whole bone having been removed in a decayed condition.'

Before the mid-nineteenth century, mastoidectomy was performed rarely and only in a last-minute attempt to save lives. The drainage of acute abscesses become more common at the start of the twentieth century when antibiotics were available. Pioneering ear and eye surgeon, Sir William Wilde (1815–76), Oscar Wilde's renowned father, began the era of modern mastoidectomy ('Wilde's incision', a retro-auricular incision into the mastoid bone), the development of which continues to be a life-saving procedure.

Pauline's life hung in the balance that night and the doctors did not hold out much hope that she would survive the operation. Yet the next day she was in less pain and able to sit up and talk to her family. Dorothy had rushed back from Belgium to be at her side in a show of sisterly support. The candle had not gone out.

The same report documents Pauline's quite miraculous recovery:

On Thursday morning the doctors found the pneumonia and pleurisy had disappeared during the night. As Pauline described it 'Why, I can breathe now, yesterday I wished I could die.' Her temperature, which was 104 on Tuesday, went down steadily after this and the poison poured out of the wound for the next three days, but the pain was only felt when it was dressed. Three days after the operation she was able to sit up, laugh and talk, and have chicken for dinner. On the sixth day the discharge stopped and the temperature was normal.

Pauline had been incredibly lucky, but the operation had weakened her lungs permanently and active sport was a thing of the past. It also affected her future flying career. She continued to recuperate well and was soon back to her usual self, much to the relief of the whole school. Music became her focus and so, in her final school year, she was a solo violinist in the senior school orchestra and appeared in a fine performance of Joseph Haydn's *Toy Symphony*. A quieter end to her active school life, but perhaps a reflective and appreciative one after what she had endured in hospital.

Her serious illness had strengthened her Catholic faith, which was to be a comfort throughout her life. The year before, on 16 July 1926, she had made her first Holy Communion and fully embraced her chosen religion. Beechwood had nurtured her and held her close during the dark hours of her operation – in return she remembered the school with affection and dipped her wings in a friendly salute when she later flew overhead.

LEAVING SCHOOL, LOOKING AHEAD

Pauline stayed actively engaged with her old school for many years after she left. She led Beechwood's first Girl Guide pack and was president of the Old Girls' Association during the 1930s. She was fondly remembered for attending an old girls' meeting in 1946, accompanied by her fiancé, whom she was proud to introduce to her peers. They both went to Beechwood after their marriage to give lectures on the ATA and the RAF respectively. It was a place Pauline was always drawn to and where she always received a warm welcome.

Her potential was recognised while still a pupil, and her photo still hangs proudly in a sun-dappled Beechwood corridor. Pauline stands centre back in her school group photo of 1928, staring resolutely at the camera, ready for her future. Her presence is felt as soon as you enter the school, thanks to the large red plaque next to the school entrance sign, a welcome addition to the wall in 2015, courtesy of Tunbridge

Wells Civic Society and Tunbridge Borough Council. She is their most famous old girl and appears in their school's history, *Calm Amidst the Waves* – they were rightly proud of her subsequent career as one of Britain's first female aviators, who 'showed the world opening up for females in a way never experienced before'.

Robert and Dorothy did not get to hear about their daughter's early flying lessons straight away, however, as she kept them quiet, scraping her own money together to feed her dream. She had been completely bitten by the bug after a flight at 18 with aviator Captain Hubert S. Broad who was visiting Tunbridge Wells as part of a national tour. She knew immediately that she wanted more of the sky, inspired no doubt by pioneers such as Winifred Spooner and Amelia Earhart. Flying became hugely popular in the late 1920s and 1930s, the golden decade of aviation, for those with connections and money behind them, but it was not the career choice Pauline's parents were expecting.

Upon leaving school at 18, Pauline explained the reasons behind her early career decisions in her typically straightforward and humorous manner:

> Certainly it was not the novelty, nor the adventures and dangers, not the glory which then attached to flying. I must explain too, that having been stricken by a pernicious ailment which barred me from active sports at seventeen, and having besides the desire to earn my living, flying appeared to be the ideal 'sedentary' occupation!

Note her determined desire, at this age, to find a paying occupation and one at which she quickly excelled, early mishaps notwithstanding. She goes on: 'This decision followed an attempt to send me to a finishing school in Paris, from which I ran away.' This is illuminating. Her parents clearly had a husband hunt in mind, a good marriage, a family. Pauline wanted more than that. She explained: 'I had tried to interest myself in a number of things – Greek mythology, photography, writing verse, hunting and playing the violin. I also went through a London "season", was presented at Court, did all the things expected of a debutante, and was bored to tears by all of it.' Her self-awareness reveals a strong thinker who masked her depth in light-heartedness at times, particularly in her poetry. But she was certainly not going to opt for an easy route to marriage, and the life that was expected of her. She wanted to direct her own future:

> I am still interested in mythology, photography, riding to hounds – in fact, in everything, but at 19 my thoughts turned to flying and I decided to do it seriously. I was convinced that aviation was a profession with a future and determined to earn my living and make my career a *paying proposition*.

She had to, initially, as her father cut off her allowance when he knew her career intentions. So Pauline found ways to fund her lessons, while overcoming his opposition. Her independent spirit and drive kept her going, setting herself goals and achieving them.

Pauline may not have made huge fortunes in the air, during the summers that followed, but she proved that she could earn a living at what she loved doing best. She went on to inspire many other women to do the same, leading by example.

COMING OF AGE

On her 21st birthday, Robert Gower presented his younger daughter with a Spartan two-seater aeroplane with a Cirrus III engine. Did he want to be seen as the great provider at this point? Or had he simply come to accept Pauline's single-minded passion and wanted her to fly in safety? Her elaborate tales of too many forced landings may well have done the trick! Her mother may have also influenced his decision.

Claudia Parsons, in a key article on Pauline and Dorothy Spicer, who were fellow members of the Women's Engineering Society (WES), in the spring 1948 edition of *The Woman Engineer*, considers his gesture from all angles. Born in August 1900, Claudia would have influenced her readers as an engineer, traveller and writer. She was also the first woman to circumnavigate the globe by car. A highly respected alumna of Loughborough University (1919–22), she graduated with a degree in Automotive Engineering, one of just three women on a course of more than 300 men. She would be tickled, perhaps, to know that there is now a 480-room hall of residence in her name, as well as an annual lecture that aims to raise the profile of women working in Science, Technology, Engineering and Mathematics (STEM) subjects. Both of which keep her memory, influence and achievements very much alive.

The WES was founded on 23 June 1919 by a small committee drawn from the National Council of Women, created during the First World War to find work for women to release men for the armed forces. Founding members included wives of prominent engineers such as Lady Parsons. This group of influential women had government backing to support women engineers who, by the end of the war, were pressurised to leave the workforce to release jobs for the returning men (a similar scenario happened at the end of the Second World War). They founded WES to resist such pressure and to promote engineering as a rewarding job for both sexes.

The society's journal, *The Woman Engineer*, was launched in the society's first year and has been published regularly ever since. The first annual conference was held in 1923 and has been cancelled only twice since – during the Second World War, and in 2020 due to the Covid-19 pandemic, although it was still held virtually. Notable members have included Dame Caroline Haslett, Professor Daphne Jackson and Amy Johnson.

In her article, Claudia recognised Pauline's own pioneering spirit, reinforced by the 'exuberance and confidence of youth and a very decided will to conquer'. She saw the birthday gift as a key moment in Pauline's career, but that her father's intentions were perhaps somewhat pragmatic:

I used to ponder this parental gesture, which, so early as 1931, might have seemed to many to be rash and courting trouble, and reflected how often really enterprising acts were well rewarded and that here was one that had laid the foundation stone of two successful careers. … One rather gathers … that the hand of Sir Robert Gower was forced rather than held out eagerly with the gift of a two-seater Spartan plane. The gift was advanced only in the face of the inevitable, and as a safety measure.

Robert Gower had moved on from his initial reaction to his daughter's flying career, when he immediately stopped Pauline's allowance, and perhaps recognised his own fierce Gower determination propelling her towards the sky. It was only a matter of time; she'd financed her training through giving violin lessons to unsuspecting pupils and would have found a way to secure some wings soon enough.

Pauline outlines the significance of the birthday present in her book *Women with Wings* and celebrates it as the key to their business opportunity. She is direct in her appreciation and does not hint at any underlying agenda on the behalf of her father. She opens Chapter 3 on a high:

All that we now wanted before we could really start our business was an aeroplane of our own. To our unutterable joy my father gave me one for my twenty-first birthday. It was a two-seater Spartan and it did not cost very much; but to us it was the finest aeroplane that had ever been built.

She goes on to say that her late arrival at meals and artfully exaggerated accounts of rather too many forced landings (not always the fault of the plane) had caused some distress in the family household and motivated Robert's gift. Neither father nor daughter were necessarily averse to a little deception, and perhaps there was an arched eyebrow on either side, but we only have Pauline's side of the story! It shows her talent at using subtle direction to achieve her aims, a skill she was to use successfully in the ATA. She must have the last word here:

Thank heaven he knew little about Air Ministry regulations and aviation generally. Had he thought twice about the matter I doubt if he would have credited my stories. However, whether he believed them or not, in self-defence he bought us an aeroplane which at least had a certificate of air-worthiness.

This very welcome gift was the catalyst: 'Directly we got the machine we started work.'

Pauline and Dorothy had laid their plans, while using hired aircraft to take up their first few willing passengers. Now they were ready to put them into action.

2

STAG LANE –
LEARNING TO FLY,
BREAKING RECORDS

We soon decided that it would be immense fun and very profitable
to go into partnership together.

Pauline Gower

It started with a hoax. And a press opportunity. Pauline Gower and
Dorothy Spicer met in 1931 at Stag Lane Aero Club in north London
and subsequently set up the first all-women air-taxi business. They
broke records, achieved significant firsts for women in aviation and had
many airborne adventures along the way. They became firm friends,
there for each other when the ground came rushing to meet them, or
when they needed to fly each other home after tragic family events.
But mostly they shared a successful and harmonious working partnership and only once nearly came to blows when they had to decide who
should write the account of their adventures.

Perhaps if the reporter who visited Stag Lane one cold February day
in 1931 had been older, or less gullible, their story might not have got
past the introduction. Pauline thought him 'a nice young man' who
smelled of soap, but journalism was clearly not his natural calling. She
was always a good judge of character, which helped her succeed in many

situations. Pauline and Dorothy made up a story in jest, of plane travels to exotic imaginary places, and the journalist went off to write it up. Somewhat red-faced they telephoned the newspaper office to explain their hoax, but the story had already been printed. But another journalist was dispatched to seek the true story … and they decided that perhaps they should work together and make their flights of fancy a reality.

They were young, ambitious, ready for the sky, and had foreshadowed their own business future. Pauline charts their ground-breaking career that followed (she won the argument as to who would write their story) in the entertaining *Women with Wings*, published in 1938 after six summers spent together. She does not hesitate to log the near misses, the scrapes with danger and the sheer chance and circumstance that kept them on course, as well as the times she flew off course in dangerous weather, or with passengers whose eccentric behaviour led to plenty of just-in-time moments. She and Dorothy took it all in their stride.

Pauline could have taken a very different flight path. Her wealthy background ensured that she did not really need to earn her living, which may have sent her in the opposite direction. She could have followed her schoolgirl interests in music and the arts, while waiting for the right husband to cross her path and make a suitable marriage.

In a series of articles for *The Australian Women's Mirror* in 1934, Pauline summed up how it all started. Quite simply: '"I am going to learn to fly." Boldly I made this assertion over the breakfast-table one spring morning a few years ago.' Easy to imagine the silence that followed, the scrape of a knife on a plate, the settling of a spoon on a saucer. Dorothy Gower's initial silence. 'My father barely looked up from his paper. "Where's the money coming from?" he grunted. "I shan't pay for you to break your neck." My mother merely looked pained and said she hoped I would do nothing of the sort.'

Pauline was not daunted and most likely finished her cup of tea with a flourish. A splash of tea on the white linen tablecloth. 'From the first I realised that parental support either financially or morally was out of the question, but by dint of scraping together every penny I possessed and not spending anything on clothes I managed to save enough to learn to fly.' A lesson there for anyone with determination and a willingness to wear the same outfits!

Her first flight was on 25 June 1930 at the Phillips & Powis School of Flying in Reading, chosen because the lessons were cheaper than flying from Stag Lane. She flew for forty-five minutes in a Gipsy Moth G-AAJW; interestingly her instructor was called Mr W. Giddy. Nevertheless, she flew 'straight and level' and was no doubt ready for the next lesson as soon as she landed. It did not take long – on 6 August she made her first solo flight, after just seven and a half hours' instruction, this time in a Moth G-EBTG. Pupils from Beechwood had watched her first solo – one onlooker remarked that her 'teeth chattered with nervousness' – and were relieved when she landed safely. Another triumph for their old girl!

Pauline needed a hundred hours' solo flying to acquire her pilot's 'B' licence. This would allow her to take up paying passengers and fund her flying. Without her parents' knowledge, she 'mortgaged' a £100 coming-of-age pot and used this for lessons, in a hired Gipsy Moth. Perhaps this added to the fun, and the heady excitement of earning her wings. She also gave violin lessons to anyone who thought she could play (typically self-deprecating, considering she had played solo in the school orchestra) to help towards the cost of lessons. It was starting to come together.

There were some fine role models to spur her on. One aviation pioneer of the 1920s who received less attention than most in later life was Connie Leathart from Northumberland. She was one of the first women in Britain to be awarded a pilot's licence and fly over the Alps in a De Havilland Tiger Moth. She was remembered, by a young Colonel Michael Bell, as a fearless woman who would invite him into her flimsy Bristol Grasshopper and undertake a series of death-defying stunts. Pilot, passenger and ancient biplane made it down in one piece every time. Colonel Bell recalled those flights clearly, with a smile, even when he had reached his century! He described Connie as 'very plain, not much to look at, very stout and square', although he forgot to mention her pipe and her trademark Eton crop. The pair remained great friends throughout their lives and Colonel Bell would visit her Cumbrian cottage and discuss the old times over her favourite whisky and Woodbines.

Like many of the early women pilots, Connie Leathart was determined and dedicated to the cause: her pilot's licence. She learned to fly at Newcastle Aero Club in 1925, infamously landing upside down on her first solo flight. Yet two years later she had achieved her licence and the sky was hers. Fearless and feckless, she didn't live for 'firsts' – just the joy of flying and the freedom it gave her. Paving the way for later pioneers, she became great friends with Amy Johnson. Very different women, but with the same love of wings, speed, excitement. And courage in abundance. Connie was to cross Pauline's path when she decided to join the ATA in late 1940 – a more than adequate recruit with 700 hours in sixteen types of aircraft. Her story is remarkable, just one of the many stories of courage in the air.

LONDON AEROPLANE CLUB, STAG LANE

This was where it all began for Pauline and Dorothy, six years after Connie's upside-down solo flight: a mile off the Edgware Road in north London, near Hendon Aerodrome, and closely linked to the early aviation pioneers. The airfield had become a popular flying club and played a key role in the growing aircraft industry.

The commemorative plaque, unveiled on the site in 2001, reads: 'Site of Stag Lane Aerodrome founded in 1916 by the L and P Aviation Co., then, from 1920, Home to de Havilland Aircraft & Engineer Companies.'

The land for an aerodrome was purchased by the London & Provincial Aviation Company in October 1915 and the company used the aerodrome for flying training during the First World War. From humble beginnings, the de Havilland Aircraft Company was founded on 25 September 1920 in two rented sheds at Stag Lane.

Pauline was 10 at the time; in just a few years the place would come to take on a huge significance as the start of her training, the catalyst for her airborne adventures with Dorothy and the many records they broke between them. It was a relationship central to Pauline's life and one that defined both their careers. The natural, carefree photographs of them during their summers together shows the strength of the bond between them, their excitement in what they were doing and their absolute love of and commitment to their planes (all of which had names).

Stag Lane Aerodrome was sold and replaced by a housing development in 1933; the last flight was a de Havilland Hornet Moth in July 1934. Pauline later imagined that her spirit might still haunt the land! (*AERO*, May 1935, referenced in Chapter 4).

The time that Pauline and Dorothy spent there was formative to their careers and the start of their successful partnership. They were both bitten by the same bug: one choosing the sky, the other preferring work on the ground. Pauline for one was only going one way: 'By the time I had obtained my "A" certificate the harm was done, my appetite was whetted, and I knew that it would be impossible for me to give up aviation.'

This is a familiar story, the 'eagerness for the air' is a common, addictive drug. Those without easy means worked hard to pay for their training, as they do now. Learning to fly has never been a cheap pastime. Pauline used her resourcefulness and determination to keep going and find a way to make it work. Her natural resilience was key to her successful and enduring leadership later in her career. Yet right from the beginning she knew what she and Dorothy were up against: 'It was not easy at first, nor in fact has it ever been easy – this life that we had chosen. No-one would take us seriously. People ragged us and did their best to hinder our training.'

At the aerodrome they would often hear male voices say: 'What do these bloody women think they are doing here.' Not surprisingly, given her upbringing, she was more shocked by the language than the sentiment. But neither stopped them going back for another flight.

Pauline made records, hitting the headlines again in September 1930, at Reading Aviation School, after becoming the first woman there to gain her licence. Not only that but she had qualified in half the time it had taken most male pilots there. It was the start of a string of firsts. She admitted, a year later, that initially she had been sick every time she went up, but gradually became used to it, which must have been a relief. Flying did wonders for her appetite, and it was also 'the most marvellous thing' for her complexion. Pauline certainly accentuated all the positives!

She also continued her other interests, finding time for one of her first loves: music. She took part in a concert at Eastbourne School of Music on 26 July 1930, performing two violin solos, 'Slumber Song' and 'Elfin Dance' (Haydn Wood). Music was always important to Pauline.

WHEN PATHS CROSS

Meanwhile, in 1928 a young woman had travelled south to London to take up a new secretarial role in a city law firm. One weekend she took a bus ride to explore her local area and stumbled across Stag Lane Aerodrome. She missed another couple of buses while she watched planes taking off and was hooked. Amy Johnson went back to her rented room knowing what she would do next. Just one year and much hard work later, she became the first woman in Britain to achieve her Ground Engineer 'C' licence, in December 1929, and went on to become a fully qualified 'A' Ground Engineer in March 1930.

In a manner that has echoes of Pauline and Dorothy's 'hoax', Amy Johnson then planned a 'stunt' to get herself taken seriously as a woman pilot. And one who meant business. She told a newspaper reporter that she intended to fly solo to Australia. She adopted (for her worried mother) the motto 'Be Careful', bought a second-hand Gipsy Moth, which she named 'Jason' after her father's company trademark, and left Stag Lane for Croydon Airport on 4 May 1930. Her famous solo flight and return to celebrity status and a CBE from King George V has been recorded in detail, particularly by biographer Midge Gillies, who reflected the popular song of the moment in her sub-title, 'Queen of the Air'. Amy was just 26 and had only ever previously taken a two-hour flight to her home city of Hull. She was a madcap and ambitious woman who had a strong influence on Pauline. Stag Lane was where it all began: 'Here I met Dorothy Spicer and Amy Johnson … We were all staunch friends.'

They all spent a memorable weekend together, which Amy recounts in detail in her foreword to *Women with Wings*. At the 'beautiful old house near Tunbridge Wells … Dorothy and I are guests … Pauline does the honours as hostess, gracefully and efficiently presiding at table'. She alludes to the home of father and daughter, the shadowy absence of a mother figure. They spent the 'crisp winter's morning' horse-riding, under Pauline's 'expert instruction'. A trip to nearby Hastings was next on the agenda, 'where, after an invigorating walk along the sea-front and a morbid discussion on Eastern atrocities, we storm the pier with its penny-in-the-slot machine'. It is Pauline who makes off with the most prizes and Amy jokes that they are 'afraid to be seen with someone whose hands are absolutely crammed with packets of cigarettes and sweets'. The evening passed enjoyably too, listening to their hostess perform on piano accordion and banjulele, a reminder of Pauline's talents nurtured at Beechwood and a love of music inherited from her mother. She made up songs, which Dorothy occasionally joined in with, and Amy notes that her soprano was a 'perfect partner to Pauline's lower notes'. Interestingly, she concludes her foreword as observer, a neat summing up of what made her friends tick: 'I played the part of spectator, admiring not only these social arts and graces, but the utterly unspoiled characters of two girls who have done more than their bit making aviation history.'

She had written to Pauline beforehand, saying she was welcome to amend anything in the text before publication if she thought fit. Her letter shows a friendly honesty: 'This foreword is my own unaided work except for the information bits I lifted. Please don't laugh at the ending & cut it out if you don't like it.'

Yet the ending stayed, and Pauline was equally complimentary about Amy's talent and drive: 'Amy has always been a good friend of ours, and I think we both recognise in her the splendid qualities of courage and enterprise which have helped to make her one of the finest pilots in the Empire.'

'ENTERPRISING GIRLS'

This 1931 newspaper headline referred to Pauline and Dorothy's blossoming partnership and went on to list their achievements as 'Two Keen Flying Girls'. Accompanied by a photo of them at work at Stag Lane, with Pauline kneeling on a work bench and Dorothy absorbed in mechanics, both in overalls with their familiar neatly waved hair, the article sets out their early aspirations. Miss Spicer, they said, is studying for her Ground Engineer's Certificate, likely to be the only other 'girl flyer' to achieve this apart from Miss Amy Johnson, while Miss Gower is studying for her 'B' Pilot's Licence which will allow her to fly commercially. The only other woman to hold this at that time was Miss Winifred Spooner. There was a twin determination, natural talent, and a necessary edge of competition in their shared ambitions.

Amy Johnson neatly summarises their partnership: 'Two young girls working together in perfect harmony who found that the secret of conquest consisted merely in hard work carried through with light-hearted zest and a cheerful philosophy.'

She generously lent them a plane for their first trip to the Continent, so that they could attend a meeting of the International League of Aviators in Paris. They set off in the two-seater Gipsy Moth with some motoring maps, marked with their route, and bags of optimism. Literally. They 'took it in turns' at the controls, from the back seat, while the passenger sat upfront with the luggage. Pauline admits this was 'a highly dangerous business' – especially as, while flying, their suitcases were allowed to rest on the stick. She flew the first lap, to Paris, and they had their first 'misadventure' shortly after clearing customs at Heston. Trying to ease back the throttle, she was puzzled why it would not budge, even after a 'hearty wrench'! She called through the earphones, in a huge panic – 'Dorothy, the throttle's bust! What shall we do?'

Dorothy was cheerfully reassuring. She had just got one of their suitcases resting on it and, with a bit of luggage manoeuvring from the trusty engineer, they managed to use the throttle, but only from the front seat! Pauline muses on this early journey in *Women with Wings*: 'The trip over the Channel was an unqualified success.' She continues, perhaps with a smile: 'We have often reflected since that in those early days of our flying experience a very special Providence must have looked after us. It makes our blood run cold now to think of the awful things we used to do – and get away with.'

All went well until they were ready to land. As Pauline was flattening out (more commonly known in aviation as flaring or rounding out), Dorothy let another case drop on the stick – the pilot in the back avoided a fatal stall, as the pilot in the front shoved on the throttle, with seconds to spare. It did not end there, of course. After they had lunch in a nearby tavern, they returned to the plane and aerodrome 'feeling fit for anything'. Just as well, as they soon got lost, approaching Paris from the south instead of the north: 'We could see the Eiffel Tower sticking up in the middle of the city, but no trace of an aerodrome we could find.'

Not easily daunted, the pair spotted another aeroplane and followed it in the hope that it was en route to their own destination, Le Bourget. It was indeed, and they landed with relief at the aerodrome without bothering to do a circuit, 'to the consternation of everyone concerned'. Military aircraft had been on manoeuvres overhead, and they had 'landed right in their way'.

They had dinner that night with some other English pilots, who drew sharp breaths when they heard how dangerously low they had flown over the Channel in their borrowed Gipsy Moth. One pilot asked what they would have done if, heaven forbid, their engine had cut out. Pauline admitted: 'I had to confess that I had not thought about that, and my partner was so overcome at the bare possibility that she nearly choked.'

This is just one of the many air-bound adventures Pauline and Dorothy had along the way, getting safely through with their natural cheerful robustness and just a hint of chance.

A DOUBLE DISTINCTION

By the summer of 1931 (my annotated copy of *Women with Wings* advises, in fine pencil, that it was 13/7/31), Pauline had gained her 'B' licence and Dorothy was a 'real live engineer' who was now capable of signing out one type of plane and engine – the De Havilland Gipsy Moth, which was the only type on her licence. Perfect! They were jubilant: 'We felt that the whole world was ours for the conquering.' The girls had worked hard, both to pay for their training and to study for their licences, and, at 21 and 23, they were surely invincible.

The *Southern Daily Echo* of 27 August 1931 places Pauline's record in context, as mentioned earlier, and headlines their photo 'A Double Distinction'. Pauline is carrying her small dog Wendy and appears in flying boots, long coat, cap and raised goggles, while Dorothy has one hand nonchalantly in her belted overall coat, calm and composed as only 'the second woman in England to receive a mechanic's "A" licence'.

In May of that year, Pauline had enjoyed success at a woman's air race in Reading. Lieutenant Colonel F.C. Shelmerdine, the director of Civil Aviation, had opened a new clubhouse and aerodrome building and Pauline competed in the ladies' handicap race for the President's Cup. She achieved a flying speed of 95½ miles an hour, coming second to Miss Aitken but, more importantly, beating Amy Johnson in friendly rivalry. The next day she and Dorothy flew to Antwerp, then onto Paris in the first of one of their many adventures.

Pauline's night-flying test, necessary to achieve her 'B' licence, was a dramatic challenge, however, and she describes it in chilling detail in her book. The fear of descending fog would have been felt equally by her pilots in the ATA; they were always at the mercy of the changeable English weather. Interestingly, she was supported that night by 'Team Dorothy' – Spicer and Gower, friend and older sister. She did four practice landings at Penshurst Aerodrome, guided by Major Travers, the club instructor. They then flew to Croydon, some twenty minutes away, and waited for her test. Pauline was glad, in hindsight, that they had topped up the tank with four extra gallons of petrol. During the two hours' wait, while other would-be pilots took their tests, Pauline gabbled nervously without remembering a word of what she had said. She had realised, for the first time perhaps:

How very large and lonely the night can be when you are going to do anything unusual in it! I wasn't cold, but little shivers chased each other up and down my skin most disconcertedly. To be alone in the air at night is to be very much alone indeed … cut off from everything and everyone … nothing is 'familiar' any longer.

That sense of looking up at the vast, dense sky, starlit or otherwise, and feeling suddenly very small. Dizzy. And that is with your feet on the ground, without the thought of taking off in a light aircraft and making your way through the darkness. Alone. The brush of eternity beneath your wings.

Pauline eventually took off just after midnight and circled the aerodrome to gain the necessary 2,000ft. She was given the signal to fly to Penshurst and her description is worthy of note, for her memory is vivid:

I was lost in wonder at the sight beneath me. It was my first experience of night flying. The sky was cloudless and the moon nearly full. In front of me the Tatsfield lights blinked cheerfully and behind me the myriad twinkling lights of London. The moon gleamed on patches of silvery water, and the beauty of it was strange and almost unearthly.

Perhaps if she was not so intent on her test, she may have composed some lines for a 'piffling poem', with the moon looming large. But there was no time for poetry. A layer of drifting mist quickly turned to a rolling ground mist that 'swept beneath me in one unbroken wave'. It soon turned to fog that obscured everything, causing her to climb again rather than attempt a blurred landing. She was just using a watch and compass, and tried to fly back to Croydon, after allowing for drift. Rockets had been sent up to light her path, but they could not penetrate the fog. Again, Pauline paints a powerful picture:

> There I was, flying round hopelessly lost, and thick mist underneath me blotting out all sight of the ground. I was alone in the air – cut off from every living being – and from all help. I must confess that I felt small and cold and sick and anything but brave!

The moon, just a few minutes earlier seen in all its glory, had now become a danger. Suddenly obscured, with a light switched off, Pauline felt like she would soon be enveloped in clouds and flying blind, without instruments. Any pilot reading this account will understand her fear that she 'should spin down and crash' without any idea of what lay beneath her.

According to her watch, she had been flying for two hours and was very relieved of that extra four gallons. Although would it only prolong the agony and delay the inevitable impact with the ground? She turned eastward, away from London, and decided to find a quiet spot, a field perhaps, in which to land. She felt like the whole world had deserted her; two hours flying, her first night flight, and no end in sight.

The next part of her story reveals much about Pauline's strength of character and lightness of touch. She remembered a 'faithful friend' who had helped her through previous difficult times. A stowaway dog, perhaps? No, a mouth organ! She 'hectically' played 'Show Me the Way to go Home' ('I'm tired and I want to go to bed' must have been very apt) but realised the chances were slim. She switched to 'The More We Are Together'. At the end of the song, she saw a light flashing through the mist. The flare path of an RAF aerodrome – Hornchurch. Her next thought, perhaps after the lightheaded giddy feeling of relief, was reminiscent of some of the ATA women pilots (Diana Barnato Walker in particular): 'Everybody was exceedingly kind, but I could not help feeling rather uncomfortable because I was minus the two necessities of life: I had neither a powder-puff nor a comb.'

Pauline's first night flight had a welcome natural break, and she spent the night at RAF Hornchurch with a shiny nose. The fact she recalled it all in such detail, including her palpable fear, shows the impact it had on her as a fresh young pilot. She worried that her 'night adventure' would not count, as she had clearly lost her course, but the length of her flight enabled her to gain her 'B' licence on 13 July 1931. She flew safely back to Stag Lane the next day but learnt that another candidate had not been so lucky. He had set off before her and got caught in the same fog; he ran out of petrol, crashed into a tree and had been badly injured. Chance and circumstance at play again.

On 1 August 1931, *The Daily Telegraph* pictured her waving triumphantly from an open cockpit – 'Miss Pauline Gower, daughter of Sir Robert Gower M.P., to whom the Air Ministry have granted the "B" aviation certificate, which entitles her to carry passengers.' Still only 20, Pauline was now the third and youngest woman in the world to obtain the prize commercial licence.

Another newspaper extended that line to 'for hire or reward', an interesting concept considering how many passengers Pauline went on to take up over the next few summers. Assisted by her forthright business partner Dorothy – a force to be reckoned with – even if they did not always feel like a successful team to begin with, shivering in their first overnight shelter without proper windows next to their plane!

Their reputation spread around the world and the *Cape Argus* was full of praise in October 1931 for the 'two English girls breaking new ground for their sex'. They outlined their joy-riding business, remarked on their qualifications and described their sleeping arrangements in a bungalow next to their flying field, with the two-seater plane housed with a farm tractor. The newspaper then detailed their day: 'They rise at dawn, put on overalls, and are busy preparing the machine before breakfast … their working of flying, which ends only when darkness falls.' One wonders which line held the most interest for Cape Town readers over their own breakfast, or perhaps it was this summary that raised an eyebrow or two: 'Their confident handling of the machine has convinced everyone of their efficiency. The majority of their passengers are men, who apparently have no qualms at placing their lives in feminine hands.' So that, perhaps, was the nugget of the article!

Pauline was delighted with her first plane, which she took delivery of on 9 August 1931. The two-seater G-AAGO Simmonds Spartan was to see a lot of flights and even more passengers, and the first port of call was a field near Wallingford where they set up for business. There was a shed for the plane and a one-roomed hut for their very basic accommodation. Business was slow at first, so they flew further afield to give joy-rides. They travelled to Cowes one day, taking sixty-eight paying customers, and were delighted with the resulting £8. Other destinations, under the newly formed 'Air Trips, Limited' included old haunts Reading and Stag Lane as well as Heston, Northolt, Banbury, Watford and Didcot. They were in business!

A PARTNERSHIP OF SKY AND GROUND

Dorothy Norman Spicer was born on 31 July 1908 at Hadley Wood in Middlesex and was two years older than Pauline. She was the only daughter of Hilda Mary Sisterson and Norman Spicer, a brilliant athlete at Cambridge and later active in philanthropy and religious societies. Educated at Godolphin School in Salisbury, Wiltshire, Dorothy went on to study at University College, London – an excellent start to any career. There is something about the steady clear sightedness of Dorothy from her photographs that speaks of a single-mindedness and, like Pauline, she followed her talents, drive and passion. They were a formidable pair with more than a glint of fun, which kept them, metaphorically at least, grounded.

Dorothy was never destined to be average. She broke all records as an engineer but was not showy or brash about her achievements. Driven to keep moving towards the next certificate, it seems, she had them all in her sight. And obtained all four. In her Foreword to *Women with Wings*, Amy Johnson endorses Dorothy's achievements:

> To secure the practical experience required, she spent six months with Saunders-Roe of Cowes, Isle of Wight, to learn aircraft construction, and a further six months with the Napier Engineering Company, Limited, at Acton, London to qualify on engines.
>
> Possession of all these Air Ministry Licences authorizes her to inspect, pass out and make major repairs to both engines and airframes. She is thoroughly competent at her job, and the highest tribute I can pay her is to say that I would fly to Australia with the utmost confidence behind an engine that she had passed out as O.K.

She broke down barriers and made huge strides for women in the field of aeronautical engineering. Pauline would have been lost (and she would have been the first to admit to getting lost, early in her career) without Dorothy's expertise on the ground, making their aircraft safe every night, before the next day's hectic schedule. Pauline paid tribute to this on several occasions. Dorothy was dedicated to the detail on her work, a true professional. Neither were afraid of hard work.

She studied hard for her exams at the London School of Flying at Stag Lane, starting at 7.30 a.m. and putting in a full day to get as much practical experience as she could. Obtaining her 'A' licence in the summer of 1931, by June 1934 she had passed the Air Ministry's 'B' certificate for inspection and overhaul of aircraft. Dorothy was, amazingly, the only woman at that time to hold this certificate. Although she typically modified it, when speaking to the press in Hunstanton: 'I am not sure I can claim to be the only woman in the world who has qualified as a ground engineer, but certainly I am the first in England.'

She was as modest as Pauline: they knew they were breaking records, but that was not their only focus. They were following their passions and talents, and the licences allowed them to go further and achieve more. They were a passport to a wider freedom.

Many of the newspapers photographed her in overalls, often carrying engine parts. The *Daily Mirror* featured Dorothy in an elegant, sideways pose in pearls and an off-the-shoulder evening dress. She was a striking woman who photographed well; but she may well have been impatient with an overlong shoot. She had planes to maintain. Dorothy's father said she had worked hard for her second licence: 'To qualify for it, she underwent an intensive course of six months' training at Cowes. There is now only the "D" certificate remaining and it is possible that she may try for that.' Possible? Inevitable!

Dorothy trained in the workshop at Saunders-Roe on the Isle of Wight for her 'D' certificate. She then took an oral examination and was questioned for an hour and a half by a panel of three. Upon successful completion, the 'D' certificate enabled her to hold a constructor's licence. This meant that, as well as being able to undertake repairs and pass planes as airworthy, she could even 'get the rough material and make them up'. She was awarded her 'D' licence at Napier Engines in London in 1935. No small achievement for a woman in her early 20s.

Pauline reveals more about her partner's character in her action-packed *Women with Wings*. We learn that Dorothy was not a morning person and did not much care to speak at breakfast time, or earlier 'she does dislike noise or prattle with the dawn'. She certainly did not enjoy having to listen to one of their landlady's old gramophone records, which punctuated their morning routine during their Crimson Fleet summer with scratchy regularity. While Pauline happily brushed her teeth to 'Here's to Good Old Beer, Mop it Down' or laced her shoes to 'Pack Up Your Troubles', the old songs made her friend scowl and 'groan in a most distressing way'. She would eat in silence, avoiding the strains of 'Tipperary', with a pained expression, and hurry back to her room. Not before she had given her more musically minded partner 'such a volume of acid abuse' if she had even started to hum along to that song! We can only assume that the differences between them made their partnership stronger. We can also imagine Pauline twinkling at

Dorothy's discomfort. She gives much away in those well-drawn scenes in her book, her prose spare yet illuminating.

The following contribution is from a contemporary Spartan owner and adds some rich detail:

Life in the Sky, 1930s Style

Anne Grant, who runs the Solent Aviatrix website to keep local aviation stories alive, introduced me to biplane enthusiast Rod Hall-Jones. He offered to contribute the following piece, to reveal the ups and down of life with a Spartan. His own historic aircraft is home-sick, and he's trying to get 'Gabby' back to the Isle of Wight where it was built, for future generations to see and enjoy. The plane would have been flying at the same times as Air Trips Ltd was in operation. His Spartan, G-ABYN, has the pilot in the front cockpit to allow easier access for the passengers and is the only one of its kind still in existence.

You can read more about Rod Hall-Jones and his ambition to find a buyer and return his historic aircraft to the Isle of Wight at www. solentaviatrix.wordpress.com.

HELEN OF TROY

Pauline Gower and Dorothy Spicer would have encountered many challenges jointly owning an aircraft such as the Simmonds Spartan three-seater 'Helen of Troy' (so named 'Because it is a Spartan, and sometimes goes wrong'), which today they would not face. To them of course owning and operating a modern aircraft only nine months old necessitated following certain rules and procedures before commence-ment of a day's flying. This is as true today as it was then; the difference being the procedures are far less involved as we have moved away from using wood and Irish linen to build aircraft. Engines do not need daily maintenance before flight, but they do need oil and filter changes every fifty hours. They also start at the turn of a key!

However, Dorothy would have been up early 'to ready' the aircraft for the day's flying and would have regularly worked well into the night to complete the day's compulsory and/or unscheduled maintenance before the next day's flying. Checking the tightness of all main nuts and bolts, the propeller to the hub and the hub to the crankshaft, check/reset the valve clearances, the list covers six checks in all, none of which would be performed today other than a visual look over the engine. At 130 hours' flying there had to be a 'top overhaul' where the cylinders would be removed and carbon build-up removed; in 400 hours the engine had to be removed and completely rebuilt.

In comparison, a modern-day piston engine will go beyond 2,000 hours before a complete overhaul. The propeller and airframe would also have taken up a lot of Dorothy's time – basically, wood and Irish linen do not like moisture and glue can break down. These aircraft were best housed in hangars, but I suspect this would have been a rare luxury for 'Helen of Troy' and Dorothy as she laboured to keep her in the air. When moisture gets into the wood it expands and, on drying, shrinks; this in turn affects the rigging of the aircraft. One day Pauline may be able to fly the aircraft straight and level with hands and feet off the controls, the next having to hold the joystick one side of neutral to achieve the same result – very tiring if doing a lot of joy-riding.

Pauline on these occasions would consult with Dorothy, who would then reach into her toolbox, select her wooden rigging tool and tweak two or more of the many wires holding the wings together. This is a very skilled art that only takes a few minutes to do, but can take many flights to get correct for the less capable.

Starting these old engines was also a bit of an art. On a warm dry day most would behave themselves. A cold moist morning could lead to a lot of frustration and the need for an aching arm to reach up and pull the prop through. Dorothy would have known 'her' engine imminently and how much prime (if any) it needed to get a quick start under most conditions. If this failed, spark plugs would be removed from a stubborn engine, heated, and quickly reinstalled to get a response.

Pauline, seated in the rear cockpit, would size up the two passengers as they were led to the aircraft: were they heavy, tall or disabled in any way? Heavy passengers and a full fuel tank would mean a longer take-off run and poor climb performance. The landing run would also be longer. A tall person would restrict an already restricted view ahead and a disabled person would likely require assistance in an emergency. As fuel was burnt off, the aircraft would perform better and she would be able to relax, but visibility would always be a concern. Taxiing on the ground, the aircraft would be zig-zagged as she first looked out one side, turned, and looked out the other to check that the area was clear. This would be repeated until she was lined up for take-off.

With full throttle and the tail up, she would get her first look straight ahead or around the head of that tall passenger. Climb-out would necessitate a series of gentle turns to ensure no one was ahead as she would rarely be alone. Others would also be giving joy-rides, and then there would be the air display aircraft keeping the crowds entertained.

To minimise the risk of collision, before the commencement of a day's flying pilots would agree on a designated joy-riding area, along with air corridors to and from. With no radios as an aid, lookout was paramount. Accidents and incidents did happen; in this respect Pauline unfortunately was not immune.

SURVIVING A CRASH

On 10 May 1936 Pauline ended up in the Coventry and Warwickshire Hospital. It was not Pauline and Dorothy's best summer by any means. They had joined Tom Campbell's Black's Air Display – a fleet of nine aeroplanes, which included a 'Flying Flea' and three parachutists. The weather was foul throughout, and Pauline describes that time as 'the most tedious and unpleasant season' they had experienced. It was their sixth summer together and the constant change and moving on from place to place, a new town every day, was wearing thin.

That day they had flown from Basingstoke to Coventry. A circling magnetic storm caused the wind to drop and chop and change direction. The first disaster was when a Scion five-seater took off full of passengers, lost a wheel in a hedge in a sudden wind change and had to land on the remaining wheel while everyone watched in horror. Luckily pilot and passengers were all unhurt, but a mechanic who tried to revive the engine had his arm broken by the propellor. It was not boding well.

Pauline was asked to start a demonstration air race, perhaps to divert the crowd's attention. She taxied into a corner of the field, two passengers on board, at the same time as another pilot took off from a different direction. They met headlong in the centre of the field. Pauline was the main casualty, her head taking the full brunt of a wheel of the other plane, which had been knocked off on impact. It was a serious head injury and, as she noted, 'people and things mixed themselves up bewilderingly in my mind'. She continued: 'After a lapse into unconsciousness I awoke to find myself in a hospital bed. I realised where I was and decided that I must look around and register my impressions so that I could later write an article on my impressions on hospital.'

She had raised herself out of bed and was swiftly admonished by a nurse. By this point, Pauline had become vague and could not remember why she had sat up. The nurse had asked if she wanted anything, and why she was sitting up instead of resting. Pauline had replied, somewhat blankly, 'I'm just registering' and the nurse had gone to fetch a doctor, leaving her to lapse into unconsciousness again. It was serious and she was operated on, 'stitched up under chloroform'. Perhaps it brought back memories of her teenage trauma. She writes about it in her typical matter-of-fact manner, but she had had a lucky escape.

Her parents reacted very differently. Robert Gower apparently had not been overly worried, on the surface: 'Of course she will pull through. My daughter has a charmed life, and after what she has been through, I think she can stand up to almost anything.' He was right, but perhaps there was a sense of willing her through. Dorothy Gower acted in her daughter's interest, cancelling all her commitments to be with her. A telling response:

> I am all for air development in every possible way, but a certain amount of anxiety must be interlarded with the enthusiasm for development when one so dear to one is involved. After all, flying is only a comparatively immature science and one can never be without a tinge of unease.

Pauline spent three weeks in hospital and another two weeks at home in bed. To some, this may have signified an end of her flying career. A sure sign to find an even more 'sedentary' occupation. A safer job behind a typewriter, writing about flying, or stationary in an office.

But not to Pauline, nor to Dorothy, who had spent those weeks preparing another aeroplane for her to fly once safely recovered. There was no stopping them!

The insurance company had paid out and provided another three-seater Spartan. Pauline was now in the front cockpit, and, within a month of the crash, they were back in business. They say you should always get back on a horse after a fall and it is no different for pilots, especially when there are passengers to ferry. But Pauline had lost her nerve a little. Her first flight in the new Spartan, up to Berwick-on-Tweed in Northumberland, was full of alarming 'what ifs' and she made a bumpy landing on arrival. She soon got the hang of the new plane and enjoyed the front-view cockpit. Life in an aerial circus went on.

3

AIR CIRCUS SUMMERS
WITH DOROTHY SPICER

I'm a star in an air circus. My partner in this adventure is Miss
Dorothy Spicer, the only fully licensed and practising woman
aircraft engineer in the world.

Pauline Gower

By 1931 Pauline and Dorothy had established the first all-women air-
taxi business. They focused on their individual talents to forge a strong
working relationship.

In her foreword to *Women with Wings*, Pauline's lively and action-
packed account of their aviation career, Amy Johnson describes what
lay at the heart of this successful partnership:

Pauline and Dorothy are two of my best friends; and I have formed
a habit of thinking that everything they decide to do is sure to be
interesting, amusing, and worth-while. Interesting because they have
both chosen careers very much out of the ordinary, which proves
them to be women of enterprise and resource; amusing because they
possess a unique sense of humour … and worth-while because the
work they do for aviation, and for women in aviation in particular,
has placed them in the ranks of the pioneers.

There is an edited version in the RAF Museum London that shows them in an even more favourable light; Amy leaves out 'nor any great skill' so that her sentence reads: 'At first, they neither of them had very much experience … but, young as they were …' She knew their true potential.

Amy herself had set remarkable, world-famous records, showing immense courage and resource, and she instantly recognised these qualities in her friends. Both women followed their course but would not have seen the full impact of their pioneering adventures in their day. They knew they were breaking records and making huge strides for women in aviation in the 1930s, but they were also living day to day and *Women with Wings* is as much about the challenges and hardships of the life they had chosen at that time, as it is the heady, fleeting glimpses of sun glittering on clouds. In sharing some of the book's adventures, hopefully Pauline's voice and legacy will be heard afresh. She has a talent for deft characterisation and getting to the heart of the matter. She does not waste words.

While Amy Johnson offered a foreword to the book, Dorothy Spicer provided the prologue ('*By* D.N.S'). Many of their friends had suggested they write about their air circus adventures and it was a natural outlet for Pauline's creativity. She also used it as a means of encouraging women to fly. In her prologue, Dorothy reminds readers: 'Our average age when we joined forces to make our career in commercial aviation was twenty. If you find these pages foolish, forgive their folly with the tolerance of the wise for youth.'

They agreed to pool their memories of their joy-riding summers, but the 'vexing question' was who should write the book – who would be 'I', and who would be the 'other fellow'. You may think they came to a calm decision, given their finely balanced working relationship, but apparently the heated argument that ensued 'shook the firm of Airtrips, Limited, to its foundations and nearly caused a parting in the ways of its two directors'. Dorothy's tongue is a little in her cheek here, perhaps. In the end, Pauline, as pilot, would have the last word and 'present the play' while Dorothy would have the role of 'ringing up the curtain'. This is a reflection on their decision-making at the outset, when they agreed who would take to the air, and who would be the ground support.

In five short pages, Dorothy outlines their hard-working partnership – 'we learnt early to take the rough with the smooth' – her contented days training at the aircraft company Saunders-Roe and Napier's aero-engine factory, and recollected two of her more eccentric landladies, both of whom desired more interesting jobs than providing her meals. One wished to lay out the dead (she had done so for her husband, and apparently it was 'beautiful' – Dorothy had not dared to ask if he was living or dead at the time); the other to become an attendant in 'ladies' conveniences'. Dorothy rambles in a similar manner and humour to Pauline, but then brings herself up short. Her prologue done, she steps aside 'and Pauline shall tell you of the laughs and the struggles we have had since we joined the brotherhood of the skies'.

The book was launched on 7 April 1938 to glowing reviews. Literary critic of the day Harold Nicholson said it was one of the best books of the year. C.G. Grey, editor of *The Aeroplane*, speculated first on whether 'women with wings' referred to angels, commenting on their appearance and social status in detail before accepting that they worked hard to make a living in the air (not to mention driving a car, cooking and housework of a caravan, which he thought relevant to add to the review). He then became complimentary:

> Pauline Gower does not profess to be a writer. She is certainly not consciously a maker of phrases or a deliberately literary person, but she writes unusually good plain English, singularly free from journalese and without any of the irritating tricks and clichés of which most professional writers are fond. She has plenty to say and she says it in a jolly conversational way which enables one to see in one's mind's eye exactly what she saw … And although Pauline Gower does try to recall some of the miseries of touring with an air circus, her natural cheerfulness and her out-of-the-way sense of humour have let her forget most of the miseries and to concentrate on the joyous or funny things that happened. Both the girls deserve compliments and thanks for turning out such a joyful and graphic and historical book.

He got to the point eventually. Safe to say the book is a valuable historical account of the bygone aviation of the 1930s and the story is carried along by two cheerful and resilient voices of the air and ground, enhanced by drawings and poems by the principal author.

Pauline and Dorothy spent six long summers giving joy-rides up and down England, from coast to coast, and field to field. They had some hair-raising adventures in the process, perhaps not all of which are recorded. Pauline took up more than 33,000 passengers during these years, some of them unplanned: she once took up a schoolboy stowaway, hidden in the front cockpit as she unwittingly did a couple of test loops. And a spin. Once safely landed, he stumbled out looking pale and sickly, and clearly terrified. Pauline instantly demanded money he did not have for his free stunt ride; she did not suffer stowaways lightly. He came back the next day, rather sheepishly, to help wash the plane's wings and was taken up again in recompense, this time without the spins. He may well have been the inspiration for one of Pauline's 'piffling' poems, with a few years added …

A Word of Caution

He was a joyous undergrad when first he came in sight,
With fur-backed gloves and muffler too, all ready for his flight.
He asked for aerobatics (a tear-drop dimmed my eye).
I watched the pilot take him up and throw him round the sky.

That poor young man, when he came down was anything but gay:
The perspiration shone upon a face of ashen grey.
And, as he staggered on the 'drome, a worn-out, useless rag,
I heard him murmur to himself, "Oh, where's my paper bag?"

I always hate to moralize, but bear with me this time
For there's a little moral here embedded in this rhyme.
If ever you go for a flip, remember this one snag:
You may feel ill if you are looped, so take a paper bag.

It is hard to imagine now the sheer mix of headiness, excitement and normality of air circuses in the 1930s. We live in a world of health and safety – rules, regulations and compensation. All unheard of back then, when the joy of having wings led to an air-bound freedom that will never be found again. No radio communications. No navigational instruments. Just buy, beg or borrow a plane and the sky was yours. If you had the money, of course. *Women with Wings*, some of it written between heady flights, is a window onto the world of that decade's aviation progress. There was a huge amount of trust involved, in both plane and pilot. Pauline and Dorothy formed a fine blend of talent, practicality and just a little hold-your-finger-to-the-wind in a shared spirit of adventure.

The press, as always, were keen to get the scoop on the latest flying story. A special correspondent in Hunstanton, where they set up in a caravan next to their plane, discovered: 'A fair young woman in the early twenties stood in blue overalls today examining a three-seater Moth aeroplane in a field near Hunstanton town.'

He goes on to describe their working and living arrangements: 'The two have rented the field and live on their improvised field in a cosy-looking caravan. Miss Gower acts as pilot and Miss Spicer as mechanic – with the help of a boy to do the rough work.'

Even before the paper mentions their record-breaking careers, it should be remembered that this was a unique set-up in 1931 – the very first all-women air-taxi service. Striding ahead in the 1930s; two independent and adventurous women who continued to challenge themselves, while having a great deal of fun. The press called them 'remarkable', and indeed they were. Pauline's accounts in *Women with Wings* also recounted many 'just-in-time' flights, some more serious than others. Remarkable and risky.

One man vividly remembered Pauline's air-taxi career. Sir Peter Gordon Masefield, aviation enthusiast, journalist and a leading figure in Britain's post-war aviation industry, first met her in April 1932, as a 15-year-old schoolboy, at the opening of the Hillman's Airways aerodrome at Maylands in Essex. Looking back almost sixty years, when writing to Michael Fahie in 1993, he said he had the 'happiest and most cordial memories' of Pauline. 'Your mother and Dorothy Spicer – who acted as her close friend and ground engineer – were at Maylands that day doing a brisk business in five-shilling joy-rides; flying, if I remember right, a Spartan Arrow three-seat biplane. Both charming people, enthusiastic aviators and great favourites with everyone who met them.'

Dorothy's character jumps out of the pages of Pauline's book. The two had similar qualities to ensure compatibility, but equally enough of their own personalities to keep them alert to difference. It would not do to become complacent in such a partnership – they needed to keep their wits about them. Every flight mattered.

At Sevenoaks in Kent, they decided to run their own meeting to drum up more business. Action was the key to their partnership. That and the occasional mishap. Pauline was about to house their new Spartan in a nearby aerodrome, Penshurst, but did not notice a boundary light in the encroaching gloom, as it was in her blind spot. She hit the top of the lamp with one wheel and landed on the nose of the plane, with a smashed undercarriage. Just a couple of bruises for the pilot, fortunately, but the plane would be out of action for a couple of weeks and Pauline felt 'degraded' at the accident, especially when Dorothy arrived by car and saw the damage. But, true to character, 'she hid her disappointment beneath a cloak of optimism'. A valuable insight into their partnership and a fine example of Pauline's way with words.

In April 1933, Pauline and Dorothy joined the British Hospitals' Air Pageants, touring England, Scotland and Wales with a gruelling schedule. The aim was to visit 200 towns to raise money for the hospitals. Money was a big incentive for them to join, as they still owed around £300 in instalments for their Spartan and knew they could earn more as part of a big aerial circus. With fifteen well-known pilots and three parachutists, it had more crowd-pulling power than they could hope to have as a two-woman team, despite the success of the previous summer. Among the pilots were C.W.A. Scott, famed for long-distance flights, the Honourable Mrs Victor Bruce, famed for a need for speed, Jock Bonar and the experienced joy-rider E.W. Jordan. During the six months in which they were part of the tour, Pauline and Dorothy visited 185 different towns, a new place pretty much every day, and the now 23-year-old pilot took more than 6,000 passengers up in their trusty Spartan. Considering the travel between towns, this did not allow much time for rest and relaxation. Dorothy would carry out all the necessary maintenance each morning and ensure the plane was ready for the day's work. It was a huge responsibility, but they appeared to thrive among the eclectic team of seasoned professionals.

The anticipation of the crowds in each town was a reward for the hard work required by pilots and engineers to pull off each circus safely and successfully. It was a feat of organisation, attention to detail – for pilot and ground crew – and called for level-headed resilience in the face of challenges, of which there were many.

Pauline outlined their daily routine in *Women with Wings*:

> Early morning sees the engineers busy inspecting the aeroplanes, the pilots studying their maps, and the rest of the staff hurriedly striking camp. Then comes the flight to the next place on the itinerary … to arrive at the new town in time to make a fresh camp and settle in before the afternoon show begins.

This was the golden age of aviation, which is re-enacted today with nostalgic events and demonstrations to remember that heady decade. The crowds around the country came to expect ever more daring displays as the 1930s progressed, while the pilots were kept busy fulfilling their daily needs for joy-rides and excitement in the sky.

In an article for *The Chronicle*, published in 1934, Pauline said they saw the countryside in detail for the six months they were with the Air Pageants tour, in many 'peculiar places, from a lunatic asylum to a Tyneside fish quay'. She elaborated on the former. She had got into conversation, on several occasions, with one of the patients whose 'mental derangement' had been caused by lack of activity and thought outside her own interests. The curse of introspection. She had become convinced that she had been forgotten by God and so Pauline took time to help her through her troubles and bring her out of herself. She asked her to write to her daily, with news of what had happened that day – Pauline said she would look out for her letters at every morning post. This revealed her inherent kindness, her ability to bond with people and to help them through difficult times. Pauline was delighted to hear that the woman found a renewed interest in life and took up some charitable work once treated for her depression. The power of writing at work, encouraged by a poet and friendly pilot.

Each circus started with a 'propaganda' formation flight – with all aeroplanes flying over the town and surrounding district to announce their arrival. Similar, but perhaps more widely effective, than Pauline's flour-bombing of the previous summer (though without the fun!). In Hunstanton they had used willing participants in a speedboat and Pauline would 'bomb' them with flour to signal to the local holiday makers that they had arrived and were ready to take up passengers. Everyone who took part enjoyed the daily spectacle and Pauline rarely missed her target!

Advertising over, the daily circus programme would begin, and Pauline offers more detail: 'After the grand formation flight … joyriding begins in earnest. The "joy" part of this sobriquet, of course, applies to the passengers. But if they get their pleasure out of the flight, we certainly get our fun as well as our money out of the passengers.'

Although not all their passengers provided amusement. Someone on the large side, 'Teddy Brown's twin brother', for example, would not make a good second passenger when your first 'is of such dimensions that she cannot have seen her feet for years'. In 1930 British Pathé had introduced popular musician and xylophonist as 'the one and only Teddy Brown (there's quite a lot of him!)' – an introduction very much of the time.

Pauline kept her sense of humour, in contrast with Dorothy's sharp remarks on these 'weighty occasions', as she was the one who had to fix anything broken after the ride: 'I do not know whether she has ever heard the proverb, "Least said soonest mended." Judging by the remarks she makes to me when this sort of thing happens, I hardly feel she has.'

What else was on the Air Circus programme that summer? Activities unique to that decade included balloon-bursting, paper-cutting, bottle-shooting from the air and height judging. It also featured aerobatics and stunt flights, which included treating passengers to 'rolling, loop-ing, spinning, diving, and sometimes quite literally turning them inside out'. The name gives it away – circus rides in the air. 'Crazy-flying', for example, involved the pilot doing everything against natural instincts: stalling a few feet from the ground, flying (sideways) with one wing brushing the grass, flying towards an obstacle, such as a dangerous petrol wagon, and then pulling back just in time. That is all even before any mention of parachute jumps!

And there were fatalities. Two personnel were killed that summer and several seriously hurt. The rest of the crew had to carry on despite this and Pauline noted that they stayed optimistic to get through, with an 'eat, drink and be merry' attitude. A good deal of British 'carry on regardless' spirit too, if only on the surface. Pauline was thankful for her religion at times – the 'spiritual rock' that others lacked. Many of her passengers shared her Catholic faith it seems; she was surprised during the first week of the tour how many of them left rosaries, crucifixes and other emblems in the aeroplane each day. She does not mention what happened to these finds – perhaps the pilots pooled their religious resources at the end of the tour.

The afternoon performance was repeated at 7 p.m. for the 'great British public's' thrill and amusement. It is easy to imagine that once the planes had gone through the process of being made safe for the night, and some-times having to be inspected during the night in the face of strong winds, the air circus crew were more than ready for their makeshift campsite beds. But the day's flights still had to be logged, the number of passengers taken up tallied, tickets counted and more. It was a tough life, and the thrills must have at times only barely outweighed the daily repetition and sheer hard work. But Pauline writes about that summer with a character-istic enthusiasm, practicality, and the energy of youth. The resilience and determination to keep going in the face of challenges were to stand her in fine stead for the ATA operational years ahead.

Pauline recounts many flights in *Women with Wings*, and usually finds the humour in the situation. She had once taken up a love-struck parachutist, intent on wooing the girl of his dreams, Snowdrop, from the sky. This took place near Burton upon Trent in Staffordshire and the hapless suitor attempted a semaphore proposal on the way down, only to land in a slime-filled murky pond. The landing was clumsy, he was indignant, and Snowdrop was not impressed. When Pauline went over to reassure her, kindly, that he was only a little wet, Snowdrop agreed. She had not signed back any semaphore or registered any delight in the mid-air proposal. Pauline drove them back after the flight and noted in the mirror that they were not sitting as close on the back seat as they had been on the way to the airfield. A frosty silence had fallen too. She wondered if Ashby-de-la-Zouch by moonlight might help. Perhaps she thought the name might spark romance, a French flavour, or simply a diversion on the way back to Burton. The market street would have looked very much as it does today, but a moon on the rise over the ruined Norman castle might well have rescued the situation. The would-be suitor and Snowdrop shook their heads and Pauline drove on; the pull of Ashby's romantic heritage did not change their lives and they went their separate ways.

In 1931, Pauline enjoyed her first significant romance. She had met Keith Erskine, a twin and third son of Sir James and Lady Monteith Erskine, and they got engaged in February of that year. Keith's father was MP for St George's, Westminster, from 1921 to 1929 and had then retired to enter the hotel business. In 1929 he received a knighthood. A mutual interest in family politics may well have brought the couple together.

They were both members of the 'Erratics' – a group of young people 'with unconventional ideas' was how Keith described them. When pressed, Keith said they enjoyed themselves in 'an original manner' – picnics before breakfast, that sort of thing. All part of the 'season' for a certain set. The Erratics held a ball at Eccleston Square in south-west London, opened by Pauline who burst a balloon to signal the start of the unconventional evening. This was followed by the young women dancing with air balloons attached to their skirts that the men tried to burst as part of the show. There was more to come. At midnight a group of plainly dressed men ran in, each one whisking out a notebook and pen as if to signify a police raid. But no, this was all part of the fun and the 'officers' were also Erractics!

Pauline and Keith Erskine are pictured with broad smiles in the papers, in the garden of Sandown Court, and the papers' headlines ran 'M.P.'s Daughter's Flying Romance' – not the simplest of splashes. As in reportage of the 1930s, parents were placed in a society context and Lady Gower is described in the *Sunday Pictorial* simply as a 'cousin of Viscount Lee'. Readers clearly knew their viscounts.

Pauline and her fiancé looked carefree and happy; in many of the photos they are holding the small family dogs under their arms, smiling into their future. She had pasted all the cuttings into her scrapbooks, one cut out around their heads in a gesture of fun and girlish excitement.

The engagement, perhaps more of a society romance as some papers suggested, was in fact short-lived. Pauline was just 20, Keith 23; maybe the timing was not right. Another cutting from the Gower archive carries the headline 'His Flying Fiancée' and shows a similar photo, but they are pulling apart slightly, Keith turning to the left with a rather forced smile. Pauline as usual is looking straight at the camera. There is a clue in the text: 'Miss Gower intends to fly to Karachi in the spring.' No mention of a wedding date, or future location of future house. Pauline had clear ambitions and a non-flying husband might not have made for a long-standing companion.

By June it was all over. 'Broken Off. Marriage Not to Take Place.' Reading between the lines, as there is no real explanation given, it appears that Pauline was set on flying to India, a plan that her parents had publicly opposed. The paper spent more column inches informing its readers of her aviation aspirations and achievements.

Another headline ran 'Broken Off. Aviatrix daughter of M.P. Provides Surprise.' The piece goes on to detail Pauline's plans and, again, it is all about aviation. The engagement was surplus to her newsworthy interest – she was the daughter of a renowned Member of Parliament but, more importantly perhaps, she had mileage in her ambitions as an aviatrix. That, in the 1930s, was what really mattered. Engagement and romances came and went, par for the course, but women who wanted to fly solo to India? No, Pauline and her uptilted chin, cap and goggles, and clear determination of expression was what their readers were interested in. Keith Erskine and her engagement to him soon faded from the headlines.

Friends had hinted that flying would always come first, and it seemed the case, this time at least. There was no reason given for the end of the romance; the papers focused more on the fact that it was the '30th broken engagement announced publicly this year'. Commitment was a flighty thing in 1931. Instead, the press was full of Pauline's ambition to break Amy Johnson's Karachi record.

INDIA IN SIGHT

The plan to fly to India sparked instant disapproval from her parents, her father in particular. But so had her initial intention to learn to fly, and she had won him over. It just took the right words at the right time, sure signs of her early diplomatic skill. Why India?

Amy Johnson had set the bar high and her flight path even higher.

Pauline had hinted to her father of her plans and the press put it in a much louder context. Competition played a part; they wanted to beat their friend's record. The headlines declared 'Women's Attack on Flight Record' and the story added that 'two young Englishwomen are work-ing feverishly on a London–Karachi flight, on which they hope to beat the speed record created by Miss Amy Johnson'.

What lay behind their desire to go one better? The sheer confidence of youth was at play, the excitement of daring plans, the belief that they had the knowledge, skills, and determination. Amy Johnson had done it in six days, in May 1930 – they thought they could do it in two. Highly ambitious, as at this stage Pauline had only just completed her first solo cross-country flight in England, from Reading to Heston. Twenty minutes one way, thirty-five minutes back. Robert Gower was clearly not going to back her plan, despite her roundabout way of telling him. He put his foot down, which equated to no finance for the trip. Funds from violin lessons or shop work would not get them to India.

Pauline stayed determined. No sooner has she gained her licence, after a record-breaking seven and a half hours in the air, she announced her plans to fly to India. This would not be every pilot's next step! Her parents objected, as they had done to her flying. This fuelled her ambition. And her response was played out in the papers, from Glasgow to Sidcup, Nottingham to Belfast. Sir Robert Gower was a prominent figure and here was his daughter mapping her own chosen flight path. He put his foot down again. 'Banned flight' read the Glasgow *Evening Citizen*'s headline of 21 October 1931, while the *Nottingham Evening Post* carried the headline 'Wants to Fly to India. M.P.'s daughter awaits parents' consent'. Meanwhile, South African paper *The Natal Witness* of 22 October 1930 revealed Pauline's bid for freedom – 'Parents Far Too Old Fashioned' ran their headline, following up the story: 'No flight to India until she is older, says Sir Robert Gower M.P., who has forbidden his daughter, aged 20, to fly to India.' This next bit is particularly revealing: 'He says one would hardly like one's young daughter to go to India alone by train or steamer, so why fly there. "So old fashioned, this fussiness!" comments the daughter, who learned to fly in seven and a half hours.' A father–daughter spat, highlighted in public – light-hearted, or otherwise? Two strong characters certainly, but Pauline had learned how to achieve results.

Squashed between all the cuttings, which one imagines Pauline pasting in with some delight, is a short piece from the *Sidcup Times* announcing that 'Miss Pauline Gower, daughter of Sir Robert Gower M.P., has announced her intention to stand as candidate for Parliament when she comes of age'. She was clearly determined to follow in her father's footsteps and saw herself in the political arena. In October 1930, the *Kent Messenger* also reported on her political ambitions – 'A Future Woman M.P.' – saying she had already spoken in her father's place at several events in Gillingham, Kent and planned to become a candidate herself at 21. They grew fanciful about her future success:

'One of these days the voters in a rural constituency may be wooed by a charming lady candidate who descends upon open-air meetings like a bolt from the blue, and perhaps scatters propaganda leaflets as she tours the countryside in her plane.'

It was in fact one of her passengers that did an unexpected leaflet drop, nearly causing a fatal crash skilfully averted by the pilot, but the 'charming lady candidate' certainly found other ways to make her influence felt.

Was her growing political interest another way in which to win her father's approval, by following his own more traditional career path? The *South Wales Echo* surely rubbed salt into her wound. The paper's headline ran 'That Amy Johnson feeling. Girl Wants to Fly to India: Parents Say "No"'. But Amy's name would at least draw more readers and win sympathy for her cause. And they were friends, 'girl fliers' intent on breaking records and pushing themselves as far as they could go. They were young and the skies were wide.

A reporter from the *Kent Messenger* went to visit Pauline at her 'beautiful home, Sandown Court' and took the story further. 'One day the world may ring with the name of Miss Pauline Gower, the twenty-year daughter of Sir Robert Gower, M.P. for Gillingham, and Lady Gower' their piece opened grandly on 18 October 1930. Pauline was 'bubbling over' with excitement at the prospect of flying to India and her 'eyes sparkled'. She had this underlying message for her parents, as quoted in the paper: 'I hope to do a long flight before very long, at any rate, as soon as I can perfect my flying and obtain my parents' consent, which at present they are not inclined to give.'

The reporter, perhaps feeling the need to sidestep the parents, asked Pauline if she ever felt afraid of crashing, likely having several recent accidents in mind (the R101 disaster and the death of Mr Giddy, for example. The R101 was one of two British airships built in 1929, the largest man-made object ever to fly. It crashed on its maiden voyage on 5 October 1930, in a meadow in France, killing forty-eight of its fifty-four passengers). The newspaper's sub-heading was 'A Bit of a Fatalist' – quoting her response. Pauline spoke with the full confidence of her age: 'Luckily, I am not affected with nerves. I have never felt nervous in the air except on my first solo flight.' She talked candidly about her plans, her thoughts on her father's views about India – 'I hope to break his opposition down in time' – and, interestingly, her candid thoughts on death: 'I'm a bit of a fatalist, you know. We've all got to die some time, and if I did crash, I would rather die like that than any other way.'

In the end the flight to Karachi was a non-starter as essential funding did not materialise. Pauline's lack of nerves nevertheless took her safely through many more flying hours and thousands of flights, and her parents were naturally proud of all her achievements. Whether or not they read the *Kent Messenger* at Sandown Court is not documented.

JOINING THE CRIMSON FLEET

In March 1932, Pauline suffered a crash in the Spartan that put it out of action for some weeks. She was flying back to Penshurst after a busy day giving joy-rides and had missed a boundary light when landing. The impact smashed the undercarriage and, although Pauline 'landed on the nose of the aeroplane', she only suffered 'a couple of bruises' and presumably was a little shaken up despite her professed lack of nerves. Soon after the crash, she and Dorothy were invited to join the Crimson Fleet air circus at Shoreham in East Sussex and decided that it would be a good way to pay off the £300 outstanding on the plane. With the Spartan back in action and freshly painted to suit their new outfit, they joined the Crimson Fleet on 14 May 1932. Their first stop was Pembury, back in Pauline's home town of Tunbridge Wells, and they were delighted to take £30 on their first day – a fortune in their joy-riding life to date. But it was tough. They flew over 100 passengers some days and had a constant round of towns from Bath to Blackpool, flight to flight. Yet it built resilience in both pilots and ground crew and there was fun in between the flights, a sense of camaraderie as part of an air circus team.

PARACHUTES AND PILOTS

During her early career, Pauline made a huge impression on daredevil parachutist Naomi Heron-Maxwell. Initially training as a glider pilot in Germany, Naomi had broken new ground and records to become the first British woman to achieve the Silver Certificate, a significant accomplishment for any 1930s' aviatrix. Her son, Nick Thomas, found her diaries and letters decades after her death, and in 2011 published the story she had been too modest to tell. He thinks she may not have dared to write her own memoir, being in awe of major figures such as Amy Johnson, Amelia Earhart or indeed Pauline herself. Yet very much like Pauline, her son said, 'she pursued her adventures with little regard for convention. Her inspiration was her own.'

Like Pauline, Naomi was the younger of two sisters. Her sister Jean excelled at both domestic and social skills, whereas Naomi 'could not sew, nor cook and she refused to be presented at court'. Shades of Pauline, who ran away from finishing school and suffered a short London season before escaping from the tedium of it all. They both wanted to fly and make a name for themselves, challenging what was accepted, going against the grain.

They were to meet at two crucial times in their careers. The first time was when Naomi had been invited to work with the famous Alan Cobham Circus and was deliberating, while negotiating terms and conditions. Sir Alan had heard her on the radio and saw mileage in having a woman parachutist to pull in the crowds. Naomi was equally aware of her marketing potential; she had come across in her interview as assured, talented and ready for fresh challenges. She had hoped it would lead to new opportunities.

Alan Cobham joined the RAF in 1918 and after the war went to work with pioneering aircraft designer, Geoffrey de Havilland, as his first pilot. Over the next few years, he established himself as a test pilot and aerial photographer. He won several aviation prizes. In 1927 Sir Alan Cobham started his 20,000-mile aerial survey of Africa from Hamble. Then, in 1932, he established Cobham's Flying Circus which featured aerobatic pilots, wing-walkers, parachutists, and other novelty acts. By 1937, the first in-flight refuelling trials took place at Hamble. This idea came from Alan Cobham who wanted to take off with minimal fuel and heavy cargo, and then, once airborne, take on more fuel. This idea was evolved by Armstrong Whitworth in 1938, who also developed the first all-metal, four-engine airliner, the Ensign, for Imperial Airways. Fourteen of these were built at Hamble.

The Hamble Valley region, a few miles from Southampton on the south coast of England, was a rich centre for aviation, particularly around the Hamble South and Hamble North airfields. The early Hamble flyers represent a 'who's who' of the history of aviation – designers as well as pioneer aviators who created a local hub of aircraft manufacture.

From 1911, Spanish aeronautical engineer and pilot Juan de la Cierva designed and produced some of the most revolutionary designs in early helicopters, including the enormous Air Horse, which was at the time the largest in the world. To secure investment for his invention, Juan came to England and set up a company in Hamble in 1925. Some of the most important experimental helicopter work in the world was carried out in Hamble during this period when A.V. Roe built many of the world's 500 autogyros.

On 4 April 1935, three days after Naomi's mother had played an April fool's trick on her, faking a letter from Cobham to say that he 'will no longer be requiring your services owing to what he has read in the papers', Naomi had tea with Pauline at the Ladies Carlton. This meeting certainly worked in her favour as:

> She gave me any amount of tips. Among other things, advised me to insist on having this trial week included in the contract, and having the contract signed now and not after the trial week. Rang up Cobham and made an appointment with him straight away. Extracted some of Pauline's courage and toddled along to see him. He talked loud and long but conceded in the end. Rang up Pauline to tell of the result.

They appeared to enjoy an easy friendship and had much in common at that time. As well as their air circus enthusiasm, they also shared a love of climbing. This proved a welcome distraction for both of them during difficult times and when dealing with personal loss. Naomi was to meet Pauline again in 1942, when she applied to join the ATA and was accepted on the grounds of her former work in the air circus. The aviation world was a small one, especially for the growing band of women pilots.

HAPPY HUNSTANTON

Pauline and Dorothy decided to go it alone in 1934, after the gruelling schedules of the summer before with the British Hospitals' Air Pageants. At the beginning of the year, Pauline had taken a well-earned holiday, cruising on Bibby Line's passenger liner *Shropshire* and staying with her sister Dorothy and her husband in Ceylon (now Sri Lanka). Her fame now went before her, much to her embarrassment. She avoided the large crowd that had gathered at Columbo Dock, there to meet 'the famous airwoman' in person, by hiding in the ship's toilets! An amusing thought, considering the crowds she had performed in front of and the hundreds of passengers she had taken up the previous year. She was plane-sick during her stay, enjoying the sightseeing but longing to fly.

Dorothy Spicer meanwhile was hard at work studying for her 'C' licence in engineering. She spent six months of practical and theory training at the Spartan Aircraft Company at Cowes on the Isle of Wight. This is acknowledged and rightly remembered – Dorothy's legacy endures on the island. It was time well spent as she became the first women in the world to gain the qualification, in a traditionally male-dominated environment.

The third member of their party, the Spartan, was stored over the winter months with the Kent and Rollison company at Croydon Airport. It was tested in March to ensure air-worthiness and then used for some pleasure flying over the Easter break at Hatfield and later along the south coast. But what to do for the summer?

Pauline and Dorothy had toyed briefly with fulfilling their ambition to fly to India, on another record-breaking mission, but this was once again met with parental disapproval. They decided to keep on making money and stay independent but, rather than fly across country to town after town, they would hire a field and encourage passengers to come to them. They had visited Hunstanton on the Norfolk coast the year before, talked to some local residents, and were drawn to the coastline and the potential of the area.

They found an ideal spot near the railway line and alongside a marshland, known locally as 'The Swamp'. Accuracy on landing would be essential! The owners, the Searle family, were happy to let Pauline and Dorothy use the field, perhaps seeing the profitability in attracting new customers to their own catering and camping business. Instead of sleeping in a tent or a string of endless hotels, as they had done on tour the year before, a new luxury was in store for intrepid pilot and engineer – an old gypsy caravan. They cleaned it up and moved in. After all, as Pauline said, it offered: 'Two rooms quite large enough to give us all the space needed for cooking, eating, and sleeping, with a corner still to spare for a desk, and a shelf for our aeronautical reference books. So we were then absolutely self-contained – our own field, with our plane and our home side-by-side.'

They certainly look happy in this simple arrangement, with Wendy the much-flown dog there to complete the scene. The relative comforts of the caravan boded well for the summer ahead, although it did let in the rain and jam jars were lined up to catch the drops. Raincoats were also needed at night as covers. The caravan was later referred to as 'The Slum Dwelling'. Their focus, as always, was flying and it seemed that any accommodation, however basic, would suffice. They were young, without ties, and each summer held its own adventure.

However, it was not all plain flying at Hunstanton. Potential passengers were easily distracted on the way to their field by two competing attractions. South Beach Fair was the first, and Pauline and Dorothy would often watch with envy from the air the fun their prospective joy-riders were having. Rifle ranges, water-dodgems, roundabouts, shove-ha'penny tables and palm readers were all on offer. Once satisfied from the fun of the fair, visitors then came across the dog circus before they reached their waiting plane. But Pauline had a trick up her sleeve, or rather underneath her plane. Their unique form of advertising entailed painting 'Cheap Flights' on the bottom of the plane, underneath the fuselage, and flying low over the beach to attract more customers. Pauline would add some aerobatics by way of enticement. She admits it did not always work and visitors preferred the lure of the sea in hot weather.

While waiting for paying fares, Pauline took to her second passion (more of which in Chapter 4) and wrote a lengthy poem next to the waiting plane, with 'apologies to Henry W. Longfellow'. Apparently, Dorothy was not gushing with her praise when she heard it read aloud the first time. It seems appropriate to include a few stanzas here, to entice a new generation of more enthusiastic readers …

Hiawatha the Pilot

Near a large town full of trippers,
In a green and spacious meadow
Hiawatha sat lamenting,
Sobbing out his soul in sadness;
For his aeroplane stood idle,
Idle in the summer sunshine.

To the beach the crowds were straying,
Bathing in the cool sea-water;
Laughing, playing, spending money
With the sweet- and whelk-stall-holders;
Never caring, little thinking
Of the pilot sitting lonely.
Yet not lonely; for beside him
Drooped his engineer and partner,

Grieved to see no people flying
And the aircraft standing empty.

'Hiawatha!' cried he sadly
'If we do not give some joyrides
Soon, we shall not have the money
To repay our friend the farmer
For the hire of this meadow.
Neither can we buy more petrol;
For the greedy garage owner
Will not trust us any longer!'

Hiawatha sitting silent
Brooded on this information,
Facing ruin and starvation.
Heavy-lidded, cross and sulky
Sat he silent for a long time,
Thinking out a plan of action.
How to draw the crowds from bathing,
From the beach and from the whelk-stalls,
To the flying-field for the joyrides.

Then a sudden inspiration
Flashed across his mind like lightning,
And he cried out gaily, gladly
To his sorrowing mechanic:
'Hasten, gather twigs and brushwood;
Take the bark from off the birch-tree.
We will build a mighty beacon
In the centre of the meadow.
We will pour on some petrol,
So the flames will roar and crackle'…

Pauline Gower, from *Piffling Poems for Pilots*

A hoax, for sure. Imaginary, of course. Pauline scribbling away at her own slant on Hiawatha while her 'sorrowing mechanic' scoured the field for sight of customers. Perhaps Dorothy had objected to her 'drooping' beside the pilot. The poem goes on to describe a mighty bonfire that attracted the day trippers up to the field in the hope of seeing a burning aircraft (safely hidden out of sight). They had to pay to enter the field and were disappointed to see no sign of a burnt wreckage. The pilot, Hiawatha, quickly decided to put on a display and 'Climbing, diving, rolling, looping' attracted the crowd's attention and the now-smiling engineer encouraged them to 'Fly with Hiawatha'. The result may well have raised a smile from Dorothy, even if just with relief that the poem was *finally* near its conclusion!

First a lad and then a maiden
Paid their money for a joyride
Went up and came down delighted;
Told their friends the joy of flying;
Bid them all to go up likewise.
When the darkness fell that evening,
Hiawatha sat and counted
With his engineer and partner
All the money they had taken,
Crackling notes and clinking silver
In the still and dewy darkness.
   'Now my friend,' he cried exulting
'We can pay the kindly farmer,
Pay the greedy garage-owner,
And still have sufficient over
For another large instalment
Which is owing for our aircraft.'

Amusing in its biographical detail, the poem reveals Pauline's love of storytelling and humour to get through tricky situations. Money was important to their continuing partnership, and the eventual purchase of their plane and livelihood, but she puts it neatly into perspective in this poem. Interestingly, the original epic poem *The Song of Hiawatha* was published on Robert Gower's birthday, twenty-five years before he was born. Henry Wadsworth Longfellow was a hugely popular American poet of that time and Pauline would have been struck, perhaps, by his lyrical musicality and stories of myth and legend. She may well have studied his poetry at school and enjoyed playing with similar rhyming schemes. Her own tribute had a fitting inclusion in *Piffling Poems for Pilots* – there's even a follow-up, 'Hiawatha Again'!

Hunstanton certainly had its fair share of experiences for Pauline and Dorothy. As their company Air Trips Ltd was no longer in the red, the pair were feeling a little flush that second summer. Business was brisk, with many passengers wanting to be taken across the Wash to Skegness. This was a fifteen-minute flight but could take up to four hours in a car, hence the demand. The arrival of the 'Flying Flea' aircraft, officially known as the Pou-du-Ciel, owned by Monsieur Henri Mignet at Skegness Aerodrome, also proved popular. Pauline and Dorothy had by now learnt the art of advertising and cultivating the local press. Reports in the *Lynn News* about their flour-bombing arrival drew the crowds, often as many as a thousand a day, to their field.

They decided they needed a bigger plane to take more passengers and so make more money. On 1 August 1935 Pauline took a short test flight in a single-engine DH 83 Fox Moth, SU–ABG and ten days later returned to Heston and bought the plane. Dorothy, rather unwillingly as she was not an enthusiastic pilot, flew back the Spartan. She overshot their Hunstanton landing strip, carried on to nearby RAF Bircham and unwittingly attracted a crowd of airmen ready for a joy-ride or two. Pauline, ever the opportunist, had flown to fetch Dorothy with another pilot and, while he safely delivered her engineer back to Hunstanton, she took up the onlookers and presumably earned a few more fares.

However, when Pauline took up two passengers the following day, all ready for a new chapter in her new plane, the flight did not turn out as expected. Not at all. In fact, as the *Lynn News* so enthusiastically reported (the courting of journalists brought promotion of all kinds)

– 'Plane Lands in Swamp at Hunstanton' – not the most successful of virgin flights for the Fox Moth. The engine had failed as soon as they had 'rose like a bird' and Pauline had no choice but to land in the safest of places – 'The swamp be it'. The undercarriage was smashed to pieces, the wings folded back, the engine completely torn out and the passengers … well they were, to use Pauline's own words 'shot out like bullets through the resulting hole'. She was speechless with shock, winded by the forced landing and could only 'sit on the ground and gasp and goggle'. It took all her skill and control – and presence of mind to turn off ignition and petrol afterwards to avoid a fire – to land as safely as they had, but much was left to chance and circumstance. Luckily the passengers, Mr Roy Bull and an unnamed local council official, were unhurt and seemingly unperturbed. Not long afterwards, Pauline took to the air again in the trusty Spartan and gave joy-rides until the light faded over the Wash. Dorothy worked wonders on the wrecked fuselage which was dragged from the swamp by a crane … the engine and undercarriage had already been removed, and it was a sorry sight. The plane was repaired but was quickly sold on again – one swamp crash too many as far as its owners were concerned.

This is just another account of Pauline's quick thinking in the air and calmness in a crisis. She avoided a fatal crash, even if they did have to 'tear across the swamp at fifty miles an hour' to do so. It was not a stunt worked into their performance however, and the memorable first – and last – flight in the Fox Moth was not, it seems, recorded in her logbook.

The rest of the summer continued fairly smoothly, with many of their friends flying in to visit them at Hunstanton, including pilots from their days with the British Hospitals' Air Pageants. Flying was still a fantastic adventure, and they were making their living at what they loved doing best. Yet the summer of 1935 proved to be the light before the shadows to come.

A CHANGE OF MOOD

After five years of long flying days and sustained engineering work, Pauline and Dorothy planned a well-earned holiday before the next season. They had taken up thousands of passengers, travelled around the country probably at least once and come through several near-fatal skin-of-the-teeth moments in the air and on the ground. It was time for a break. Their cruise on the SS *Ranchi* set sail on 31 January 1936, just as Pauline heard that her second volume of poetry, *More Piffling Poems for Pilots* had been published. A good start to the year. Their overseas holiday was just what they needed, and their ports of call included Tangier, Marseilles, Malta, Bombay (now Mumbai) and Singapore. A welcome relief from English seaside towns no doubt! And a chance to rest and recuperate.

Amy Johnson was also recovering at that time, from a shoulder injury. She had received a letter from Pauline and had written back warmly: 'It was so sweet of you to write to me, and appreciate your cheering words very much. I have had my dislocated shoulder set, and feeling as fit as can be expected. Please give me a ring soon and come and see me.' Another sign of their enduring friendship and of Pauline's much-documented kindness.

In the summer of 1936, the Gower–Spicer team had agreed to join Tom Campbell Black's British Empire Air Display. Pauline was to be chief pilot and Dorothy senior engineer. The tour started in April at Broxbourne in Hertfordshire and quickly proved to be another hectic one. That summer was also plagued by terrible weather and accidents, including Pauline's own, as noted earlier. She described the abysmal conditions in *Women with Wings*:

> The weather we experienced during the tour was anything but pleasant. Hardly a day went by without rain and we seemed to chase the bad weather round. Often we left one place in brilliant sunshine and arrived at the next town about seventy or eighty miles away in

a rainstorm. These bad meteorological conditions made the flights from town to town very difficult and on most occasions visibility was poor.

On 1 September Dorothy received an urgent telephone call to say that her father had died suddenly in a fall from a window of his London flat in St John's Wood. She was needed at once. Pauline flew her friend as far south as she could before again hitting appalling weather conditions. She arranged a car and driver to take Dorothy to Perth railway station to continue her 600-mile journey from Lossiemouth to London. It must have been difficult to let her travel alone after such news.

In fact, Dorothy's father had taken his own life, at the age of 57, and the verdict was 'suicide while of unsound mind due to depression, sleeplessness and lack of confidence'. It was believed he was depressed due to the poor state of his business affairs – a tragedy for his only daughter to come to terms with. *The Times* described Norman Spicer as 'A man of wide reading and of great personal charm and sympathy, he was always ready to do a good turn to anyone who needed it.' His funeral was held at All Saints' Church in Finchley Road, north London, and there was a considerable attendance from friends and family.

After the funeral, Dorothy travelled up to the Midlands on 7 October to join Pauline for the last leg of the tour. It must have been a welcome distraction, not least as the famous 'birdman' Harry Ward had joined the show – he jumped from a plane with canvas wings, imitating a bird, before letting his parachute loose for a safe landing. He was a crowd-puller! The next day marked the end of their air circus days, and they flew down south together through a strong wind. Yet perhaps with some slight relief that the long travelling days were behind them, thrilling and exciting as they had been.

Their final stop together, as a partnership, was Hayling Island in Hampshire. They gave taxi trips to nearby Portsmouth and Southampton, and joy-rides on demand. But the schedule was their own. The peace, however, was not to last long.

A DOUBLE TRAGEDY

The year 1936 was to be forever imprinted on Pauline's memory. Her mother Dorothy had suffered from depression for much of her life, and this became more acute as she grew older. By her mid-50s it was believed she had developed a phobia that she had cancer and would suffer a painful and lingering death. Today this may have been classed as extreme health anxiety, alongside her prolonged bouts of depression.

There is a brief and poignant account in *A Harvest of Memories* of the tragedy that took place on 1 November 1936, All Saints' Day, which may have had some significance. Whether Dorothy Gower had that in mind or not, it is impossible to know. Fearing the worst, unable to face a painful death, she took her own life. She had sealed the windows and let her bedroom fill with deadly gas. The next morning her maid Gertrude Frost found the door locked and it took Robert Gower to break the door down for her death to be discovered.

Dorothy Gower had pinned three notes to her pillow, one for each of her daughters, and one for her husband. There is no record of what was in the latter, but she wrote to her daughters: 'A very hurried line to send you my love and all my best wishes for your future happiness and peace. Again I say you have less than nothing to blame yourself for. Try and forgive me. Your utterly bewildered and terrified but loving Ma.'

Pauline was 26, her sister 28. The pain would have been palpable, the scrutiny of those notes unbearable. Michael Fahie acknowledged that the 'suddenness and manner of Dorothy's death shocked my mother, causing a grief that was to remain with her for the rest of her life'. A certain guilt too, possibly, for all those around Dorothy at that time. Too many 'what ifs' left unexplained. Life for the family had changed forever.

On 4 November *The Times* reported the death, placing Lady Gower in a family context, saying that only two days before she had opened the annual exhibition of disabled men's handicrafts at Tunbridge Wells. Her maid had said that she had seemed very cheerful that day, although later had complained of a worrying internal pain. An inquest took place in the dining room at Sandown Court.

On 5 November, *The Times* reported a verdict of 'Suicide while of Unsound Mind' and continued:

Sir Robert Gower said that his wife had it in her mind that she was suffering from cancer, and she dreaded another London season because she did not feel fit enough for it. He did not think there was any ground for her belief. He and Lady Gower lived a completely harmonious life.

Dorothy Gower junior added her own explanation, which appears in *A Harvest of Memories*: 'My father was really very mild but could "blow up".' She recalled that there had been a mix up of messages that day between Robert's secretary at the House of Commons and his secretary at the office resulting in the chauffeur, Hodge, turning up at the wrong station – Tonbridge rather than Tunbridge Wells. It was a 'most ghastly night' and Sir Robert Gower had to walk two and a half miles home, in his morning coat and silk hat, and 'when he arrived home he was quite annoyed. Anyway, she [Lady Gower] had not been feeling very well and I suppose just thought life wasn't worth it.'

This seems like gauze over a deeper issue, perhaps, but there is no further explanation. Whatever the reason, her mother's death had a profound and enduring effect on Pauline. They had been very close, and it was a shock from which she perhaps never fully recovered. After Dorothy Gower's funeral, Pauline returned to Hayling Island on 9 November, but the season was almost over and there was not much in the way of distraction. A long solo flight or two, routes not detailed in her logbook, were perhaps one way of coping with the tragedy. She never spoke publicly about her mother's suicide, but it left a huge gap in her life.

With her sister having married and left home, Pauline had to step into her mother's shoes in many respects, handling the running of the household and accompanying her father to political and social events. Much fell on her shoulders.

4

PIFFLING POEMS FOR PILOTS AND OTHER WRITING

Flying took up most of Pauline's leisure time, aside from her family duties, but her second passion was writing. She had a strong ear for rhyme and rhythm and composed some of her poetry while flying (I tried this, as a passenger in an open-cockpit plane, but ended up dropping the pen and holding on to the seat instead). Pauline was also prolific in the time she had to dedicate to her craft. Her first collection, *Piffling Poems for Pilots*, appeared in 1934 and was launched, according to the *Harrogate Advertiser*, 'in her flying field, on the Watford by-pass' – the newspaper labelled it 'a collection of lively light verse concerning the adventures and misadventures of flying'. Sadly, Harrogate had witnessed one of the latter the previous summer, as the newspaper also reported that Pauline's visit with the Hospital Air Pageant had been 'marred' by the tragic death of a parachutist, recorded in more detail in *Women with Wings*.

There is depth to her poems, a flickering subtlety of light and shade, but mostly there is humour. A light touch, a directness of language and just a hint of irony at times. She tried some of her work out on Dorothy who, apparently, was not always the most appreciative of audiences! But may have added a dry word or two when she saw her friend struggling. The following poem from *Piffling Poems for Pilots* reveals Pauline's characteristic humour:

The Stranger Pilot

From some far continent he came
  To teach us how to fly.
We had not even heard his name.
  From whence he came, or why.

He told us of the things he'd done
  At least a hundred times,
And all about the cups he'd won
  In distant, foreign climes.

From tales he told we had to grant
  He was no 'also ran'.
With wonder we exclaimed 'You can't!'
  But he replied 'I can!'

It was a joy to tease and bait
  This pilot of renown,
And each in turn would lie in wait
  And try to do him down.

One day we caught him by the sea
  That was the last of him.
De mortuis – well – R.I.P. –
  The blighter couldn't swim.

Amy Johnson (in 'Miss Mollison's Tribute') offered a review of her 'envied' friend's achievements, saying that although the exhilaration of flying often made her want to break into song, she did not have Pauline's talent with the written word. She reminded readers of the *Tunbridge Wells Advertiser* that her friends enjoyed a successful, strategic partnership: 'Pauline flies and composes poems, while Dorothy looks after the engine and the machine.' She didn't mention the small terrier, Wendy, that often accompanied them in their plane, an integral part of the overall fun and inspiration.

In the summer of 1933, Dorothy acquired a black 'lop-eared' spaniel puppy, which Pauline was initially captivated by and bought from their hotel manageress for 25 shillings. After the first sleepless night, when the puppy had been sick over her bed several times, as the 'very young and perfectly untrained puppies can do', Pauline found herself covered in flea bites. Their next stop in that summer's air circus was King's Lynn, where they made a necessary purchase of Keating's Powder. They had lunch in their tent first, as both treated that as a firm priority. The puppy was then stood on a table and dusted in powder, with seventeen fleas as the outcome. It was Dorothy's turn to look after the spaniel that night and Pauline decided that she was content with just Wendy and so sold the puppy on to another pilot, claiming back her 25 shillings. But Dorothy had become attached, despite the fleas. The pilot gave it to her, and Dorothy promptly named her Rhua (for no obvious reason). Pauline concluded: 'She is a topping little dog and has been our constant companion since August 1933.'

Pauline's keen sense of humour cuts across all her 'eighteen bursts of facile rhyme', as the *Aeropilot* rather tartly described her collection: 'The metre runs as almost as evenly as an aero engine, and the authoress is to be commended for avoiding the highbrow.' It goes on to say that the booklet was dedicated to her friend and partner 'Miss Dorothy Spicer, which will appeal to all who know this irrepressible pair of "sportsmen".' An interesting slant and one that would have probably caused Pauline to arch at least one eyebrow.

In the early months of 1938, before the summer rounds of joyrides and circus tours, Pauline wrote her first short story, aptly titled 'The Adventure of Two Air Girls'. The main characters were called Jane Recips and Polly Rewog, their own names reflected backwards. A recipe for airbound adventures!

Pauline went on to write stories for *Girl's Own Paper*, which was published by the Religious Tract Society (later the Lutterworth Press) and which during the 1930s had a keen focus on promoting flights of fancy. The magazine carried flying stories, ran articles featuring careers in aviation for budding pilots and held regular competitions via its Skylarks Club. It encouraged its broad international readership to submit essays on subjects such as 'Why I want to Fly' or describe how to 'Make Your Own Aeroplane' and so was the perfect vehicle for Pauline's own passions. It kept an open-minded view of the emerging political situation, or perhaps tried to ignore it. But by October 1940, *Girl's Own Paper* changed its tone rather dramatically and reflected what was going on in Europe. It also introduced a new character, Joan Worralson, who was based on Pauline:

> Behold Worrals – she's emerged to do her bit in this war. She a real live character with a genuine love for planes; in fact her job means something to her. It is her whole life. She's ready to take on all personal risks in the service of her country. She's made up her mind that there'll always be an England.

This could have been an introduction to many of the ATA women – but embodied, clearly, their future leader. Flight Officer Joan 'Worrals' Worralson, who featured in an eleven-volume series from 1941 to 1950, originally at the request of the Air Ministry to help inspire and recruit young women, was the invention of 'Captain W.E. Johns', who had already captivated readers of both sexes with his series of *Biggles* books. Featuring Captain James Bigglesworth of the Royal Flying Corps, they proved hugely popular.

My 1948 copy of *Spitfire Parade* is dedicated on the flyleaf, in spidery writing: 'Lots of love to Tony on his eighth birthday. From Auntie Winnie, Uncle Austin, Richard and Pamela.' After a slice of cake, Tony would have probably flicked to the three illustrations by Radcliffe Wilson, and would have enjoyed the drama contained in the captions. The first is of two planes in action: 'As straight as an arrow sped the Spitfire, straight towards the Junkers.' The second shows an airman encountering 'an animal of the bovine species' after a forced landing: 'The ferocious-looking beast gave vent to a savage bellow.' The third depicts Ginger's 'wild and erratic' flying in combat: 'The furnace caught the Heinkel fair and square across the fuselage.' The detailed line drawings would have only whetted the young reader's appetite for action. It is worth noting the preamble, which strikes a tone similar to some of Pauline's own stories and practical viewpoint:

Biggles's Philosophy

When you are flying, everything is all right or it is
not all right. If it is all right there is no need to
worry. If it not all right one of two things will
happen. Either you will crash or you will not crash.

If you do not crash there is no need to worry.
If you do crash one of two things is certain. Either
you will be injured or you will not be injured.

If you are not injured there is no need to worry.
If you are injured one of two things is certain.
Either you will recover or you will not recover.

If you recover there is no need to worry. If you
don't recover you *can't* worry.

This is excellent all-round advice for any pilot!

On opening my copy, a flyer of the time fell out – a typed insert advertising a pension scheme from Sun Life Assurance Company of Canada. 'Dear Reader, £4,315 for you at age 55.' Presumably it was pipe, slippers and the newspapers thereafter. The postscript was interesting: 'P.S. The Cash Sum quoted on the first page applies to men – for women it is somewhat different.' Pauline might have read this with similar interest; an issue she may have later raised had she become a Member of Parliament.

The *Biggles* stories are not without their poetry; a night flight in *Biggles Flies East* begins:

The moon was up; it hung low over the desert like a sickle and cast a pale blue radiance over a scene of unutterable loneliness. Then, in the hard, black lattice-like shadows of the palms … he sprang to his feet as a strange sound reached his ears … it reminded him of the harsh confused murmur of the waves upon a pebbly beach, afar off, rising and falling on the still night air.

Pauline was often captivated by the moon, and in her account of night flying – 'My Most Thrilling Flight', published in *Popular Flying*, 1933 – she enthuses:

It was on a clear and moonlight night in June that my most thrilling flight commenced … For a few minutes I flew quite happily. This was my first experience of night flying, except for a few landings with my instructor which I had done earlier in the evening. The moon gleamed down from a cloudless sky. Just behind me were the myriad twinkling lights of London, and altogether the scene was wonderfully peaceful and beautiful.

Pauline's excitement is palpable. This is not Worrals, but real-life night flying. Maybe the lights shining over London reminded her of candles flickering at convent school, lit by the same thrill of the unknown. A poetic licence, but one I think Pauline might have allowed. This was flying at its most exhilarating, at an age when the spark of new experience was everything, especially when it involved her main passion in life. Wings and a wide, open sky.

W.E. Johns was a prolific author and editor, producing over 160 books between 1922 and 1968, nearly 100 of which featured Biggles. Following a career in the RAF, and serving during the First World War, he became a newspaper air correspondent. Johns also edited books about flying and created the magazine *Popular Flying* in 1932, a launchpad for Biggles. He appeared in the first of the series, *The Camels are Coming* (referencing the Sopwith Camel plane) in August 1932, at first under the pen name William Earle, later becoming known as 'Captain W.E. Johns'.

The author's last house, near Bushy Park in south-west London, was on the market in 2021, price on application. The estate agents were keen to reference the historic literary connections in the details. Johns had lived in the Georgian mansion from 1953 until his death in 1968. He most probably wrote his later *Biggles* novels in the landscaped gardens full of trees.

The Worrals books were hugely popular in the 1940s and 1950s but then lapsed out of print for many years. They have been republished in association with the RAF Museum – brought up to date with new illustrations and a revamped design to appeal to young teen readers – but include the same timeless tales that entertained and inspired previous generations.

There were several popular magazines for children, at least for those who could read and afford the subscriptions, but the weekly *Chatterbox*, to which Pauline Gower was a regular contributor, was the most enduring. Launched in 1866 by British clergyman John Erskine Clarke, who also founded the first parish magazine, it was aimed mainly at pre-teens. Like most Victorian weeklies, and reminiscent of children's comics of the 1960s and 1970s, issues were at first compiled into hardcover annuals, with no new material. Unlike many other Victorian children's magazines, however, *Chatterbox* was not gender-specific, but contained material suitable for boys and girls. John Clarke edited the magazine until 1902, and it continued to be published until 1955.

One of Pauline's *Chatterbox* stories was 'The Flying Farrants', in which we meet Penelope who is looking forward to the day ahead, hoping for good weather so that she can watch her RAF pilot brother Tony 'doing his stuff' in his Rapier Moonbeam. Very much a case of Pauline writing about what she knew, for better authenticity and ease of storytelling. This extract reveals a light-hearted style to engage her younger readers:

> Penelope woke early – the birds were partly responsible for that. She threw off her bedclothes and ran to the window. Yes, it was going to be a glorious day with bright sunshine and a breeze just sufficient to make the flowers nod and dance. There was certainly no need to worry about the weather.

Pauline's poet's eye for detail made her fiction rich and accessible, although firmly of its time. Her piece is the first in this edition of *Chatterbox*, followed by thirty-two other short stories in the perfect-bound hardback collection. Other titles of interest include 'The Story of the Wurlitzer Organ' by Frank Ferneyhough, 'Our Friends and Foes of the Insect Word' by Edith Harries and 'The Chums Find Adventure!' by May Sullivan. All writing contemporaries, whose work Pauline would have known and read in comparison. 'The Flying Farrants', perhaps unsurprisingly, features Toomer's Air Circus, which Tony has just joined. Pauline writes with pace to reflect the excitement of the expectant audience, and of Penelope watching her brother's first flight. The 14-year-old was envious of one of the 'girl-pilots' called – and here you can imagine Pauline searching for a suitable name – Dulcie Cockfoster. The MC of the show, the amplified Arkwright, kept the crowds whipped up with the names and planes – Looping Lewis, who gave an exhibition of 'wind-woggling', the three Snowden brothers all flying Macclesfield Majors, Charlie Pepper in a Gilpin monoplane and then – drumroll – the arrival of 'Wizz-Bang Farrant, one of the finest aerobatic pilots in the country'. Penelope was not impressed with her brother's show name and Tony was 'decidedly uncomfortable' by that stage. Arkwright continued, 'Very shortly he will take his Rapier Moonbeam into the air and throw it about the sky like lightning gone crazy.'

The story is straight from Pauline's air circus life, the prose is youthful and buoyant. She clearly delighted in telling stories and found a creative outlet that suited her own interests. Her readers would have heard about her life as a pilot, or have been told by their parents, which would have added to the thrill of her action-packed authentic narratives.

The 'Flying Farrants' takes a darker turn and, following Penelope's excitement at being allowed to watch the evening show and have a 'snack supper' at her brother's tent (she cooks the bacon and eggs), ends in a lengthy fight between Tony and another pilot, Lewis, who he had come across earlier that day. We wait, with Penelope and her brother (smoking a cigarette), while Lewis regains consciousness. He then starts to tell his story, at which point there is a pause – '(continued on page 29)' – a perfect place at which to leave Toomer's Air Circus! Light and dark at play here, like in any good story. Pauline was not afraid to include both.

One dramatic flight, which ended in murky water for both Pauline and two unfortunate passengers, was also turned into a short story, 'Death in the Swamp'. I turned to the (unpublished) typescript pages in the RAF Museum London archive with anticipation – how would she tell the story of that fateful flight? The pilot had become one Jim Garford, in a Proctor, and the landscape suggested a desert. The opening paragraph sees him at 3,000ft thinking about where to make a forced landing. Pauline clearly had that first flight in her new plane imprinted on her mind – where better to start? The crash happens quickly: 'As the tail reared up Jim closed his eyes. The Proctor described a double somersault and ended up buried with its nose deep in the dark green tangle of weeds and mud.'

Pauline had sat up in her Hunstanton swamp (August 1935) in a daze. By page two of 'Death in the Swamp' we find Jim is in West Africa and has lost consciousness after his crash landing. He wakes up in bed with a bandaged head and no memory of how he got there, or where he came from. Pauline was clearly enjoying playing with the 'and then he wakes up' narrative! As in some of her other stories, this one takes a darker turn and Jim finds himself beaten up, trussed up and tossed back into the swamp – which helped clear his memory and he recalled he was there to investigate smugglers. Of course! The story has a more upbeat ending with Jim alerting the police, helping arrest his attacker and getting some much-needed sleep: 'and as the sun rose over a sweltering West African coast, that young man climbed into bed exhausted but happy.'

WOMEN WHO FLY FOR A LIVING

As well as fiction, Pauline wrote regularly for several journals, mostly aviation related. Her writing is crisp and concise, at once objective and often intensely personal, but without being overly emotional. Pauline kept her audience in mind, although sometimes her musing becomes self-reflective as if she is working out her own position in aviation history as she writes. I am sure, however, that she would have applied a rigorous red editing pen, just as Amy Johnson had to the Foreword of *Women with Wings*. Detail mattered to pilots.

There is much to be gleaned from her magazine articles. In 1935, looking back over her first four years of providing an air-taxi service and giving thousands of joy-rides to the willing public, flying by now seemed a 'very ordinary' way of making a living, something she and Dorothy had intentionally set out to do and which had met with considerable success. Even if at times that meant scraping meals together when money was tight (luckily practical Dorothy could produce a fine dish from a few limited ingredients) or Pauline was forced to go hunting ('it sounds better then poaching') with a dog and gun to ensure a decent dinner. She was determined they would stay self-sufficient and see another season through. Both had keen appetites and square meals were essential for a hard day's flying. There is no mention in her writing of them taking many days off, save for the occasional out-of-season holiday. They had not chosen an easy career path by any means.

In an article written for *AERO*, 'Women Who Fly for a Living', Pauline expands on her route to aviation. Although her flying career now seems second nature, she realised that 'only half a dozen girls in the country' could say the same. She and Dorothy Spicer were breaking ground with every flight, every aircraft check, every day, month and year of their partnership. Interestingly, Pauline also recognised that flying may have made her 'different' from other girls; Stag Lane workshops were not the natural progression from a Parisian finishing school and being presented at court. From evening gowns, silk and perfume, to weathered overalls, engine parts and oily rags – perhaps not what the nuns at Beechwood could have foreseen for their 'glittering figure' who excelled at music, literature and sport. But Pauline was to excel, in aviation and in wartime leadership; much was still ahead.

In the same article, Pauline sets the scene for her readers; how she came to her chosen career. She appreciates that, in her parents' eyes, she was 'well-educated' and 'reasonably polished'; all the things that money can buy. Yet she senses their underlying disappointment, reflecting with humour that: 'No doubt they occasionally allowed themselves to look forward with pride and joy to the day when, eyes blurred with paradoxical tears, they would see me lead my victim from the altar. But things do not happen like that.' Clearly Pauline was not dreaming of lace dresses and wedding cake. Her mind was on higher aspirations. Cirrus and wingspan; airspeed and acceleration. She continues: 'To the alarm of my parents I appeared determined to knock off that expensive polish and behave in a way generally unworthy of my upbringing. I decided to don overalls and learn to fly.'

The quiet rebellion that led her to climb every tree at Beechwood, push rules and boundaries. It was not just a career; it was her way of life. And one which Pauline pursued with characteristic spirit and self-acknowledged determination.

The *AERO* article of May 1935 outlines in detail their first four summers: the taxi business (in which they quickly had to learn about the business side as much as the flying itself), the air circuses, British Air Hospital Pageants and, finally, Hunstanton – Dorothy, Pauline and her faithful terrier Wendy – 'settling down to one of the busiest and most enjoyable summers' of their career. They were their own women during those two summers in Norfolk; flour-bombing with abandon to attract customers (a highly successful advertising ploy), living in a caravan in their rented field and, despite much mixed weather, happy in what they were doing. Living in the moment. The final phase of their adventurous partnership.

By the end of that first summer, Pauline had broken another record without even trying. She had taken up more passengers than any other woman in the world – at that stage between 17,000 and 18,000 people. Most of them virgin flights!

She was clearly addicted, or she would have stopped at five or six thousand, perhaps. As she explains in the article: 'I have had all these experiences, and the feeling of exhilaration when speeding through the sky at a hundred or so mile an hour has never left me.'

Pauline thought that seeing England by air, at that time, was enough for any traveller. She much preferred 'a patchwork of fields and woods' over Kent, for example, to London's indeterminable suburbs. These, she thought, were 'one of the least pleasant experiences of one's life'. In fact, the suburbs set her off on a whole train (plane?) of thought about the nature of England and aviation progress. Pauline's writing often muses on historical context – she views the bigger picture – and how the world might look in years to come. She is aware, even in her 20s, that the pioneers of her generation will influence pilots of the future. With a poignant prophecy, she predicts:

> In twenty or thirty years' time I can picture myself being looked upon in very much the same light as one now regards the retired captain of a windjammer. I shall be invited to aeronautical dinners as a sort of curiosity. Young pilots employed in making rocket-like ascents from Hyde Park with some up-to-date contraption which can transport a hundred businessmen to Paris in half an hour will listen and laugh as I make my little speech about the 'good old days' at Stag Lane and Croydon.

Pauline has placed herself firmly in the history books, without knowing, of course, how she will be remembered. I have quoted extensively from this article, because it conveys much through her voice, a first-hand account which cannot easily be read elsewhere. Any pilots reading will appreciate how she foresaw changes to come. She continues: 'When I use such expressions as "taking off" or "flattening out", or mention that I flew an old bus whose cruising speed was 85 miles an hour, they will howl with delight. But I am sure I shall return home as convinced as ever that "those were the days".'

The remainder of that article, rich in detail and anecdote, reveals her writerly curiosity and, again, her tendency to fast-forward to future memories. Perhaps she was a fan of T.S. Eliot and his fascination, morbid or otherwise, with time passing. Pauline says: 'Association is a curious thing. There was a particular smell about those workshops; not unpleasant, but unique.'

Whenever she encountered that smell, she was instantly transported 'back at her bench at Stag Lane, with all its familiar surroundings'. This was her early, enjoyable training with an exciting career ahead, pre-war and pre-worry.

As a keen rider, Pauline may well have recalled certain horses by the unmistakable smell of leather and saddle soap, the dust of damp straw on a stable floor. A final quote from this article reflects her focus on the nature of time, progress and what lies ahead: 'If in years to come, inhabitants of the houses built on that aerodrome [Stag Lane] complain that they are being haunted by a ghostlike figure in overalls and a spanner in her hand, there is no doubt whose spirit it will be.'

The RAF Museum London holds many of Pauline's personal papers and pilot's logbooks as well as her writing archive. I was fascinated to discover nearly six chapters of an unfinished novel. All good writers should have at least one of those. Like her father, Pauline pasted all her press cuttings into bound books, with the first page name plate of 'Miss Gower' with 'Sandown Court, Tunbridge Wells' (bottom left) and '205 Ashley Gardens, Westminster, S.W.' (bottom right). There is much crossover coverage, but Pauline's archive is naturally focused on her own achievements, record-breaking activities and more. She has annotated some cuttings, in a neat flowing script, marking on which occasions she had sent details to the papers. It must have been quite an occupation, to keep track of her local and regional press coverage – she was a woman of national interest! Society photographs are in abundance, too, and many of her at ease with a smiling Dorothy Spicer, often in overalls. They were a photogenic pair, natural and unassuming.

In 1938 Pauline pasted cuttings about Dorothy's wedding to Flight Lieutenant Richard Pearse into her scrapbooks. The couple had got engaged on 2 March that year, and were married at Holy Trinity Church, Brompton, London just over a month later, on 26 April. Pauline was chief bridesmaid, along with Dorothy's cousin, Anna Spicer, at what was a lavish affair, with 300 guests at the ceremony and reception. The four-tier silver-white gown and three-tier cake with a Tiger Moth aloft were equally noteworthy in the press. Pauline would have rarely seen her friend without a spot of engine oil here and there; this was high glamour. Dorothy and Richard made a handsome couple leaving the church and enjoyed two weeks motoring on honeymoon before settling in Farnham, Surrey. A new chapter lay ahead.

5

CAREER MOVES – POLITICS, SOCIETY AND AVIATION

Tomorrow we may all be flying – today there are endless possibilities for the enterprising.

Pauline Gower

Pauline took an interest in the political world from her late teens, no doubt influenced by her father's long parliamentary career. She had accompanied him to many events, especially after her mother's death. Very much like Sir Robert, who had a 'phenomenal drive and activity', she was always busy with one engagement and committee or another, between flights and flying seasons. Perhaps after her brush with death at 17 she wanted to fill her life, to make every single day matter. A natural diplomat, Pauline's strength lay in knowing intuitively the best way to progress a project, or get an idea across, to achieve results.

She threw herself into causes, as she had pursued her interests at Beechwood; her chief and most abiding passion being the promotion of women in aviation.

Her first significant political work was with the Imperial Junior League. The 'Imps' were formed by the Conservative party in 1906 to encourage 'practical political work' among the younger generation in parliamentary divisions in the country and across the empire. The social side to the organisation was an important way of keeping members involved and entertained. Dinners, music concerts and afternoon teas were all marked in Imps' diaries.

Pauline became the president of the Imps branch in Gillingham, Kent and was delighted to see so many attend their first proper meeting in October 1929. Earlier that year, in April, she had been credited with reviving the Gillingham branch – she had 'taken the matter in hand and by reason of her bright and charming manner, coupled with her great enthusiasm, is making many friends'. Pauline rarely, if ever, made enemies. Some months later, *The Chatham, Rochester and Gillingham News* also credited her skills, if not her gender: 'The Chairman said how pleased she was at the progress the branch was making …' She also had a message from her father; Sir Robert Gower had wanted her to pass on 'how keenly interested he was in their work, and he hoped to be able to attend one of their functions shortly'. Interesting to see the father–daughter political team at work in their home county. Pauline resigned from the Imps in 1937 to make time for all her other commitments.

As the daughter of a busy and prominent MP her calendar was always full. She accompanied Sir Robert on constituency engagements and social events, in addition to opening fetes (formerly her mother's role), awarding prizes and chairing a range of meetings. They were both invited to the coronation of King George VI on 12 May 1937; Sir Robert made it into Westminster Abbey while Pauline was able to view proceedings from her allocated position on Pall Mall. Her involvement in these engagements was beneficial to her later role in the ATA, when she dealt at high level to persuade, influence and make an impact.

WOMEN'S ENGINEERING SOCIETY

Pauline joined the air section of the Women's Engineering Society (WES) in 1931 and was a long-standing active member. She gave talks to members, wrote articles for their journal *The Woman Engineer* and was a staunch advocate for women in aviation. In 1935 she was appointed a council member, and in the summer of 1937 both Pauline and Dorothy gave talks at the WES fifth annual meeting. They were also key speakers at the Junior Council of London and National Society of Women's Service – a lively debate followed the topic of 'Civil Aviation and the part women are playing'.

CIVIL AIR GUARD

In 1939 Pauline was appointed a commissioner of the Civil Air Guard, a brand-new scheme set up to subsidise the training of pilots through civilian flying clubs. It applied to anyone between the ages of 18 and 50, male or female, who had passed the 'A' licence medical. The Civil Air Guard was run by five honorary commissioners, four male and one female, F.G. Miles (wife of the aircraft designer), to represent women pilots. It was met with much enthusiasm and many applications – 34,000 in the first two weeks, of which 4,000 were enrolled. But then came mutterings of excluding women pilots, followed by proposed exclusion, to which some of the more aggrieved women raised their voices – and were heard. Lord Londonderry said that while experienced women pilots, navigators and ground engineers would not be exposed to fighting risks, in any future combat they would be found a useful role. This was progress.

C.G. Grey, renowned editor of *The Aeroplane*, took a firm stance:

We quite agree with her [Lady Bailey] that here are millions of women in the country who could do useful jobs in war. But the trouble is that so many of them insist on wanting to do jobs which they are quite incapable of doing. The menace is the woman who thinks that she ought to be flying a high-speed bomber when she really has not the intelligence to scrub the floor of a hospital properly, or who wants to nose round as an Air Raid Warden and yet can't cook her husband's dinner.

Often quoted, it is important to remember the voices and opinions of the day. Before readers – then and now – have the chance to recoil in disbelief, he balanced his argument: 'There are men like that too so there is no need to charge us with anti-feminism.'

Grey caught the mood of some who thought women had no role to play in the workforce, let alone in aviation. The headlines in early 1940 continued this theme to some extent, with a strong suggestion that the women were taking jobs from the men. This was not long after the Depression and tensions simmered below the surface. Pauline's diplomacy would smooth the way for the women's inclusion, and for their contribution to be duly recognised. One strategic step at a time, the secret of her leadership success.

Pauline continued to take on new commitments in 1938 and her diary was always full. Her energy was duly rewarded with honours and appointments. In August of that year, she was promoted to district commissioner of Girl Guides and in September she was elected a fellow of the Royal Meteorological Society. It did not stop there, for in November she was appointed by the king to the Venerable Order of St John of Jerusalem, a royal order of chivalry first constituted as such by royal charter from Queen Victoria in 1888 and since evolved to become the Order of St John. Meanwhile her regular speaking engagements in aviation circles attracted the attention of Sir Kingsley Wood, Secretary of State for Air, who invited her to sit on the Gorrell Committee. Being Pauline, she accepted and became the only woman – and the youngest person – on the committee, but took it in her stride. After flying more than 25,000 passengers by that stage, she knew 'something about aviation' and felt more than qualified for helping to make decisions on the number and safety of aircraft used for advertising banners, and noise pollution issues. They also decreed that aircraft should not fly near London Zoo to avoid distress to the inhabitants.

Of course, Pauline kept flying too, taking an instructor's course at West Malling Flying Club in Kent, which she passed in November 1938. This was a busy year and perhaps she took on too much. She caught severe pneumonia and had to spend some weeks in a nursing home. Another reminder that her lungs had been weakened from her serious school illness. This time she needed a trip to Switzerland to recover, early in the new year, but she did not really slow down much afterwards. Her old word 'sedentary' did not seem to be in her nature.

ROYAL RECOGNITION

In 1942 Pauline Gower was invited to Buckingham Palace to receive a Member of the Order of the British Empire (MBE) for her impressive work as Commander of the Women's Section of the ATA. She had been delighted when she had had the letter from Downing Street, and hugely surprised at the honour. True to her nature, she did not consider it on personal merit, but was quoted as saying afterwards, when asked why her name had been put forward: 'Search me! I take it as a recognition of the work the A.T.A. women are doing.' Sir Robert Gower would have been rightly proud of her recognition, being highly decorated himself. It would have added to the family honours.

FIRST WOMAN ON THE BOAC BOARD

May 1943 marked another significant high point when Pauline became the first woman in the UK to be appointed to the board of the British Overseas Airways Corporation (BOAC), which administrated the ATA. A new board had been formed following several resignations, with Viscount Knollys as chair, and Pauline was appointed soon after, the first woman board member of a national airline. Another significant first in her aviation career. Pauline was asleep in her caravan she used near the ATA headquarters when, unusually, the news was brought to her in the early hours of 26 May, with a hand-delivered letter from Sir Archibald Sinclair, the Minister for Air. Somehow, this fits with Pauline's slightly unconventional side, especially as the messenger on a motorcycle ended up in a bed of nettles – a story surely reminiscent of her air circus days.

Pauline took her job as BOAC director seriously and put in many hours at the London offices alongside her leadership of the ATA women's section. She undertook every role with energy and dedication, but the dual responsibilities at this time took their toll on her health.

6

LEADING WITH IMPACT – AIR TRANSPORT AUXILIARY

The Air Transport Auxiliary (ATA) – otherwise known as 'Ancient and Tattered Airmen', 'Always Terrified Airwomen' or 'Anything to Anywhere', depending on the point of view or the mood of the moment – was a civilian organisation founded at the outbreak of the Second World War to ferry planes between factories, maintenance units and frontline squadrons. It was vital to the success of the RAF, even more so as the war progressed. There were 1,245 ATA aircrew, including 164 women pilots and four female engineers, who came from more than 25 countries for the chance to 'do their bit'. ATA pilots had no instruments or radios and were at the mercy of enemy aircraft and the ever-changing British weather. The chief danger. One in ten lost their lives. By the end of the war, ATA pilots had ferried 309,000 aircraft.

The ATA was the brainchild of Gerard 'Pop' d'Erlanger, director of British Airways. In 1938 he foresaw that, with commercial planes likely to be grounded, there would be a surplus of pilots with 'A' licences, with plenty of flying hours under their belt and nothing to fly. He knew that they would not all be eligible to join the RAF in the event of war, either due to age restrictions or physical limitations. Yet their skills could form a vital and reliable support network. D'Erlanger approached two key decision makers: Harold Balfour, the parliamentary under secretary for

Air, and Sir Francis Shelmerdine, the director general of Civil Aviation. He proposed gathering a pool of experienced pilots, each with at least 250 flying hours, who could support their country by transporting mail, medical supplies and officers, and work as an air ambulance if needed. It was a logical and entirely feasible idea for which he was given the go ahead, and the task of organising the whole thing.

Pauline Gower was the driving force behind the women's section, which she was asked to set up in September 1939. The First Eight, as they became known in the avid national press, were recruited on New Year's Day 1940, initially to fly training aircraft such as Tiger Moths, but in July 1941 women were cleared to fly operational aircraft – all fighter types including Spitfires and Hurricanes, and twin engines such as Mosquitoes and Wellingtons. In hindsight, that sounds like a simple route from A to B. But it needed Pauline's determined leadership, extensive flying hours and experience, and her grit and determination to make the journey for her women pilots a successful one.

Women pilots were initially based at Hatfield in Hertfordshire, with an all-women's ferry pool later established at Hamble near Southampton. Here the main objective at first was to clear the aircraft from the nearby de Havilland factory, although Hamble also delivered planes for the Fleet Air Arm to Worthy Down, Gosport and Lee on Solent in Hampshire. Later pilots were posted to Cosford, White Waltham and other ferry pools as needed.

Thanks to Pauline's leadership and diplomacy, in 1943 women achieved equal pay as men of the same rank for equal work. This was another significant landmark, making the ATA one of the first equal opportunity employers; not something widely known or remembered. Four of the First Eight received MBEs, as did Pauline, and two women were awarded certificates of commendation.

Pauline's leadership role in the ATA was testament to her strength of character and influence; women's lives rested on her decisions, as did the safety of valuable RAF planes that had to be moved from A to B, quickly and efficiently. She had to recruit the best, train those with potential and keep them all flying safely and the planes intact.

In June 1938 Sir Francis Shelmerdine wrote to Air Commodore the Honorable W.L. Runciman, managing director elect of the new British Overseas Airways Corporation (BOAC) and by July, Runciman replied to the air commodore that d'Erlanger seemed the best man for the job, and they should proceed. Any snags would be ironed out beforehand.

Gerald d'Erlanger was given access to the list of people with 'A' licences and set to work selecting suitable candidates. By 1 September 1939 thirty applications had been received, 'mostly of good quality' and Runciman suggested that they were flight tested in Bristol. Those appointed to what was soon to become the ATA were to be paid at the rate of junior officers in British Airways at the time – about £350–400 per annum. Note this salary was for the male pilots; the women who were eventually allowed to join were initially paid 20 per cent less. Once established, with No. 1 Ferry Pilot's Pool (RAF) at Hucknall near Derby and No. 2 Ferry Pool at Filton near Bristol, by August 1940 the ATA was put under the operational control of the director of equipment at the Air Ministry, Air Vice-Marshal A.G.R. Garrod.

At first the mixed pools worked, but tensions arose between civilian and military personnel and so discussions and negotiations continued at top level. By December it was decided to split the two and d'Erlanger secured White Waltham in Berkshire as the first civilian ferry pilots' pool.

As war drew closer, Pauline knew that experienced women pilots could greatly help the war effort and free up men to fly. She had long championed the important role of women in aviation, through articles and in public talks, and stressed that women had a key part to play and should be taken seriously. At first the idea of women joining the ATA was turned down. Obstacles cited included finding appropriate accommodation, and securing transport and petrol for their cars. There was also the question, yet to be proven, of whether the fairer sex was actually capable of flying all types of aircraft …

On 21 September 1939, Pauline had proposed, at an interview with the director general of Civil Aviation, with d'Erlanger present, the formation of a women's section of the ATA. The conclusion from that meeting was that it would depend on demand, but that d'Erlanger could look at recruiting twelve pilots if he could find that many with the necessary qualifications. It was also decided that the women's section should quite rightly have a woman in charge and Pauline was selected for the job. Her extensive flying experience, her 'A' and 'B' licences and her 'time in the hard school of joy-riding' made her a suitable candidate. But, of equal importance perhaps, she had not intentionally courted fame – 'She has never been a stunt pilot with all the publicity which is attached to that role.'

It did not go to plan immediately as senior members of the Air Ministry were in opposition to women being attached to the RAF ferry pools. Pauline, ever persistent, chased up the response to her September meeting and received a letter in return from Francis Claude Shelmerdine, director general of Civil Aviation, apologising for the delay. Central Flying School was not equipped to train women, as had been previously mentioned in their discussions, and the RAF had dug in their heels when it came to employing women. Shelmerdine recommended that the experienced pilots Pauline had in mind took other war work while they all waited for the inevitable, that the 'so-called war develops into a real war'. By November, it was clear that 'real war' was likely and that the ATA's role would become a real and permanent one. It was decided to form a small pool of women to ferry Tiger Moths – the cheaper training planes that they could not 'break'. And, perhaps, the job that 'the RAF was all too willing to off-load'. Pauline had broken down defences, aided by a turn of events. It was a start.

The initial terms on offer were not music to Pauline's ears, although she was most likely playing the long game. She could appoint only eight pilots, not the twelve that she had at first requested. More might be required later, at a pool at Reading (and they were, by April 1940), so at least there was scope to expand. The Treasury, likely run and staffed by men at that time, she was told, would insist on a percentage reduction for women pilots despite them being employed to do the same job. Eventually, this was agreed at the sum of £230 per annum with an additional £8 per month flying pay – 20 per cent, or £80 per annum, less than the men. And while the male pilots had some financial assistance for accommodation, the women would have to pay for their billets out of their own salaries. Equality was still some way off.

A NATURAL LEADER

Many of her peers thought that Pauline was the best person for the job. Mary Ellis described her as a 'genuine pioneer and the very highest of achievers' – she was serious and committed, with a high level of planning and organisational skills.

Writing to Michael Fahie in 1992, it was clear to Monique Agazarian, who joined the ATA in 1943, that Pauline was the obvious choice to lead the women. Together with Margot Gore, commanding officer of Hamble Ferry Pool, they thought that: 'nobody except Pauline would have been in a position to or would have had the right contacts in her own circle which included cabinet ministers etc., and most important she had the charm and firmness to carry through her resolve!'

It was that same spirit of adventure that led her to climb all the trees at Beechwood, the same drive that, at 21 and in receipt of her first plane, led her into business with Dorothy. If she had a mission, she would follow it single-mindedly. The ATA was her biggest mission. As Pauline said in a BBC interview: 'We are a small group of women pilots with a job to do. We are just helping, along with others, to win the war. Our job will be unobtrusive. But it is going to be well and efficiently done.'

The women selected had 200 or more flying hours and a strong desire to keep flying for the war effort. They were tested by a BOAC instructor, McMillan, who later became the ATA's chief flying instructor. Then they had to wait, minus their logbooks, for Pauline's decision. Once all eight were tested and accepted, as Rosemary Rees recalled, 'then the storm of publicity burst and quite a bit of fury'.

THE FIRST EIGHT – MAKING THE HEADLINES

The pilots of the RAF's most exclusive squadron reported for duty yesterday. They are eight girls … dressed in neat navy suits, with golden-braid wings on breast pockets, forage caps and fur-lined boots, these girl pilots took their seats in the cockpits of four RAF trainer planes and showed the men a thing or two about flying.

Daily Mirror, 11 January 1940

All eyes were upon them at first, many critical. The press had a field day – *women*, in *planes*? Pauline Gower was the first woman to be allowed inside an RAF plane, let alone fly one. The press photographers went to take photos of the First Eight, as they were quickly called, on a sunny 15 January, posing in their heavy Sidcot suits – only worn that first bitter winter of 1940 – and asked them to scramble from a Tiger Moth for a photograph. *Run*, in that heavy gear? The photographer did not catch them properly the first time, so they had to repeat the whole process, smiling at this stage despite the weight of the parachutes slung over their shoulders and their 'creaking flying suits and new stiff fur-lined boots'. It was a press sensation for many reasons. Only Pauline was allowed to talk to reporters. The women had been briefed upon joining not to take part in any press discussions; national safety and security seen to be operating at all levels.

Headlines ranged from 'ACE Women Pilots' to '8 Girls "Show" R.A.F.', which continued: 'The pilots of the R.A.F.'s more exclusive squadron reported for duty yesterday. They are eight girls. No orders were shouted to them as they went to their machines. Their leader addressed them as "Miss This" or "Miss That" and added "please" to her requests.'

Pauline knew that politeness went a long way and was clearly seen as a leader from the start. The *Daily Mirror* played close attention to what they were wearing, naturally, and said that once in the RAF planes they 'showed the men a thing or two about flying' – whipping up that mood of apparent non-sexism from C.G. Grey: 'They are four wives who have husbands in the Forces', continued the *Mirror*, 'and four bachelor girls who prefer flying to boyfriends. Most of them have owned planes of their own, and most of them still have cars.'

Class, family background and marital status all summed up in two short sentences. Other reports over the next few weeks would bring them more to life. They had a huge amount of aviation experience between them. They also had 'an appalling burden of responsibility' on their shoulders – this was an experiment that had to work.

Those First Eight were as follows:

Winifred Crossley

A stunt pilot before the war with C.W.A. Scott's 'Flying for All' Aerial Circus, Winifred (Winnie) Crossley had also spent five years towing banners for aerial advertising as the only woman pilot for Air Publicity Ltd, Heston. One such banner, flown over Whitehall in 1937, read 'Give All Civil Servants Pensions'. Winnie and her twin sister Daphne were both aerobatic experts and owned a DH Gipsy Moth I. Serving in the ATA from 1 January 1940 to 30 November 1945, Winnie rose to flight captain and was the first woman to fly a Hurricane, on 19 July 1941, from Hatfield.

Margaret Cunnison

Born in Haddington, East Lothian in 1914, Margaret Cunnison (m.Ebbage) was the first Scottish female flying instructor. In 1933 she entered a competition in the *Evening News* and won lessons with the Scottish Flying Club. She gained her 'A' licence in Scotland and her 'B' licence in Kent. Margaret gave joy-rides to holiday makers in Ettrick Bay and worked as a flying instructor at the Strathtay Aero Club in Perth. She became the leading instructor at Hatfield and later signed off the American women ATA pilots at No. 5 Ferry Pool near Luton. As an instructor she mostly few light aircraft.

Margaret Fairweather

Daughter of Lord Runciman, Margaret (Margie) Fairweather was a hugely experienced pilot by the time she joined the ATA with more than 1,000 hours. Born on 23 September 1901, near Newcastle upon Tyne, she bought her first plane in 1937 and was an instructor in the Civil Air Guard at Renfrew. She married ATA pilot Douglas Fairweather and was the first woman to fly a Supermarine Spitfire. Tragically both she and her husband were killed in 1944; Margie while landing a Percival Proctor on which her sister Kitty was also on board. They were survived by their baby daughter, Elizabeth.

Mona Friedlander
Ice hockey international star turned pilot, Mona Renee Vera Ernesta Friedlander took up flying as a cure for boredom, as she told the press, and in three years earned her private, commercial and navigator's licences. Her parents funded only the first so she found a job towing advertising banners before offering her services to anti-aircraft units, flying at night so they could practise target range and direction. A far cry from her education at London's Royal School of Arts. Mona flew thirty-two different types for the ATA, including twenty hours on Wellingtons. She was known to be accident prone, although exonerated on all accounts.

Joan Hughes
Joan Lily Amelia Hughes MBE was born on 27 April 1918 and flew for almost fifty years. She obtained her licence by 17 and was the youngest of the First Eight at 21, with 600 hours. In March 1943 Joan completed a Stirling bomber conversion course and became the only ATA pilot to instruct on all classes of aircraft. She had many suitors but stayed single and dedicated herself to flying, instructing thousands of pilots and later starring in films – she doubled as Lady Penelope for a *Thunderbirds* film, flying under a motorway bridge and ending up in court on seven separate charges.

Gabrielle Patterson
Educated in Paris, Berlin and Vienna, as her family moved around Europe, Gabrielle Ruth Millicent Patterson gained her pilot's

'A' licence in 1931 and competed at Reading alongside Amy Johnson, Pauline Gower and Dorothy Spicer. She became the first woman to gain an instructor's licence and was married with a son by the time she joined the ATA. As leader of the National Women's Air Reserve, she taught Margot Gore to fly. She continued instructing after the war as commandant of the Women's Junior Air Corps. Gabrielle died in 1968 and her ashes were scattered over White Waltham.

Rosemary Rees
Born on 23 September 1901, Rosemary was already a skilled pilot when she joined the ATA. She had gone solo in seven hours and purchased a Miles Hawk Major. As a girl she learnt French and German from her governess, took dancing lessons in Chelsea but never went to school. She was deputy to Margot Gore at Hamble and was annoyed that the women were initially paid £8 less than the men. Post-war she bought a Percival Proctor and launched a charter service. Rosemary was awarded an MBE in 1945 and five years later married Sir Philip du Cros and settled in Devon.

Marion Wilberforce
One of seven, Marion's father was John Ogilvie-Forbes, 9th Laird of Boyndlie, Aberdeenshire. She obtained a degree in agriculture in 1922 from Somerville College, Oxford. In 1932 she married Robin Wilberforce who spent six months in a monastery first deciding between a life of god or marriage; Marion was waiting at the gates when he came out. She served for five years in the ATA, as deputy commander of No. 5 Ferry Pool at Hatfield and commander of No. 12 Ferry Pool Cosford, and in 1944 trained on four-engined bombers. Marion gave up flying, reluctantly, at 80 when she sold her second Hornet Moth.

★★★

In the early weeks of 1940, during the phoney stage of the war, the women were under intense scrutiny from both press and public. They had to prove their worth with each flight and deliver each plane in one piece. If they were nervous in the early days, Pauline did not show any qualms. She was fine, said Rosemary Rees, 'she tackled the big powers' and when faced with those who said women could not fly 'fast, complicated, heavy, fighting aircraft' because they were not 'built or conditioned for it' Pauline simply shrugged and replied, 'Of course they can, just try them and see.' She'd spent the last few years proving that women could make a living in a male-dominated environment and encouraging women to learn to fly. She was not going to let prejudice get in the way now.

The First Eight were initially nicknamed the 'Attagirls', which didn't exactly please Pauline. She always referred to the pilots in her command as women. 'Women in this service are treated exactly like the men. That is one of the things for which I have fought.' She was justly proud of the pilots in her charge, later saying: 'Every day they handle tens of thousands of pounds' worth of Lancasters, Hurricanes, Mosquitoes, Blenheims, Spitfires, and all the rest of our aircraft.'

Statistically, the women had fewer accidents than the men; there was more pressure on them to deliver the expensive planes intact. Even if at times their nerves were shot, or they were exhausted from the endless ferrying and travel between airfields, or they had to sometimes carry hot water bottles to ward off period pains (not widely reported), they had to keep going. There was an extra weight on their shoulders, especially at first when they had so much to prove. The First Eight bore the brunt, but their collective expertise led the way for more women to be able to join the ATA, just at the time when they were needed most. After a few months, another five women were recruited after successful flight tests – Margot Gore, Philippa Bennett, Lettice Curtis, Audrey Sale-Barker and Lois Butler. They had fewer flying hours on arrival but were quickly initiated to the team of early pilots ferrying Tiger Moths and other light aircraft.

When Michael Fahie researched his mother's life in the early 1990s, Commodore Diana Barnato Walker MBE, at that time president of the ATA Association, sent him contact details of some of the women who had known Pauline very well: 'These were five of the very first eight women pilots recruited. Due entirely to your mother's persuasion in the right quarters.'

Pauline selected her women on the grounds of number of flying hours and experience and then proceeded with recruitment.

Letters of appointment from Senior Commander Pauline Gower were sent out on 11 November 1939, in which she laid out the following qualifications needed:

1). Women age 22–45
2). Minimum of flying hours – 250
3). Candidates should be the holders and of A and B licences.
4). Candidates will be required to pass practical flying and although 'A' Licence medical standard should, in most cases, suffice, in certain instances a further examination may be required.

Admission was to be on a competitive basis and those accepted would serve as second officer and receive a uniform. Their contract at that stage would be with British Airways. Pilots admitted would be required to 'fly light aircraft on general communication duties' which clearly changed during the first year of the war. Pauline signed herself as 'Officer in charge Women's Section A.T.A.' and added an interesting postscript – 'Under no circumstances whatsoever are communications or interviews to be given to the Press without previous authority of the Company.'

NO. 5 FERRY POOL HATFIELD

These first eight women were billeted around the Hatfield Aerodrome and were based in a small wooden hut on the airfield. It was a notoriously freezing winter, and they were flying open-cockpit training aircraft, mostly up to Scotland. Long arduous trips, which could take several days in bad weather, interspersed with short delivery trips to Lyneham in Wiltshire or Kemble in the Cotswolds. They would only know on the day where they were going and initially Pauline took details over the phone, before a more established system was in place. They had fur-lined Irvin jackets and leather flying boots, and they certainly needed them that winter! Yet every plane was delivered safely.

In her autobiography *Happy to Fly*, Ann Welch clearly recalled her first day in the ATA:

> I reported to No. 5 ATA Ferry Pool at Hatfield on a cold 11 November 1940 to find the aerodrome and buildings dulled with camouflage and netting. After a brief, apprehensive interview with the famous Pauline Gower, Commandant of the unit, I was handed over to Margaret Cunnison for a flight test on a Tiger Moth.

She goes on to describe the early days, the freezing open-cockpit flights, the hazards of following another pilot on her first few long trips. And the potential dangers wrought by weather, always waiting in the wings.

Rosemary Rees felt the cold to an extreme and would layer on her coats and scarves to fend off chills. Before the war she had even made a 'coat' for her plane, but that was more to fend off pigeon droppings in the hangar. But on those endless trips up to Lossiemouth or Cumbria, especially that long, hard winter, she was often so cold she had to be helped stiff and freezing from the plane. She would send someone else to drop off her chit, or delivery papers, but after a while the duty officer demanded to see 'that fellow Rees' in person, so she had to take off one of her layers in order to climb down from the cockpit, thus revealing her gender. Tea was the eternal saviour, there for comfort, but mostly a welcome means to defrost your hands. That and the electric fire that was usually turned on in the worst of the winter weather, just as the taxi Anson arrived with a group of frozen pilots. It was always a team effort.

EQUAL PAY FOR EQUAL WORK

Pauline Gower has been much credited with achieving equal pay for her women pilots for equal work, a first in England at that time and a clear reminder of her tenacity. As mentioned, her pilots started off earning 20 per cent less than men, something that was not always mentioned in the press when they were complaining that the women were taking the jobs from men (instead of praising them for delivering planes to the men). The women were taking equal risks and ferrying the same amount and types of planes. Pauline pushed the right people at just the right time, as was her way. Naomi Heron-Maxwell detailed in her diary:

> Thursday, 22 April 1943. Two men from the Treasury came down to see whether we should have the same pay as the men instead of 20% less as we have now. Apparently they don't believe we do more than two thirds of the amount of work the men pilots do. Idiots! They only have to look at the statistics to see that we do exactly the same work as the men, neither more or less, in other words just what we are given to do.

They must have had to go away to reconsider, for it did not happen overnight: 'Monday, 24 May 1943. Saw in the papers that as from the 1st of next month women pilots are to get the same pay as the men. Hurray!'

Jackie Moggridge's daughter, Candida Adkins, told me: 'Pauline campaigned hard for equal pay, it wasn't just an easy conversation here or there. She was a born politician.' Joy Lofthouse said that their 'big wheel' got them equal pay, she wasn't sure if she insisted on it, but it happened.

In fact, Pauline used all her contacts, including those at cabinet level, to achieve equality. The process was not without its challenges, as Mary de Bunsen acknowledged – after all women had only just been allowed to fly RAF planes at the start of 1940, this was another huge stride forwards. One that Pauline had long campaigned for. Mary said:

> We fought our own battles in the field, but Pauline Gower fought them unremittingly at headquarters and – like most people in high places – got very little thanks for it. We owed a great deal to her diplomacy and sense of timing, for she had to know how and when to fight or to give ground.

Equal pay remains an issue in many industries and women still strive for workplace equality. It was a triumph for Pauline to achieve it when she did, but it was right that male and female ferry pilots were paid the same. They carried out the same duties, took the same risks, flew in the face of dangerous weather without radio, but with equal amounts of courage and dedication. And the women had much more to prove from the very beginning.

FERRY PILOTS NOTES

To back up their training, or in case pilots needed essential details of some of the many types they might encounter in any one day of ferrying, they were issued with dark blue guides containing handling notes for each plane. These ring-bound ferry pilots notes were invaluable and just the right size to fit into flying jacket pockets or tuck into the top of boots. It was a treasonable offence to lose them, as they would give away valuable information. There are several accounts of pilots using them to confirm take-off speeds and airspeed indicators, and then mugging up on how to land – while still circling!

Ann Welch, an extremely careful pilot, did just that. She was just back from leave and found herself at White Waltham. Needing to get back to Hamble before the sun went down, she was offered a Blackburn B-25 Roc to fly herself back. Not having encountered that type before, she sat in the cockpit reading the notes, finding out how to take off. Once safely in the air, she read up on how to land and 'never had a moment's worry nor a moment's wonder as to how something worked – it was all THERE.' It's hard to imagine flying a new plane, as dusk was falling, while reading a small ring-bound notebook (with a small font) on how to do something so vital for both plane and pilot. Ann made a safe landing, and all was well.

RANKS AND CLASSES

ATA ranks ranged from cadet to commodore: 1st officer, 2nd officer, 3rd officer, flight captain, captain, commander, senior commander and commodore. Gold stripes denoted rank and were worn on different background colours to differentiate areas of activity. Hence flying staff wore dark blue; engineering, technical and maintenance wore purple; medical were red; operations wore white and administrative were green. Although civilian at the outset, the ATA very much followed military lines of organisation to keep it regulated and suitably recognised.

The ATA had six different classes for wartime aircraft: class 1 light single-engined; class 2 advanced single-engined; class 3 light twin-engined; class 4 advanced twin-engined; class 5 four-engined; class 6 flying boats.

Thanks to Pauline's influence, the women were approved, in stages throughout the war, to fly all types except flying boats. It was thought overnight travel with men onboard would be imprudent, although in many cases the early ferry pools had no facilities for women and they had to cover for each other using the men's toilets, or find alternative, outdoor solutions. As this was wartime, they got by.

MADE TO MEASURE

Although it was a civilian organisation, uniform was worn to provide ease of recognition and was based on the RAF design and pattern. It was dark blue, with gold badges and the ATA allowed pilots to use a military tailor to make them to measure. Some of the early women pilots, with money behind them, had gone to Savile Row for theirs and sported the occasional red or green satin lining, as a gesture of style, or individuality. If it did not show, it could not be frowned upon. By 1941, more pilots were using the ATA-designated tailor, if with some rather unusual fitting sessions. Being only used to measuring men and finding that, for example, First Officer Gore and First Officer Bennett were in fact women, they had a unique approach when it came to measuring chest sizes. Two elderly tailors at that time, Mr Pert and Mr Hix, were fine when it came to recording length of sleeve, but when it came to bust, rather more rounded than they were used to, Mr Pert would throw the tape measure around a female back, catch it in mid-air and then hurriedly make a note of the number of inches, which was dutifully whispered into his colleague's ear. Of course, trousers were also needed, which called for a change of position. Mr Hix was designated to take over the tape measure and he was fine until it came to estimating from crutch to ankle, which he did with, one can imagine, a rather red face. Probably equally red on receiving a sharp note, after delivery, from the two women. The trousers were 4in too long and were returned with chalked instructions and a reprimand.

Being accepted by the ATA, after flight tests, and passing enough training to earn the uniform fitting was a mark of achievement. It was a proud moment of recognition.

3pm Appointment at Austin Reed

The devil was in the detail, every little detail.
I scanned myself in the mirror, head to toe,
automatically straightened my blue jacket,
smoothed down my already smooth hair,
checked my wings were firmly in place.

I sensed so many people watching me
behind the polished mirror, watching

and waiting for me to fall, to crash land
or just to give up and go home, raise a family.
I drew myself up to my full 5'2" – no way!

We were made to measure at Austin Reed,
tailored to aviation perfection. It was truly
our made-it moment; we'd proved ourselves
in flying hours and cross-country sorties,
we were ready to conquer the skies!

Alison Hill, *Sisters in Spitfires*

One of the most illuminating and well-drawn accounts of ATA life, flights and characters was written in 1956 by Operations Officer Alison King. Dedicated to 'Those Friends Lost in A.T.A.', her book *Golden Wings* has the sub-title 'The Story of Some of the Women Ferry Pilots of the Air Transport Auxiliary' and is a fine testimonial to her colleagues' bravery, dedication of service and breadth of personality. King sets out first how the ATA was formed and declares with enthusiasm: 'ATA was the glorious experiment that came off.' Finding the pilots, training them to fly without wireless in all kinds of weather, 'converting' them onto all the new types in stages – it was a huge achievement of leadership and organisation. She reminds us that:

> at the peak a pilot could and did fly any one of well over 100-odd types in any one day – perhaps four in one day, from a four-engined bomber to a new type of fast jet, and then a pre-war light aircraft with a third the approach speed of the jet flown but an hour before.

By the end of the war, around 309,000 aircraft, from bombers to fighters, from training planes and flying boats, had been delivered by the ATA ferry pilots.

The huge range of aircraft flown is what amazes modern-day pilots. That men and women in the ATA coped with the sheer number of different types and variety each day. They were trained exceptionally well, and a high level of efficient organisation lay behind the operational success, but the ultimate responsibility lay with the pilots, to keep climbing into the cockpits and delivering the planes. Each day, every day, throughout the war. They might have been playing bridge five minutes before the weather cleared (which was taken seriously by those who played and those passing by who stopped to weigh up who was winning), or having endless cups of tea in the mess, but they switched to pilot mode as soon as they reached their planes. Focus on the detail, calm and professional; there was a job to be done.

Alison King has a natural talent for conjuring personalities with her crisp prose. She wanted to write about the women – 'good or bad, right or wrong', she felt the need to explain – as she worked closely with many of them and knew them so well. She knew it would be an important first-hand account, and from the ground.

Like many others, Alison held Pauline in high regard: 'Pauline herself, as head, was a person of great force, clear thinking and by all standards most efficient and knowledgeable. She had the ability to suddenly become warmly human, able to joke with anyone immediately after she had told them to do better or else.'

So that was the secret of her success! Her photos did not deceive, Pauline was a strength to be reckoned with, but one to rely on. As all her women pilots did. Alison King recognised too that such leadership is tough. 'At times too she would come down from her inevitably lonely position to find someone to be companionable with, to talk things over with, to tell a few jokes to and listen to theirs.'

Mary Ellis had been in awe of the 'big white chief', as she described her, recognising her aviation success of the 1930s, and the records that she had broken by the time she reached the ATA. At her interview, she had been nervous and expected a certain level of formality. She soon realised that Pauline was 'most pleasant with a wonderful sense of humour'. Mary was delighted, if a little daunted, to be accepted on the spot. Pauline had clearly seen her potential and revealed her own winning personality in the process.

Pauline's natural humour, evident in her lively accounts in *Women with Wings*, did not desert her in this vital wartime role. Humour, light or dark, kept people united in the face of danger, loss, tragedy. Part of the wartime spirit, but part of Pauline's nature as friend, daughter, sister, commanding officer. Humour was a vital ingredient in wartime endurance.

THE LIFE OF AN ATA PILOT

No day was ever the same, although they tended to run along the same lines. Arrive at your ferry pool at 9 a.m., collect your first set of chits, usually laid out on a table earlier that morning by the operations officer. Or a hatch would open and there would be the papers. All planes scheduled from HQ White Waltham the night before, all deliveries logged on the blackboard in the ops room. Efficiency grew as the war progressed and the ATA swelled in numbers; there were taxi planes – usually Ansons – where before there had been overnight trips, travelling back on cold dark trains. A seat if you were lucky, a parachute in the aisle if not, or (it had been known) a quick nap in the luggage rack, space allowing.

Your first flight of the day might well be a plane you had not flown before. Often the excitement mounted as pilots looked for a Spitfire on their chit – the plane of desire for many. You collected your ferry pilots notes with all the details you might need for that type of plane – take-off and landing speeds, stalling issues, engine details and much more. All neatly typed, all the detail there, but compact! Much was left to the pilots' own ingenuity and skill up in the air; you just had to keep a cool head. And there was no one else up there with you to lean on or ask for advice – it was completely up to the pilot to make a successful delivery, a safe landing. Many of the planes had just left the factory; the ATA men and women were pretty much test pilots. And all eyes were on them to land those planes safely – they were expensive and vital to the war effort. This initial intense pressure was there in the press coverage but had to be ignored once airborne. You just had to get on with the job in hand, and the flying enjoyment – experienced by so many of the women – was a bonus.

Once you had collected your notes and an area map if available, tucked into your flying boots, and checked the weather with the Met, you would sling a parachute over your shoulder (they were heavy!) and prepare yourself for the first flight of the day. (No proper practise in using the parachutes, of course, but they made good cushions and were reassuring in weight and presence.) It might be a short hop in a Tiger Moth, the early training aircraft, to a nearby airfield, or a longer flight to deliver a Mosquito, a Hurricane, or the prize chit, a Spitfire. These planes were only possible for the women to fly once Pauline had paved the way in her diplomatic yet firm way, and they were allowed to climb up into twin engines, and on into four engine bombers, once they had passed the necessary training.

You would more than likely get a lift to where you needed to collect your first plane, settling into the companionable Taxi Anson flown by a fellow pilot. It was often full of women knitting, unbeknown to anyone looking up and seeing it fly overhead! Such were the odd, small details of a world at war. You would take delivery of your plane, often the first of several ferried each day, every day, and fly it to wherever it was needed. Once safely landed, you would let the actual details seep out of your head. Apart from your logbook, you did not need to retain too much information; that way lay danger. Everyone knew that 'careless talk costs lives'.

Back to your ferry pool for your next chit, or a quick cup of tea from the mess if time allowed. If there was a longer wait, or the weather turned, you could join the girls in the rest room, take time to read the newspaper, cut out a dress pattern if you had sewing in mind, or take out some knitting. Therapeutic at the best of times, and practical, it also took your mind off the loss of friends or family, or thoughts of danger ahead. There was often a game of bridge set up, and always someone to chat to and swap news of the latest new plane. You were in this together. This was often the lull before the next flight, whatever that might have in store. If you were lucky, and flew as carefully as you had been taught, even more carefully because you were a woman and had so much more to prove, you would land safely at the correct destination (and if you did not, then quickly find your way to the correct airfield and be on your way; with no radio, it was possible to do so without too many becoming aware of the 'diversion'), deliver your chit and wait for next flight. But the weather, as sunny as it might look through the mess window, could change at any time just as it could up in the air. You had to be on constant guard, watch for the clouds lowering, the skyline disappearing, the patch of light ahead.

Hush

Those silent moments,
  Before the rain,
    Scanning the skies

Hoping for a gap
  In the clouds, know
    It's closing in.

Rare moments flying above,
  Illicitly, gaily, not knowing
    If you'll find that gap

But hoping, praying
  You'll arrive long before
    The storm breaks.

Alison Hill, *Sisters in Spitfires*

On 'washout days', which were frequent during those long wartime winters, the pilots had to sit around in the mess waiting for the weather to clear but be prepared to fly at any moment. They would set up a game of bridge, read or sew; resourceful, as ever, in using their time productively, even if it called for several cups of tea to punctuate the washout hours.

Ann Welch joined the ATA in November 1940, after a short and successful interview with 'the famous Pauline Gower' and was based at No. 5 Ferry Pool Hatfield. She described the day-to-day pilot's life in detail, and emphasised the role played by the weather:

> Next morning three of us from Brooklands sat on the tables in the watch office swinging our legs, talking, and waiting for the rain to stop. During the afternoon a few more aeroplanes came in from the sunnier south. Winnie Crossley and Lois Butler landed from Hatfield in a Dominie to collect Hurricanes for squadrons in Kent, and gave me the latest gossip, then soon afterwards the daily batch of new Hurricanes arrived, and by four o'clock there were fourteen of us waiting for the weather further north to clear. We drank more tea. Then, quite suddenly the first gleam of clearing skies appeared out to sea on the western horizon. Immediately there was frantic activity, with everyone wanting their machine started first.

It was a job of fits and starts around the all-important weather, often the greatest danger to all pilots. And when they were airborne, it was a feat of keeping their eye on the changing nature of the skies to predict, if possible, if it was safe to make the trip, or to keep flying if the weather took a turn for the worse. Much was left to the discretion of the pilots once they had taken off, much more was unknown – the weather was an ever-present threat to their safety.

LIVING FOR THE MOMENT

Wartime was grey, bleak and full of cruel, everyday tragedy that became a way of life. Rationing, shortages, hunger. Blackouts and air raids. Huge loss of life. Nothing was the same as before. There was no knowing if tomorrow would come around, or if you would see friends or family again. You lived for the moment, seized any fun that came your way. Wartime jobs were no different and the ATA pilots took their dances and nights out when they could, despite the long flying days. Or perhaps because of the long flying days.

The press highlighted the glamour of 'the flying girls' and some of the women gave them plenty of stories. Reading many of their accounts of life in the ATA, it was clear that there were opportunities to enjoy a dance or a meal whenever they could afford the petrol coupons, perhaps pooling resources to do so. It was a chance to meet men, to dress up, to dance and dream. They were young – life had to be found, romance too!

Society girl Diana Barnato Walker would often dash up to London for a night out at a club before getting the early morning train back, a quick change and a day's flying ahead. Taxi-driver brothers Bert and Ozzie Jenkins would look out for her at Hyde Park Corner and get her to Waterloo station in time for the 4.20 a.m. train to Eastleigh. Diana would walk or drive back to her digs in Hamble as it was getting light, dreaming of the encounters of the night gone by, the fun and laughter that would help her through another few flights. The brothers never let her down and Bert would greet her with 'Good morning my little butterfly!' Diana might or might not have time for breakfast before the next day's flying and recognised the stamina of her age at the time. She wrote in her memoir, 'I pine for my youthful energy.'

The blackout added a sombre air to London nightlife. Cars had metal hoods on their headlamps which only allowed a slit of light through and there was no street lighting. You had to know your way around and pick your way carefully. Diana always changed into a long evening gown for her London leave days. She would be taken out to dinner and would invariably end up at the Orchid Room or the '400' Club – 'I spent so much time in smoky nightclubs that it is a wonder it did not shorten my life. I never thought flying would.'

Molly Rose OBE first met her husband at a dinner at the Master's Lodge, St Catharine's College, Cambridge. She had been invited along with two other girls and twenty-three male undergraduates. Bernard Rose, up for his fourth year with a Bachelor of Arts in Music, and studying a MusB, was clearly smitten. They met again shortly afterwards, in November 1938, at a dance arranged at the same lodge. Bernard knew he would arrive late from conducting a university orchestra and had left her, purposefully, in the safe hands of a friend. Molly was unaware of this and thought the stand-in, Harry McQuade, very good looking, and they danced well together. But then Bernard had arrived in his dinner jacket, and they had danced and talked all night. He made her feel special somehow, she recalled. Bernard also climbed a lamppost with aplomb afterwards, once he discovered he had locked himself out of St Catharine's. After a year's courtship and a telephone proposal, which did not really come as a surprise to Molly, they were married on 23 December 1939 at Hove Parish Church. When I spoke to Molly in 2015, she told me that everyone loved music at the time, particularly Glenn Miller's 'In the Mood'. It was a song that took her straight back to those wartime years.

Spitfire Dance

Halfway between runway and romance,
mind trained firmly on the here and now,
that patch of sky ahead.
In limbo waiting to take off, sometimes dying
to land, it was a feat of balance, keeping
a weather eye on social ops.
He'd asked his dark-haired friend to look out
for her, dance after dance, claiming her
when he came off duty.

She'd approached the floor with caution,
wondering if this particular flight signalled
the start of the rest of her life.

Alison Hill, *Sisters in Spitfires*

Molly and Bernard Rose were married for fifty-six years. Her flying years had been important to her, and vividly recalled, but she immediately left the ATA once Bernard came back from Oflag 79 at Brunswick in Germany, where he had been held prisoner after being ambushed at Villers-Bocage in June 1944. It was time for a new chapter. Bernard returned to music, firstly as a music teacher, organist and choir master at Queen's College, Oxford. In 1957 he moved to Magdalen College in Oxford – as a teacher in music and organist and master of the choristers. Bernard remained at Magdalen until his retirement and Molly joined Bernard on tours with the choir all over Europe and America. They had three sons, and first lived in Bampton, Oxfordshire, then Appleton Manor to be nearer Oxford after Bernard had a major road accident, before returning to Bampton. Molly became a magistrate in 1957 and served her local community for thirty-five years. In 1983 she was appointed a deputy lieutenant for Oxfordshire and in 1989 received an OBE for her services to charity work. Molly only flew once again after the ATA, taking over the controls of a Cessna Citation business jet by invitation of the pilot. Fifty years after the end of the war, she flew it safely to their destination. Although she had never sat at the controls of a jet before, her ATA training and experience clearly proved its worth.

The first of the twelve American women hired by the ATA was Dorothy Furey (later Bragg), born in 1918 in New Orleans. Flying for her was 'an interesting interlude'. In 1940 she went along to Maynard School of Aviation and found Mr Maynard. She had no money at that time, during the Depression, but he readily took possession of her 'beaten up Ford' in return for flying lessons. It was a done deal and two years later she had her commercial licence and began to teach others.

Once she had been told about the ATA, and been recruited, she arrived in Liverpool (via travels in Harlem, which she found charming with 'the best fried chicken she'd ever tasted') with Jackie Cochran and was met by Pauline Gower at Liverpool.

Dorothy was renowned for always being prepared for a night out, as the poem below reveals. After the war, she went on to breed race-horses, managed a 550-acre farm, and in her 70s took up scuba diving. She also married four times and had five sons. The Spitfire was her favourite plane.

A Touch of Silk

I packed my parachute
I packed my evening gown –
what more did I need?

My 'Gone with the Wind' dress
I called it, essential for a girl
dashing about in a plane.

We never knew when glamour
might beckon – a dinner, a dance,
so I packed in just in case –

patting down the soft red velvet
cushioned against the tough
parachute straps of silk & security.

Alison Hill, *Sisters in Spitfires*

Brooklands in Surrey had been the scene of much pre-war flying and planes, including for Pauline and her friends, and planes were ferried there during the war. There is a painting in a corridor, just outside the elegant Bluebird Room (once used by Malcolm Campbell to create the plans for his famous land-speed record-breaking car), entitled 'A Tribute to Women Aviators'. The painting portrays Pauline seated at the centre surrounded by some of the women ATA pilots with their signatures alongside. Painted in 1991 by Roderick Lovesey (1944–2002), it was unveiled at White Waltham a year later to great acclaim, with some of the ATA women in attendance. It was loaned to Brooklands by Victor Gauntlett (1942–2003), former chairman and chief executive of Aston Martin, in March 1999. There was a limited edition of prints, and Tom Page (of the international Fine Art Bureau, Interesting Things for Interesting People) had one sent to Michael Fahie afterwards. He said the picture of his mother was intended as 'the essence of women pilots' valiant endeavours in wartime and subsequent charter and commercial aviation'.

I was lucky enough to read poems from *Sisters in Spitfires* next to Hurricanes and Wellingtons. The following poem also recalls some of the glamour of those days. It was written on the clubhouse balcony at a Brooklands '1940s Relived' day, while scanning the crowds suitably dressed for the occasion.

Brooklands Swing

They're in the mood – swirling
the dance floor, hands skimming
hips, scarlet lipstick glossing, all
eye-linered nylons & vintage chic.

They're hovering at the stalls,
clustering rails, rummaging
period pieces, yellowing maps
offering up roads still to travel.

From the clubhouse balcony
classic cars slip into easy mono
as Diana wafts by, Lettice strides
the other way, ready for the sky.

Spring sunlight dances back into
Brooklands, crowds lap nostalgia,
the glitz & glamour of bygone days
cheering races, applauding flight.

Alison Hill, *Sisters in Spitfires*

Diana and Lettice were two very different characters, and after the war Lettice described her former colleague as a 'very junior pilot whose imagination these days tends to run away with her'. That is why they are treading their different paths at Brooklands.

Another ATA pilot who certainly had her moment of glory was Maureen Adele Chase Dunlop. Born on 26 October 1920 in Quilmes near Buenos Aires, she had her first flying lessons in Britain at the age of 15. Immediately bitten by the bug, Maureen went home and joined the Aeroclub Argentino and two years later had her licence. Her father, an Australian farm manager, had volunteered with the Royal Field Artillery in the First World War, which inspired her to 'do her bit'. In 1942 she sailed across the Atlantic with her sister Joan; she joined the ATA in April, while her sister joined the BBC. Posted to Hamble, Maureen logged 800 hours and was trained to fly Spitfires, Mustangs, Typhoons and Wellingtons. Her favourite was the de Havilland Mosquito. A press photographer from the popular photojournalism weekly *Picture Post* (which was published between 1938 and 1957) snapped a perfect cover image of Maureen, which greatly appealed to its almost 2 million readers when it landed on doormats and newsstands on 16 September 1944. Maureen was 24, fresh-faced, and destined to stay that way.

The Cover Girl

Maureen Dunlop was caught
on the cover of Picture Post
stepping fresh from a plane.
A breeze ruffling her curls,
she graced every breakfast
table, set many hearts aflame.

It was a perfect press moment,
unscripted, and they knew it.
She was forever that girl from
the plane, one hand to her hair
cap and goggles in the other,
an image of carefree glamour.

She'd told the photographers
she was busy, had a Barracuda
to put away, but then smoothed
her hair, smiled as the sun flared
her youth, her golden bracelet,
and there she was – cover girl!

Alison Hill, *Sisters in Spitfires*

The extensive press coverage did not do the ATA any harm, and quite likely increased the country's admiration for the work of all ferry pilots, men and women. Maureen Dunlop flew throughout the war with the ATA then returned to Argentina. She became an instructor, worked as a commercial pilot and flew for the Argentine Air Force. Like Pauline, she also held a partnership in an air-taxi company and actively flew until the late 1960s. Another inspirational role model for women pilots.

THE POWER OF THE SPITFIRE

It is still a thrill for many to watch a Spitfire flypast – the distinctive sound of the early Merlin engines, the sleek ergonomic design, the agility in the air. Several of the ATA women were taken up again in later life, equally thrilled to return to the cockpits, during peacetime, when they could enjoy the planes for everything they symbolise. Not forgetting the speed!

Diana Barnato Walker enthused: 'They were lovely aeroplanes … they were part of you … when you moved it moved … so light and dainty … beautiful things to fly.'

Joy Lofthouse had a much-publicised flight in a Spitfire at the age of 92, on 8 May 2015 to commemorate VE Day, and was thrilled to experience the iconic plane again after seven decades. She considered herself lucky as she took the controls and was calm, smiling, not at all ruffled. The iconic Spit was deep within her memory, her fingertips recalled the lightness of the controls – 'the nearest thing to having wings of your own and flying'. She remembered that they were tricky to handle on the ground – you had to avoid lifting the tail too high as the propellor could easily clip the ground. This was a familiar story. Joy was not used to voices over the airways, however, and found that distracting; with no radio control the ATA pilots had been able to concentrate fully on the task in hand. Joy had loved the silent world of her own and said it was the only place where she used to enjoy singing as she didn't have a great voice!

Spitfires were much easier to control in the air, but Joy added that the take-off and landings were important to get right.

Molly Rose agreed that the Spitfire responded to the lightest possible touch, and it was very much a lady's plane: 'You could dance with a Spitfire.'

Mary Ellis, who delivered 400 Spitfires while in the ATA, firmly agreed. 'Up in the air, on your own, you could play with the clouds. So delightful and lovely. I can't tell you how wonderful it was.' It was not the technical details she recalled so much, although she emphasised that they were particularly light to fly. It was the speed – fast and furious. As she told her biographer Melody Foreman, she thought they were the most beautiful aircraft, the nearest thing to wearing wings and becoming a bird.

Mary's house was full of Spitfire memories, and with planes taking off all day from Sandown Airport next door, where she was managing director from 1950 to 1970, and the UK's first female air commandant, her whole life was full of wings. She also loved the sound of a Merlin engine overhead, smiling at me with a twinkle as she recalled her many Spitfire flights. She showed me all her memorabilia, a word that does not do lifelong memories justice. Mary had put the wartime years in context but was nevertheless enjoying the recognition that had come late in life. The helicopter flight with the handsome pilot – her words – when she had been offered, and accepted, the Queen's seat. She had respected and appreciated her commanding officer as they all did – as a natural leader. Mary also remembered her kindness, which was again recalled by many in her command.

Pauline was the perfect person for the job; she quietly proved her worth, a gradual approach without upsetting the men. I see that from her photo above my desk, a cool, calm gaze that says: 'and why not?' 'Push barriers, you won't know until you try.' That was her reasoning when it was suggested women could not fly heavy twin-engined bombers, or the Spitfire they all loved with one voice. 'You could dance with the clouds,' said Mary Ellis with a far-away look. 'It was just lovely.'

In her book *Spitfire Girl, My Life in the Sky*, Jackie Moggridge is effusive in her respect for Pauline, describing how, when they first met, she quickly put her at her ease. Jackie was just 18, determined to fly, and had made a long and arduous journey from Pretoria in South Africa to England to do so. She arrived at Hatfield Ferry Pool feeling like she was 'entering the portals of a new boarding school'. These women were assured and diffident, they sat with 'awe-inspiring confidence on the edge of tables or slouched past in the narrow corridor, parachutes slung over their shoulders'. Movie stars in the making, years later, with cigarettes of course. Imagine walking into that pool, young and green, not understanding the nuances of the British language and culture, the looks that only they could understand. Pauline was not like that at all. She was expecting Jackie, welcomed her to her office and to the ferry pool. Although she did ask for an alternative name when hearing Jackie's surname, Sorour – 'We can't call you that. Sounds much too tragic. What other names …?'

She helped the nervous Jackie relax in a stressful situation; she could have pulled rank and applied the clipped British voice that would have made the situation much worse. Instead, she kindly put the younger woman at her ease with her characteristic friendly grin. 'You mustn't be shy. We are all newcomers here.'

Candida Adkins went on to say, when describing Jackie, her mother, that flying was very much a job and they were all very matter of fact about the whole experience. But at the end of the day, literally, they all enjoyed it, the fun and excitement of so much flying, despite the sheer hard work and long days. Candida stressed how much fun they had, up in the air, alone and free, simply 'doing their bit'.

Joy Lofthouse, like many of the women pilots, couldn't wait for her first Spitfire: 'Such a wonderful aeroplane. The nearest thing to having wings of your own and flying that I've known.' She agreed, like many others, that the flying was easy. It was the take-off and landing that required concentration. These were expensive planes, and all eyes were on the women to deliver them safely. But if fun was to be had along the way … well, why not?! And who was to know, with no radio control, if they once or twice dipped over those clouds?

Mary de Bunsen wrote about her own pre-war flying and the challenges she faced along the way in her entertaining autobiography, *Mount Up with Wings* (Hutchinson, 1960). Mary contracted polio aged 4 which left her lame, had a congenital heart condition, poor eyesight and had endured countless operations since childhood. Her opening chapter, 'One in Ten', is a sharply observed account of flying to America for pioneering heart surgery. When she arrived at the hospital, which was a complete culture shock, she tried to read Nancy Mitford's *The Pursuit of Love*, by way of distraction. Her young surgeon, Dr Bailey, had been amused to see it open on her bed when he did his pre-op rounds. He read a passage aloud and passed the book around to his grinning team, before checking on the state of Mary's ankles. She liked him instantly. Reflecting that she was now part American, after three pints of donated blood, Mary slips in a paragraph (her mind flitting back to her first American encounter) that deftly sums up the ATA experience:

> In the Second World War I had been a ferry pilot, doing the necessary but non-combatant job of moving aeroplanes about between the factories, squadrons, flying schools and maintenance units. The few hundred cheerful scallywags with whom I did this work were mostly men, too old or otherwise unfit for operational flying. Most of us had flown with clubs before the war, scraping up the money to do a few hours a year, and we were blissfully happy being paid to do the thing we most enjoyed.

Mary had met Pauline before the war and remembers her natural kindness. Mary had had problems with a medical, with poor eyesight, and also failed her first height test. This involved climbing to 6,000ft and landing in a glide within 150yd of a mark. She had made what she thought was a 'perfect touch down' but then another Tiger Moth landed at right angles to her own path and clipped her tail. She was not really to blame but had been failed anyway. The same day 'an odious little grey horse' had bolted with her and she had nearly been thrown off. Not daunted, she passed her second test and received a resounding 'good show' from Pauline, who had been watching. Mary was despondent still and explained about the failed medical. Pauline told her to go and see her own doctor, who was more used to the idea of women pilots. This worked and the Air Ministry was satisfied that she could see *and* fly – she passed both tests and a licence was duly granted. Mary was very grateful to Pauline and glad to join her in 1941:

> ATA had its own standards, and a pair of spectacles or a limb or two missing was no bar to a reliable pilot. In fact the crocks were probably as safe as anybody, for they could not afford to make mistakes, and few of them ever put a foot wrong.

Mary summed up the continuous pressure the women encountered in the ATA; and they flew with more care and attention, and with fewer accidents, because of it. Mary's aviation story was a remarkable one, from girlhood teas in Dorset with leading poets, to four years ferrying anything to anywhere, from the taxi Anson to the twin-engined Mosquito in which she liked to hum Bach fugues as she flew. Mary disliked society's expectations of marriage, but had a real passion for the air, for her part in the sky.

Taking Tea with Thomas Hardy

I was shy, but it was not as bad
as matchmaking – I liked to think
I had some literary credentials!

And Thomas didn't mind a fig
if I was near-blind or lame;
I was just a young girl perched
    on a tapestry wing-back.

But I could sense he was trying hard
to remember my name and how
I fitted into his landscape.

I tried to imagine his books, his desk,
his pen, hoping I may inspire a line or two,
the angle of my cheek or my face in repose.

Before I found planes I dived into books
hid deep beneath their pages, as later
I skimmed the feathered clouds
    solo in my Cirrus Moth.

Alison Hill, *Sisters in Spitfires*

POETRY OF FLIGHT

The Spitfire – in all its many designs and marks – has inspired countless poems, paintings, plays, exhibitions, films and even a musical since its design in 1936 by R.J. Mitchell. The Spitfire embodies history, passion, power and so much more. Nowadays it evokes nostalgia and instant recognition: Spitfire flypasts always turn heads. All the ATA women agreed that it was 'a lady's plane' and the sleek design and snugness of its cockpit inspired even the most practical to play with words.

The somewhat formidable Lettice Curtis declared: 'To sit in the cockpit of a Spitfire, barely wider than one's shoulders, with the power of the Merlin at one's fingertips, was a poetry of its own.' While the more flamboyant Jackie Moggridge enthused: 'A few seconds later I found myself soaring through the air in a machine that made poetry of flight.'

Jackie wrote poems on scraps of paper, or the back of chits, one of which I was glad to publish for the first time in the anthology *Fifty Ways to Fly* (Rhythm & Muse, 2017). Her daughter Candida had found it in her attic, which she said was stuffed full of papers and flying memorabilia. She told me that her mother had not been so keen on the technical side of flying, and hated maths, but took much pleasure in dancing, singing and the joy of the moment. Jackie wrote on the way back from airfields, as Pauline had written between flights, once stopping by a lamppost to finish her sparkling poem 'I'm Longing to be a Pinup'. Other times she wrote appreciative poems to engineers, by way of thanks for ensuring the pilots' safety in the air. Her tone was light and joyful, as was her character, but the one below, written in 1942, hits a more sombre note, looking back on her full and adventurous life.

The Last Flight

When I must set the compass for my flight –
the last and all alone.
Which bearing is the best all through the night
to reach the great unknown?

Will wind allowance matter in the void
through which I have to go?
Or navigation error be allowed with faults?
I do not know.

How can I tell the distance and the time
or weather on the way?
Or estimate the height I have to climb
until I land some day?

Pray that the Master Pilot of us all will
check my course to steer
And not allow my wavering wings to stall
when I take off from here.

Jackie Moggridge, *Fifty Ways to Fly*

When Monique Agazarian applied to the ATA, not once but several times, writing every three months in her typically determined style, she was finally interviewed by an amused Commander Gower. Monique had 'stretched' her height to fit the bill – pilots had to be at least 5ft 6in tall, preferably with an aptitude for sport – Pauline was aware of this but did not let on. Monique was delighted to be accepted and in a letter to Michael Fahie (13 February 1992) is full of praise, recalling the meeting in detail:

> Having passed the medical and 'intelligence' test I was ushered in to meet Commander Gower. I found myself in front of a charming and very beautiful woman who seemed to have a certain amount of trouble holding back laughter. Apparently the doctor had told her of the antics I had got up to trying to stretch myself to meet the height requirements for the job! She put me at my ease, telling me that we had both been educated at the Convent of the Sacred Heart, telling me what A.T.A. was about, and when she found my only question was 'am I in' told me at once 'Yes'.

This directness can be seen in many of Pauline's photographs, particularly in the National Portrait Gallery series.

Monique continued:

> When the ATA was formed Pauline realised that the experienced women pilots should also use their skills if possible to swell the pool of pilots needed to back up the services. Since women had not previously been considered in this role, Margot [Gore] thinks that nobody except Pauline would have been in the position to or have the right contacts in her own circle which included Cabinet Minsters etc., and most important she had the charm and firmness to carry through her resolve!

Monique's daughter Lou-Lou Troup was happy to elaborate:

> Mummy was a great storyteller about her life during the war and she frequently told the story of how she really wanted to join the ATA. She wrote and applied on a regular basis, always changing her experience from no flying experience to many hours on various aeroplanes – so when she finally got her interview, the interviewer commented on what a varied flying career she had had so far!
>
> She also told the story of part of her actual interview - she knew that she was not tall enough, but she had been told by a friend that if she lay out flat on the floor for a minute before her height was measured, she would be at least an inch taller. When they wanted to measure her height, she asked if she could lie out flat on the floor – she did and she was the right height!

During the research for *Sisters in Spitfires*, an old friend Elizabeth Harrison MBE told me she had met Monique Agazarian on a coach trip to France. Born in 1923 in Belgium, Elizabeth escaped during the war and later worked with the SOE (Special Operations Executive) for many years, reuniting families. A talented sculptor, she designed a monument for a war memorial in Valençay, France. She told me that she had drawn the design on a napkin over a lunch event at the RAF Club, the way of some of the best projects, and it had been accepted. She and many others subsequently made an annual pilgrimage to the memorial. Monique Agazarian had attended the unveiling on 6 May 1991; she had never travelled by coach before that trip and shared stories with Elizabeth on the way to France. Some of the details from that coach journey, and meetings between the two women in London, feature in Monique's poem from *Sisters in Spitfires*. 'Model Pilot, Model Lawn' alludes to her Catholic schooling which, like Pauline's, had a significant bearing on her life. Both schools were part of the Sacred Heart group, which had similar outlooks, producing strong women and highly skilled pilots in these two cases.

Model Pilot, Model Lawn

*The Sacred Heart sisters found her a delightful
child but very pleasure loving. Peter Pan inspired
dreams of flying, lent her silver-tipped wings.*

*Her passion for planes began in the back garden,
in an old Sopwith Pup her mother found at auction;
Monique and her brothers happily flew the world.*

*From volunteer nurse to ferry pilot, Monique stood
taller for the ATA, borrowing an inch or three
for her medical, flying Spitfires with ease.*

*She ferried cigarettes once or twice too, stashed
in an overnight bag or down by her parachute,
a welcome favour for those waiting to fly.*

*Long after the war she manicured her window box
with nail scissors; a friend's flight of fancy adding
a miniature blue Spitfire set into the grass.*

She'd flown all types of front-liners in the war,
yet did not take a coach trip until May 1991.
Why be driven when you can fly?

Monique wanted the sound of a Merlin engine
at her funeral – arriving, passing, fading –
lingering essence of her energy, her vibrant life.

Alison Hill, *Sisters in Spitfires*

Flying clearly stayed in the family, as Lou-Lou Troup told me:

Although I am the youngest of three daughters, I was the only one interested in learning to fly – so I did, at the same age as Mummy had started her *ab initio* training with ATA – and after six months I had flown two types of aeroplane while she had flown considerably more! I was always enthused by her love of the Spitfire, which she said was the most magnificent and wonderful aeroplane to fly and so as a surprise for my 60th birthday, my beloved arranged for me to have a flight in a two-seater Spitfire (Mummy would not even contemplate that as she said it was clearly a one-person plane!). It was one of the most exciting and memorable experiences of my life. It was a perfect Battle of Britain day – a blue, blue sky with some puffy clouds here and there. The pilot who took me up knew about Mummy and her history of being in the ATA and he encouraged me to talk even when we were taxying. As we took off I unexpectedly burst into tears (and I am now as I write this...) as my head was filled with emotion and thoughts of all those who had flown this amazing aeroplane (including Mummy's brother) to make sure that our land was safe and free. The all-round view of the sky was incredible, and I was bowled over by the performance of the Spitfire. The pilot asked me if I wanted to fly her and I was hesitant, but soon realised that this was such an easy plane to fly, and I flew her with a little more purpose and verve – it was an absolute delight and the spitfire responded to even the smallest of commands. I was literally in heaven for the twenty minutes or so that I flew the Spitfire and to top it all, the pilot did a victory roll on the way back to Biggin – just amazing. The only problem is that I want to do it all over again!!

Another testimonial, this time from Rosemary Rees, one of the First Eight, sums up Pauline's character in a fine brushstroke:

Pauline Gower was asked to form the small women's section. She had done a great deal of joy riding at Alan Cobham's circus for some years so could be called an experienced pilot, but far more importantly, she was intelligent and thrusting and could browbeat, in the nicest possible way, the Ministers and Air Marshalls who held our future in their hands.

Richard Poad, chairman of the Maidenhead Heritage Centre, where many ATA diaries and archives are held, has described Pauline as a 'consummate politician' who always took a 'softly, softly' approach; one flight at a time, access to a new type of plane at a time, but always pushing forward to get more freedom for the women pilots, more responsibility and, in 1943, equal pay for equal work. She had learnt much from her father's political career, but she brought her own skill and diplomacy to the table to achieve her goals. She was determined to succeed.

Lettice Curtis was another pilot ready to make her mark. Her no-nonsense attitude comes across in her memoirs and in archive video clips; she was a force to be reckoned with, if not the warmest. It was thought she knew Pauline well, but one photo perhaps tells a different story. They are sitting in the cockpit of an Avro Anson and the distance between them is tangible. Their smiles are somewhat strained. Lettice perhaps had the ambition to be 'top dog' although she always talked about Pauline with respect and admiration. In a letter to Michael Fahie in 1992 she said: 'I didn't know your mother that well but there are a few still around such as Joan Hughes and Margot Gore who would no doubt have known her pre-war. Also Sir Peter Mursell who as Chief Instructor would have known her when she was "upstairs" at White Waltham.' Interesting that Lettice points out the rank and the level of operations at the pool, with that one word. She herself was a blue stocking, way ahead of her time at Cambridge and later in aviation, and she found some of the wartime flying restraints tedious. But her detailed *The Forgotten Pilots* tells the story of the women pilots' incredible bravery in a world without instruments, dodging balloons they dared not mark on maps: 'Because of the balloons, you simply couldn't afford in many areas to fly on until a river, railway or what have you turned up.' She made it sound so effortless.

Lettice revisited a Tiger Moth in her 80s and told the owner enthusiast that she had 'adored' the compass. Adding that it took at least a day to get from Hatfield to Lossiemouth, Scotland, and with at least two stops to refuel. They did not plan where to land, she said – it really was a case of finding an airfield in the right place at roughly the right time. And then getting the train back, often alone and travelling through the night, jolting through the dark and unfamiliar countryside, as I imagined below. Just seeing the cockpit had brought so many memories back for Lettice, despite her long post-war career in aviation. Those early Tiger Moth flights must have been imprinted on their minds, if not their maps.

A UNITED FRONT

Record-breaking American pilot Jacqueline Cochran knew that American pilots could bring valuable skills and experience to the ATA effort. She selected twenty-five of 700 potential pilots in a thorough and extensive screening process. They were trained in Canada before making the 'big and voluntary decision to leave their own wide shores for what might be a tottering island', as Alison King so vividly recalls. It was a cultural experiment that took some time to achieve the desired results.

Pauline, Kitty Farrer her adjutant, and another senior pilot, went to meet and greet the first five recruits when they docked at Liverpool in spring 1942. Alison imagined how the conversation might have gone (perhaps it had been relayed to her in the ops room afterwards or over-heard); the polite questions and answers that would have only given half the truth. As she concluded: 'British reserve! American bewilderment! Not the best mixture for a good beginning.' She goes on to describe how Pauline was ready to 'stand them all to a jolly good dinner' and had suggested they go to her hotel later that evening 'if they felt like it'. British women would have taken this as an official invitation from the woman in command. The newly arrived American pilots were no doubt tired after an exhausting journey, with the inherent fear of their ship's attack, and did not have much energy for dinner at Pauline's hotel. So they took her literally: they did not 'feel like it' and did not turn up, which was probably not the best start. There were other dif-ferences, of course, which became more apparent as time went on, but they added to the mix of the ATA pilots, in background, culture, lan-guage and outlook. They also added a certain spark, as Mary de Bunsen recorded in her memoir:

> Before long they started to use women pilots, and our multi-national, multi-racial band of brothers and sisters included a lot of Americans of both sexes. I remembered the American women for their inex-haustible energy, their bottomless capacity for whisky and parties and most of all for their kind hearts.

Joy Lofthouse recalled that it was 'quite a League of Nations' and English was certainly not the only language spoken in the mess. She saw it enriching the day-to-day life in the ATA and a long way from her bank clerk job in Cirencester. Her daughter said that she 'loved the mix of women and talked about them all gathering in different corners of the mess, either chattering away in Polish or cutting out dress patterns or, in her case, playing bridge. Joy learned to play bridge in the mess while waiting for the weather to lift. She used to watch the experienced ones and then when one woman was called to get her flight "chitty" Joy would take over her hand. Bridge became one of the great joys of her life and she played regularly until six months before she died.'

Pilots joined the ATA from more than twenty-five countries, including Denmark, Poland, Chile, Argentina, Canada, New Zealand, the US, Australia and South Africa. The women worked alongside each other day in day out and made the most of the chance to experience other cultures, a curious richness to wartime life. Margot Duhalde arrived in Liverpool in April 1941 and spent the first five days detained in London as a suspected spy. She had learnt to fly at 16 with the Air Club of Chile in Santiago and her journey to Hatfield, reporting for duty on 1 September, was an eventful one. On her first flight, with no grasp of the English countryside from the air, she crashed in a snow-covered field in north London and was arrested. She spoke no English and had no papers but did remember the name of Pauline Gower and was released. Once back at the ferry pool, Margot was directed to spend three months in the hangars learning more about Tiger Moths and the English language, by which time she had picked up some rich vocabulary. A posting to Hamble followed, where she was known to all as 'Chile' and became good friends with Maureen Dunlop from Argentina and Jackie Sorour from South Africa. All three women had made incredible journeys to fly with the ATA and do their considerable bit for the war effort.

Londoner Ann Welch, who later achieved considerable success with gliders, became friends with Polish pilot Barbara Wojtulanis who, she said, flew Spitfires with ease, but never mastered the art of pedalling on two wheels. This is their poem from *Sisters in Spitfires*.

Out of the Silence Came Chopin

We'd been practising in poor weather –
our wings clipped we turned to two wheels,
running along the peri track, Barbara wobbling
at my side, never quite getting her balance right –
*   it was so different in the air!*
We grinned through gritted teeth, but it was
not to be and her cycle gave way to the Spit,
graciously bowing out of the duel.

Grounded again, just before Christmas,
we passed Winchester cathedral wreathed
in snow, lit only by the stars. Chopin's
Revolutionary Study cascaded through the silence
from a distant piano and Barbara was rooted
*   by strains of Polish hope.*
The music ended as suddenly as it arrived,
leaving us shrouded in the snow-bound night.

Alison Hill, *Sisters in Spitfires*

In October 1942, a year marked by sheer hard work for Pauline, Eleanor Roosevelt, along with Clementine Churchill, paid a visit to White Waltham ostensibly to inspect the twenty-two American pilots now serving in the ATA. The women were lined up on the tarmac in front of Hurricanes, Wellingtons and Spitfires. The heavens opened and the VIP guests received an umbrella, while the pilots were not so well protected. It was an auspicious occasion for First Officer Lettice Curtis, who was photographed sheltering under a looming Halifax bomber. The press led on the story the next day 'Girl Flies Halifax' – it was only a matter of time. A blast from the siren and a bombing raid on a nearby airfield during the after-lunch speech from Eleanor Roosevelt did not dampen the spirit of the occasion – women were about to fly all types of aircraft in line with the men. Lettice was shortly put on a conversion course to fulfil the headlines, becoming the first woman to fly a Halifax. Pauline's diplomacy and determination had achieved results, and more was to come.

AB INITIO TRAINING

By 1943 there was a growing need for more pilots to ferry many more planes. All those with 'A' licences who wanted to join had been signed up and were busy flying. Joy Lofthouse was accepted on one of the first courses for novice pilots, after seeing an advertisement in *The Aeroplane* magazine. She describes in detail the thorough training that made the ATA such an efficient and successful organisation, after the early days of the war that is, when the girls 'had really roughed it'. First came nine days of technical ground training: how a plane worked, combustion engines, navigation (map reading) and the hazards of the English weather – vital components for successful ferrying.

Once they had passed an exam at the end of the nine weeks they were allowed in a dual-control plane. They learnt the basics – taking off, turning left, turning right, climbing, descending and landing – and then, after ten to twelve flying hours, they were allowed to do a solo circuit – the 'Big Test'. Once safely passed, and most women did as they had been taught well and respected the planes they had to land, the training moved onto forced landings, getting out of a spin – 'more adventurous things', as Joy recalled. Next came twenty-four cross-country flights, getting yourself safely from A to B, and using all the training to best effect. Once those were behind you, and you had not lost your nerve in the process, the proud moment had arrived. Getting your wings and being fitted for your uniform at Austin Reed. Then came progress: the next type, the next plane, women flying operational aircraft.

Alison King, operations officer at Hamble, like many, attributed this progress to Pauline: 'Each new type had to be fought for. For, whatever women had done in the past, they were still not necessarily thought to be quite capable of taking the next step. Pauline's sense of timing, though, on any scheme was perfect.'

FROM TIGER MOTHS TO HURRICANES

As she told the young Jackie Moggridge, Pauline had her sights set firmly on the horizon from the start. They might have begun with the yellow training planes, but she knew her women pilots were capable of flying twin-engined and four-engined bombers. Some men were adamant that women were not capable of handling such monsters.

Imagine, women controlling big planes! They could, of course, with the right training. Women could ride prancing horses of sixteen hands or more – why should they not be able to handle aircraft without any equestrian testosterone?

Pauline met with the right people at the right time, a diplomatic voice in the right ear, so that her women soon progressed from the training Tiger Moths. In May 1941, Lieutenant Colonel John Moore-Brabazon became Minister of Aircraft Production. He visited Hatfield shortly afterwards to have lunch with his old friend Pauline, primarily to discuss the possibility of women flying bigger and faster aircraft. A photograph opportunity, with him surrounded by a group of women pilots, was referred to in the press as 'Brab's Beauties' and all eyes were on the outcome. This was Pauline in charge and progression was on the cards. She had long had the end-goal in sight.

Once the women had passed through the central flying school at Upavon, they were converted onto advanced training aircraft, a step up from Tiger Moths, such as the twin-engined Airspeed Oxford and the Master. Sound and speed were the key differences, the roar of progress. In July 1941, women moved onto their first operational aircraft, which represented further progress, thanks to Pauline's instigations. Seven of the thirty women flying at that time were selected to make a circuit at Hatfield. Winnie Crossley, one of the First Eight, became the first woman to take off in a Hurricane. It was a big moment and the other pilots watched nervously as she did a quick circuit and made a neat three-point landing. As the onlookers let out a collective sigh of relief she stepped out and simply remarked to the six other waiting pilots: 'It's lovely darlings, a beautiful little aeroplane.'

There was a celebratory dinner at the L'Ecu de France restaurant in London afterwards – this was a huge triumph for the pilots. They pooled their petrol coupons to drive up to town and raise a glass to future success.

The Halifax was next. Lettice Curtis had paved the way soon after Eleanor Roosevelt came to lunch at White Waltham, and it was not long afterwards that women were 'converted' via the necessary training to fly 30-ton four-engined bombers. Air Service Training at Hamble had informed ATA that they would be doing a modification on the American Fortress and Cunliffe Owen at Eastleigh, in Hampshire, and were expecting a Halifax contract. The time was right. Women were needed. Pauline looked to her best pilots.

In early 1943, Lettice was passed out after the necessary number of successful landings (at least ten) and cross-wind landings and delivered her first of almost 400 four-engined bombers. A formidable pilot indeed.

Next Margot Gore proved the point, quietly, confidently and without fuss. She had had her conversion training at RAF Marston Moor Bomber Station in Yorkshire, where there was a small ATA Class 5 Unit to provide the necessary instruction. Margot did a mere three and a half hours' dual control, and the same amount solo. Then she was back at Hamble and ready for her first Halifax. Alison King sums up: 'All difficulties were overcome, as they had always been overcome, and some hundreds of four-engined bombers were delivered in good order.'

The Spitfire was, of course, the ultimate prize. The snug cockpit, effortless agility and lightness to fly were some of its attributes, which made it the perfect plane for women pilots. Many could not wait to get that chit, as Ann Welch recounted:

Then came the moment I longed for. I was given my first Spitfire. It was a new Mark VB AA746, its camouflage paint unscratched, waiting at Lyneham to go to a squadron at West Hampnett [now Goodwood]. I had read the Pilots' Notes, been warned about the ease with which a twitchy first take-off could be achieved by over-use of the sensitive elevator; but like everyone else I still twitched into the air. But once there the Spitfire's delight in flying gave me sheer pleasure … [it] was perfect and when I came into the circuit at my destination, she floated back on to the ground like a feather.

As she taxied in, exultant at her first Spitfire flight and perhaps even more at the successful landing, she saw two flights of Spits roar into the air in formation, like a swoop of starlings, off to France. Ann wondered if the one she had just delivered would be flying off to the same desti-nation the next day. Once delivered, they had to put the planes out of their mind and focus on the next flight.

WARTIME LOSSES

One in ten ATA pilots lost their lives in service, fifteen of them women, mostly due to the changeable weather and unforeseen haz-ards. The very nature of the job had a daily element of danger and risk, but in fact pilot error accounted for relatively few fatalities. As in all wartime work, those left behind had to carry on, day in day out, and emotions were rarely on display – it just wasn't done. Even years later, some of the women were reluctant to talk about friends they had lost. The ATA Association annual reunions would have helped keep their wartime bonds alive, for all those who attended over the post-war years, and would have provided fitting occasions to remem-ber lives lost.

Amy Johnson joined the ATA in May 1940 and, despite some initial misgivings about the nature of the work, she fitted in well. She had written to her father the year before saying that if she had played her cards right, she could have had Pauline's job, but the powers that be had made it clear that they wanted someone who attracted less press and public attention. Her tone was disparaging: 'I'd much rather work in a proper commercial aviation company with men pilots, than be one of a team of women … being given the crumbs to keep them quiet. They're not really doing much, and the pay is very poor.'

It certainly wasn't her usual record-breaking round of dazzling adventurous flights, but it was an essential job, which she undertook with dedication. Pauline had invited her to join soon after setting up the women's section, but Amy had taken some time to consider her options. As well as considerably less pay, the routine daily flights were a far cry from her former much-publicised adventures. She may have hankered after the commandant role, but she showed no ill-feeling to her old friend once she joined. Operations Officer Alison King spoke only warmly about Amy's time in the ATA and the contribution she made. She dedicated a chapter to her, perhaps knowing that in years to come Amy's name would be remembered as a true pioneer of the 1930s and a wartime ferry pilot. Naturally there were reservations at first when she joined Hatfield; when she landed at an RAF airfield 'embarrassed yet determined' airmen were there waiting for her autograph, closely followed by squadron leaders and wing commanders. Yet Alison affirms that: 'She fitted into Hatfield like a hand in glove and made a lot of friends.'

Amy Johnson broke many records in the 1930s. While working as a secretary, she discovered the London Aero Club at Stag Lane and found her calling. An instant attraction to aircraft. She gained her 'A' licence in July 1929, just before meeting Pauline and Dorothy, and became the first woman in Britain to qualify as a ground engineer. She went on to achieve worldwide fame and (often short-lived) fortune, although Alison King thought they brought her neither happiness nor peace. Her ill-fated marriage to record-breaking pilot Jim Mollison, who also joined the ATA, brought equally dramatic highs and lows. Theirs was a notorious and well-publicised partnership of high flights, fast living and much drink-related drama, which finally ended in divorce in 1938.

Amy was rarely out of the press after her first sensational solo 11,000-mile flight from London to Darwin, Australia, in just under twenty days, in her two-year-old Moth she named 'Jason', the Greek-inspired symbol of her family's fish business in Hull.

But the pressures of fame took their toll on her health. She had committed herself to a forty-town tour across England, organised by the *Daily Mail*, in return for the sum of £10,000 – 'the largest amount ever paid for a feat of daring'. Her health broke down, the tour was cancelled, but she was allowed to keep the money.

On 5 January 1941, aged 37, Amy made the headlines for the last time. She was one of the first ATA pilots to lose her life, in circumstances still surrounded in some mystery. At 11.49 Amy had taken an Airspeed Oxford V3540 from RAF Squires Gate Blackpool to Kidlington in Oxfordshire. She had decided to put down the day before at Blackpool, en route from Prestwick, due to bad weather and had stayed overnight with her sister. Despite her reputation for reckless flying, Alison King remembered Amy as being practical and taking breaks as necessary until the weather cleared – 'It's sensible to be sensible' was her famed Northern attitude.

Yet she didn't arrive as planned.

Alison King recounts how she had flown with Amy to White Waltham, not long beforehand, and had met up with some other pilots in the Mess. Amy was kind enough to ensure Alison was included in the conversation, which had turned to the death of a pilot the day before. On leaving White Waltham, Amy had turned to Alison 'with her quick, brilliant smile' and had said 'half lightly', 'You know, that'll be me one day.'

On that day, Pauline had known instinctively that something was wrong. An atmosphere had descended on that cold, foggy afternoon at Hatfield; people were not meeting each other's eyes. Nothing tangible, not yet, but all was not well. Pauline came of out her office with a white face. The Admiralty had been on the phone. Two bags had been found in the Thames Estuary, marked 'A. Johnson'. Alison offered to phone around for any news, but Pauline advised caution, they didn't want the story getting out. As Alison recalled, Pauline lit a cigarette and 'squared her shoulders in the typical way of hers' but her voice 'had faded into hopelessness'. Calls to Prestwick Operations, where she had first taken off, did not offer much hope either. Pauline had tried to reassure Alison and told her to keep on trying, with a smile that 'struck her with new sorrow, so forced it was'. The press was already on the scent, putting a call through to the Hamble, but no calls came from Amy Johnson.

That afternoon, HMS *Haslemere*, part of a wartime convoy passing through the channels of the Thames Estuary, had seen a parachute descend, followed by a silent aircraft. The ship immediately changed course and went to the aid of a figure in the water that they could see was a woman. Members of the crew tried to rescue her with ropes, before the lifeboat was launched, but she was thrown under the stern of the ship, out of reach on the strong current.

The captain, Lieutenant Commander Walter Fletcher, dived into the icy water to save what was believed to have been a second figure. The lifeboat eventually reached him, but he was unconscious and died a few days later from shock and hypothermia. Amy Johnson had been swallowed by the sea and her body never recovered.

It can only be surmised that Amy had got lost in the fog, already above cloud, waiting for a gap that never materialised. She was more than used to overcoming hazards and challenges on her 1,000-mile solo trips, but this four-and-a-half-hour flight for the ATA, as just 'one of the girls', in worsening weather and with fuel running out, was to be her final challenge.

On Such a Day

Our hearts sank when we guessed
the worst or dared to let ourselves imagine …

On such a day, we stayed on the ground
not wishing to tempt fate.

On such a day we looked upwards
almost at the same minute, the same hour.

We couldn't help ourselves, automatically
scanning for any signs of life.

On such a day we stretched aching limbs
pinching our flesh raw while

waiting for news that never fully surfaced.
We knew in our hearts that she was gone.

Alison Hill, *Sisters in Spitfires*

Pauline had been a loyal friend to Amy and did not doubt her skill as a pilot or that she had in any way disobeyed ATA regulations by picking up a passenger without clearance – just one of several rumours that surrounded her death at the time. She had the difficult task of informing Amy's parents while quashing any rumours surrounding her death. Her obituary, written as both friend and commanding officer, was published in *The Times*. These lines show the strength of their friendship and of Pauline's natural leadership:

> Although I appreciate her brilliance as a pilot, the attributes which went to make her a character were to me more impressive than her wonderful feats in the world of aeronautics. Those who knew Amy Johnson intimately saw her as an ordinary human being, keen on

her job, brilliantly successful but always accessible. Many have been assisted, encouraged and cheered by her.

Pauline, perhaps also wishing to dispel further rumours about her friend's contribution to the ATA, made it perfectly clear in her conclusion:

> She settled down to her new life with all the eagerness and enthusiasm of somebody who obviously had her heart in the work and was anxious to do a good job for her country. Whatever the circumstances, however she was feeling, the job was done; and the conscientious manner in which she carried out her duties was an inspiration to all those who worked with her.

Within a few weeks of her death, the WES established a Scholarship in Aviation for Women, which Pauline immediately sponsored. She also spoke at a Women with Wings lunch in August, which served to raise money for the Amy Johnson Memorial Fund, but also provided a platform for Pauline to once again quash the rumours that Amy had been carrying a passenger on her fatal last flight.

Margaret Fairweather, one of the First Eight and sister of Pauline's good friend Kitty Farrer, also lost her life in tragic circumstances. She had recently had a baby, and sadly lost her husband Douglas Fairweather, fellow ATA pilot, in a crash three weeks before the birth. On 4 August 1944 she was flying a Percival Proctor with Kitty and Mrs L.H. Kendricks from the Ministry of Aircraft Production as passengers. The plane suffered engine failure and Margaret made a forced landing in a field, which would have been successful apart from a hidden ditch that caught the undercarriage. She was thrown through the windscreen and died from her injuries the next day in hospital, aged 42. Margaret is buried in Dunure Cemetery, Ayrshire beside her husband. They were the only ATA couple to share a Commonwealth War Graves Commission headstone. Kitty broke her leg and spent almost two years in hospital, on and off, recovering from the crash, while Mrs Kendricks escaped unhurt. Accidents such as these were stark reminders of the ever-present risks of wartime ferrying.

Mary Ellis, based at Hamble under Alison King's watchful operations eye, was a close friend of fellow pilot Dora Lang and they were billeted in the same house. They used to play backgammon together while waiting for the weather to clear and their next flight. Dora was killed on 2 March 1944 when her Mosquito reared up and crashed on landing. The two women had previously had a near miss on the same landing run, on a short flight from Chattis Hill, near Southampton. Dora had written in her friend's autograph book, 'And the next time we land on the same aerodrome, on the same runway, may we both be going in the same direction!' After Dora's fatal accident, Mary reported for work but was told by her commanding officer to take two days off. 'I didn't talk to anyone about it,' she said afterwards. 'It was just too sad.' Mary was back ferrying soon after, focusing on the plane in hand. It would not do to dwell on death, not while flying.

Dora had been giving a lift to flight engineer Janice Harrington and the crash came literally out of the blue, a tragic end to what had started as a sunny day:

Mosquito Tears

Yet in that moment before the stone drops,
akin to a horse rearing at rustling paper
or lashing out in a sudden temper,
their Mosquito bucked upon landing,
reared up and burst into flames. Those left
behind tried to stop the darkness from
descending, as they watched the draped
coffins through flickers of late autumn sun,
as they tried to comprehend.

Alison Hill, *Sisters in Spitfires*

Dora and Janice are buried alongside each other at All Saints' Cemetery, Maidenhead in Berkshire, where there are seventeen war graves, representing six different nationalities. There are other ATA memorials at White Waltham, Ringway, Ratcliffe, Whitchurch and Hamble. The latter was unveiled on 10 July 2010, the 70th anniversary of the Battle of Britain, attended by ATA pilots Margaret Frost, Annette Hill, Joy Lofthouse, Rosemary Seccombe, Freydis Sharland and Mary Ellis, with fellow pilots Peter George and Peter Garrod. There is a photo of the unveiling that I had in mind when I visited the aluminium Spitfire statue in May 2021. It sits proudly on Aquila Way, with Spitfire Way alongside.

First Officer Honor Isabel Salmon, granddaughter of Sir Isaac Pitman (developer of the universal shorthand), was ferrying an Airspeed Oxford from Hamble to Calne in Wiltshire on 19 April 1943. She was flying alongside a Spitfire, which flew back to Hamble as the weather suddenly deteriorated. Her plane crashed into high ground near Devizes. Honor was 30 and had been married for less than two years to Major Henry Salmon.

Other women who lost their lives to their wartime work included Canadian Elsie Davison, the first woman ATA pilot to be killed, along with her instructor, on a training flight at RAF Upavon in Wiltshire. New Zealander Jane Winstone, who had learnt to fly as a schoolgirl and accompanied record-breaker Jean Batten in her Gipsy Moth, died on 10 February 1944 when her Spitfire's engine failed at 600ft. She had been based at Cosford and was one of five women from New Zealand to join the ATA.

In St Paul's Cathedral, where the ATA Association lays an annual Remembrance Day wreath, there is a memorial to the undying memory of the 158 men and fifteen women of the ATA who lost their lives, with the words: 'Remember then that also we, / In a moon's course, are history.' (From the poem 'Passage' by John Drinkwater.)

Life in the ATA had to go on, just as it did everywhere else. But each loss was marked in a particular manner in the ferry pools, and those who had been close mourned in their own way. Emotions were never on display, but all the women remembered those close to them. Post-war reunions would bring them closer in recalling those lost in service.

PAULINE GOWER

Moving Up the Blackboard
For Operations Officer Alison King

The call came, the one we all dreaded
when her voice would change, her eyes
take on that strained, faraway look.
She'd carefully cover the mouthpiece,
nod over in my direction and I'd lower
my eyes, try to stop my stomach falling.
Another one down, details as yet unknown.
Other lives and histories would be forever
changed by their loss, that we knew.
But for now we had to log the details
find a way to move on through the war,
to keep doing our bit up in the skies.
Even before she'd replaced the receiver
I'd wiped the blackboard, filled in any gaps.
It was good for morale, it had to be done.

Alison Hill, *Sisters in Spitfires*

Wartime losses and the ongoing management of pilots and boosting of morale took their toll on Pauline's health. Hers was a huge burden of responsibility and it could be lonely at the top, as Alison King noted. From spring 1942 her natural cheerfulness, which had seen her through so many situations with resilience and good humour, gave way to periods of depression and poor health. In August the ATA doctor, Archie Barbour, advised a complete break and so she took a short holiday in Devon. She did not fully rest, however, but wrote an article for *The Woman Engineer* ('No women ferry pilot need worry about the equality of opportunity with men') and undertook various speaking engagements. Very much like Robert Gower, it seems that Pauline was unable to keep a clear diary; she had too much to fit in, too much she wanted to give. It was not a job she could easily abandon. Pauline was a dedicated leader; women pilots and their progress in aviation were her life's work.

2

Pauline Gower (seated right) in her final year at Beechwood Sacred Heart School in Tunbridge Wells, Kent. She was actively involved in the school for many years after she left, tipping her wings whenever she flew overhead. (Maidenhead Heritage Trust, MAIHC 2010.106.36)

Beechwood Sacred Heart School. Pauline is said to have climbed all the trees in the extensive grounds, also making her way down from a second-floor window for further adventure. (Author)

Posing in a Gipsy Moth at Stag Lane London Aeroplane Club, with Marjorie Lamb in the front cockpit, c.1931. Stag Lane was the catalyst for Pauline's pioneering flying career. (Maidenhead Heritage Trust, MAIHC 2010.106.64)

Pauline Gower met Dorothy Spicer at Stag Lane in 1931 and they formed a long-lasting partnership. Their story began in the oily workshops and hangars, two women in overalls in a traditionally male domain. They are pictured here using a drill press. (Maidenhead Heritage Trust, MAIHC 2010.106.37)

Pauline and Dorothy in the hangar at Stag Lane in February 1931, working on a DH 60 biplane. (Maidenhead Heritage Trust, MAIHC 2010.106.39)

Pilot and engineer are joined by Pauline's faithful dog Wendy, who flew over 5,000 miles with them over several years. (Maidenhead Heritage Trust, MAIHC 2010.106.67)

Pauline and Dorothy in March 1932, pictured in front of *Helen of Troy*, their new three-seater Spartan G-ABKK, at Stag Lane. (Maidenhead Heritage Trust, MAIHC 2010.106.46)

The crowd gathers in anticipation for a popular British Hospitals' Air Pageant show, 1933, with a low-flying Avro 504N G-EBVY. The *Daily Sketch*, the 'premier picture paper', had their sponsorship prominently displayed on the sound equipment van. (Maidenhead Heritage Trust, MAIHC 2010.106.84)

'The Barnstormers walk' in front of a Fox Moth G-ACCF. Pauline captioned the photo: Drury, Phillips, McIntosh, Morton, Jordan, self, Scott, Bonar, Rollason – some of the team of pilots she spent many weeks with during the British Hospitals' Air Pageant in 1933, a summer of travelling shows, displays and adventures. (Maidenhead Heritage Trust, MAIHC 2010.106.82)

Pauline studies a map for her next stop with the British Hospitals' Air Pageant, 1933, with fellow pilot L. Weston at Ross on Wye, Herefordshire, in front of her three-seater Spartan *Helen of Troy*. She flew over 300 tours that summer, with nearly 2,000 take-offs and landings without incident. (Maidenhead Heritage Trust, MAIHC 2010.106.89)

Signed photo of Pauline Gower, given to First Officer Jackie Moggridge and kept proudly in her ATA archive for many years. (Reproduced with kind permission of her younger daughter Candida Adkins)

A striking portrait of Dorothy Spicer, painted in 1934, by Edward Halliday. (Reproduced with kind permission of his daughter and artist, Charlotte Halliday.)

Pauline and Dorothy with actress Evelyn Laye at the opening of the show at Hayes, Middlesex, 1933. (Reproduced with kind permission of Tim Spicer)

On 1 January 1940 the First Eight joined the ATA to the immense interest of the press photographers. Women pilots ferrying planes? The newspapers had a field day. (Photo courtesy of Tunbridge Wells Library)

The press photographer didn't catch the First Eight properly the first time, so they were asked to scramble from the Tiger Moth again, carrying heavy parachutes! Taken 10 January 1940 at Hatfield. Left to right: Pauline Gower, Winifred Crossley, Margaret Cunnison, Margaret Fairweather, Mona Friedlander, Joan Hughes, Gabrielle Patterson, Rosemary Rees and Marion Wilberforce. A formidable team! (Photo courtesy of Tunbridge Wells Library)

Pauline briefing two of the First Eight women pilots Winifred Crossley and Mona Friedlander at Hatfield Ferry Pool. Maps were all important in the absence of aircraft radios; routes had to be planned in detail in advance. (Maidenhead Heritage Trust, MAIHC 2010.106.8)

Pauline in a serious discussion with Lieutenant Colonel John Moore-Brabazon, 15 January 1941. She was pushing for her women pilots to fly a wider range of aircraft, including operational. (Maidenhead Heritage Trust, MAIHC 2010.106.1c1)

ATA women at Hatfield, May 1941, following a visit from Lieutenant Colonel John Moore-Brabazon, Minister of Aircraft Production. Left to right: Constance Leathart, Lois Butler, Margaret Cunnison, Pauline Gower, Jackie Sorour, Honor Pitman, Ann Douglas, Anna Leska, Barbara Wojtulanis, Winifred Crossley, Lettice Curtis, Patricia Beverley, Audrey Sale-Barker, Audrey Macmillan, Rosemary Rees, Kitty Farrer. (Photo courtesy of Candida Adkins)

The heavens opened the day Eleanor Roosevelt came to visit White Waltham on 26 October 1942. Pauline presents a group of ATA pilots as part of the tarmac inspection. (Maidenhead Heritage Trust, MAIHC 2011.46.68)

Pauline Gower married Wing Commander Bill Fahie at the Brompton Oratory, London, on Saturday, 2 June 1945. She is pictured here arriving at the church with her father, Sir Robert Gower. Her post-war bridal outfit was a mid-length pink dress and a blue-feathered hat, with a rare glimpse of a pair of heels. (Maidenhead Heritage Trust, MAIHC 2010.106.12)

Pauline and Bill leave the church after their wedding ceremony through a guard of honour. A proud moment for all the ATA women. (Maidenhead Heritage Trust, MAIHC 2010.106.145)

'Happy Hunstanton' weekend in September 1995 to celebrate the launch of *A Harvest of Memories: The Life of Pauline Gower MBE* by her son Michael Fahie. Some of the ATA women pilots were present at the 300-strong launch event. (Photo courtesy of aviation bookseller Brian Cocks, who drove Diana Barnato Walker in his vintage Bentley to watch the flour-bombing display, echoing Pauline's well-timed advertising stunts of the 1930s)

Pauline Gower's sons Paul and Michael Fahie unveil a memorial to their mother in 1995 in Hunstanton, Norfolk, where she gave over 3,000 passengers joy-rides during the summers of 1934 and 1935. (Photo courtesy of aviation bookseller Brian Cocks, who attended the launch)

Joy Lofthouse and Mary Wilkins Ellis attending an ATA memorial service at White Waltham on 2 September 2017. (Author)

ATA memorial at White Waltham, the spiritual home of the organisation. (Author)

7

CIRCLE OF INFLUENCE – WARTIME CONNECTIONS

Pauline had a long-lasting influence on many of the 168 women of the ATA, pilots and engineers, and everyone remembered her in a positive light. The secret of her success lay in her strength of character, natural good humour, and an ability to empathise while retaining the position of leader. She overcame many obstacles along the way with a natural optimism and resilience. Her influence was felt by many in her sphere down the decades.

I strove to find anything out of character. And the only untoward incident I did find said more about Pauline's desire for speed and adventure than anything else! On 23 January 1936, a 'Standard four-seater saloon car' had been spotted by one PC Daniels driving over the speed limit at '36 to 38 miles an hour' along Farnborough Common Road, near Locksbottom in south-east London. The *Kent and Sussex Courier* continued: 'He overtook the defendant and gonged her car.' He told the driver she had been speeding and Pauline said, 'I suppose that means a summons?' She then asked him to say her speedometer was not working – a request that could have made her position worse. Pauline did not attend court in Brompton, but her advocate pleaded guilty on her behalf. She was fined 30 shillings and the matter was closed.

Fellow motoring enthusiast Mary Wilkins Ellis, then 101, remembered Pauline fondly, with real affection and sparkle. I was lucky to have coffee with Mary one Sunday morning in 2018, in her sun-filled conservatory, and to meet some of her lifelong friends. She did not need prompting about her former senior commander: 'Pauline was lovely. Very kind. If you ever had a problem, she would sort it out.' Mary handed me a plate of wafer biscuits, as delicate as she seemed, perhaps recalling the cups of tea she had shared with Pauline during their years working together. An antidote to all manner of crises and personal losses. I kept the patterned paper napkin from that meeting, folded into a chapter about Mary in an ATA book, as Robert Gower had folded wedding serviettes into his scrapbooks, preserving memories.

Mary was enjoying much media attention at that time; her autobiography *A Spitfire Girl*, as told to Melody Foreman, was published in 2016, and she had made television appearances and enjoyed helicopter flights to anniversary events. She was in demand! Her memory was sharp and Pauline's crucial role never forgotten: 'Without her incredible determination in the face of all sorts of prejudice and political opposition, I would never have had a chance to use any of my flying skills to help Britain and pilot a wealth of military aircraft including of course the Spitfire.'

I met Mary for the first time in 2017, at an ATA Association memorial service at White Waltham. After the wreath-laying ceremony, and a poem in memory of all those who had served in the ATA, read by ATAA Secretary John Webster, I spotted her sitting on a nearby bench, chatting to Richard Poad, chairman of Maidenhead Heritage Centre and her old friend, fellow ATA pilot Joy Lofthouse. Mary's niece, Rosemarie Martin, had introduced us previously so that I could send a copy of *Sisters in Spitfires* to her long-term home on the Isle of Wight, next to Sandown Airport.

Mary Ellis had written to thank me for the book and signed her poem that day at White Waltham. I was honoured that she thought the poems 'wizard' and took that as high praise, recognising the familiar RAF term, relishing the now unfamiliar adjective.

It seems appropriate to add Molly Rose's comments, as they say so much about the ATA women. In November 2015 she wrote:

Many thanks for sending me to the copies of *Sisters in Spitfires* and thank you also for maintaining the modesty that we all felt concerning our own small contribution to the war effort. I do hope you had fun in gathering the information together and then in writing the poems. We certainly are having fun reading the poems.

The ATA Association memorial ceremony over and the photographs taken, Mary suggested they go and find a cup of tea. 'That sounds like a jolly good idea!' Joy laughed, ready to catch up on any news over one of their favourite drinks, and walked with Mary to where the cups were waiting. Mary smiled at me, sprightly and elegant at 100, and accompanied her friend inside. Such commemorative events are important, not just to keep wartime memories alive, but to keep people connected and present, creating new memories to pass on to future generations. Associations too are necessary to keep connections alive.

Joan Hughes, the youngest of the First Eight, started to fly at the age of 15 and, two years later, was the youngest female pilot in Great Britain. Before the war she was an instructor in the Civil Air Guard and became the only woman qualified to instruct on all types of military aircraft in service as the most senior ATA pilot. She eschewed marriage in favour of the sky, reasoning she could not dedicate herself to both. Joan was a first-class instructor, and her reputation lives on after an amazing fifty-year career, not least in the fact she starred in the 1960s film *Those Magnificent Men in their Flying Machines*, doubled as Lady Penelope, flew a Tiger Moth under a motorway bridge and landed in court on seven separate charges (she got off lightly). Joan was 5ft 2in and formidable in the air; her ready smile seen on many photos. She eventually retired in 1985 with 11,800 hours crammed into her logbook.

When Pauline's son, Michael Fahie, wrote to Joan during his research in 1993, she recommended books by Judy Lomax and Wendy Boas. She concluded her letter with these lines about his mother: 'We all loved her and without [Pauline], the women pilots of ATA would not have got off the ground. She was a super CO and had the greatest possible tact and was marvellous at giving us all such superb encouragement.'

Judy Lomax attended the launch of *A Harvest of Memories*; she knew that Michael 'should and could do it' and offered to review the book. Another loop of time.

Pauline was also remembered for her personal touch with the women pilots. Although she was seen as a 'serious and rather self-effacing person, who obviously felt the weight of her responsibilities at the time', American ATA pilot Roberta Sandoz Leveaux, who had been stationed with 'an extraordinary collection of women' at Hamble, told Michael Fahie about his mother's sensitivity in dealing with her worried parents far away from their daughter:

> I recall her warmth, patience and kindness, and the amount of time out of her demanding schedule which she devoted to a request from my parents. They had wired her with a worry about their only child's engagement to an Englishman. Your mother asked me thoughtful, sensible questions … which encouraged me to think beyond romance … and relayed to my family that the match had not been undertaken lightly, and that my intended was '… of good family and excellent regiment.' Considering the pressure of the times, that was surely a beyond-the-call-of-duty effort!

Roberta's parents need not have worried; Pauline's sensitive handling turned out for the best, as she and 'that fellow' were happily married for almost sixty years.

At 29 Pauline was not much older than many of the women in her command, and some were her seniors, yet she brought her human touch and common sense to the role and found time to deal with issues that mattered. It may have been her natural empathy as a leader, or the knowledge that if the women were happy in themselves, they would be safer in the air. That she deemed paramount; that and the safety of the planes. All were her responsibility at all times.

'She taught Mummy the facts of life!' Candida Adkins exclaimed over the phone, her enthusiasm for Pauline's part in Jackie Moggridge's wartime sex education still evident. Candida has kept her mother's role in the Second World War and ground-breaking aviation career alive by giving talks around Britain. Her mother broke the sound barrier, flew Spitfires to Burma and, as Captain Jackie Moggridge, was one of the first five women to win her RAF wings in August 1953 – a significant achievement. Jackie was just 18 when she made her way from Pretoria, South Africa, to follow her dream and later fly with the ATA. She had ridden a motorbike at 15 but wanted to take to the sky soon after. 'And why not?' as Pauline would have said. Jackie was green, a 'fledgling', and it showed. She tried hard to fit in, noting the clipped accents of the confident older women around her, but it was Pauline Gower who put her at her ease. She reacted kindly to the young pilot's nervous manner, 'like a mouse ready to flee at a harsh word', at their first meeting. 'You mustn't be shy. We are all newcomers here. You are awfully young … You can take care of yourself?'

Jackie Sorour, as she was then, was completely in awe of the pioneering pilot who held many international records, now commandant of the Women's Section of the ATA, and said 'yes' without much awareness of what she was being asked. Or the implications. She had got this far; she could bluff her way through. Jackie was then told to pop into the office any time and to call her 'Pauline' not 'Ma'am'. At that first impressionable meeting, Jackie noted the 'glint of battle in her eyes' as Pauline informed her that they were currently only ferrying light aircraft such as Tiger Moths but 'they would by flying the heavier stuff soon if I have any say in the matter'. Which of course she did, to positive effect.

Candida Adkins, Jackie's younger daughter, offers more insights into Pauline's influence in her interview in Appendix II, adding weight with her summary of character and legacy. I first met Candida at White Waltham, at the BWPA's Diamond Jubilee in 2015, then again at the unveiling of the Amy Johnson bronze statue on a wet and windy day in Herne Bay, Kent, in September 2016, when she was helping to straighten the ATA Association flag blowing off course. Candida keeps her mother's achievements very much alive through her talks, website and events, and her contribution to this book is greatly appreciated.

Her attic is full of her mother's memorabilia, and cap and uniform come out for these talks, bringing her wartime role sharply into focus.

Monique Agazarian had further high praise for her senior commander:

> She was determined that women should be allowed to ferry the full range of military aircraft … Some of the other women felt she should apply sooner, but there was a great deal of opposition from the RAF at the idea of women being capable of flying powerful military aircraft. So she waited for the right moment, and instead of bludgeoning her way in, she asked the CO of the training flight if he thought his instructors, who were known to be the best in the world, would be able to take on the challenge of training her women ATA pilots up to the standard?

A clever and perceptive means of setting a challenge to achieve the desired result and, perhaps, reminiscent of the way in which she let her father know of her flying ambitions. Softly, subtly, but with intent.

Richard Poad, chairman of the Maidenhead Heritage Centre, has described Pauline as a 'consummate politician' who always took a 'softly, softly' approach; one flight at a time, one new type of plane at a time, but always pushing forward to get more freedom for the women pilots, more responsibility and, soon, equal pay for equal work.

Peggy Lucas remembered Pauline clearly. In 1993 she told Michael Fahie:

> Everyone I met in ATA, from pilots to mechanics and ground staff, had a great respect for your mother. She always seemed very calm, cool and collected, and one can see by her correspondence at the beginning of the war, she was very clear thinking and succinct. Of course, all we latecomers to ATA were in awe of her, after all, she had our destinies in her hand: on her decision depended on whether we were accepted or not and whether we stayed in!

Another keen horsewoman, Peggy had learned to ride on donkeys on Ealing Common as a young girl and in 1949 became the British Horse Society's first fellow. She joined the ATA after the Battle of Britain led to a much greater need for pilots and flew mostly Spitfires. Without navigation systems in place, she recalled – as many of the pilots did – following railway lines to keep on course. Peggy continued flying after the war and, at the age of 84, qualified as a helicopter pilot.

Margaret Ebbage (née Cunnison of the First Eight) knew Pauline from the outset of the ATA and, writing in 1992, remembered her as 'a delightful person, very honest and straight in her dealings with people and full of fun'. Margaret had kept both volumes of her poetry, the second of which, *More Piffling Poems for Pilots*, Pauline had presented to her husband, a surgeon who was stationed at Hatfield House when they were at Hatfield Aerodrome. Carefully preserved for almost fifty years, Margaret had offered the collections to Michael Fahie during his gathering of memories. Another clear example of the high regard in which contemporaries held his mother, decades after her death.

Diana Barnato Walker MBE, who herself ended the war with a hugely impressive logbook and many airborne adventures, was another pilot inspired by Pauline: 'I didn't meet her until I joined the ATA and, because she was a few years older than I and had such a remarkable flying record, I was somewhat in fear of her.'

Operations Officer Alison King described Diana as 'fine boned, clear cut, and, with all her money, strangely unspoilt'. Diana's lively autobiography, *Spreading My Wings* (Grub Street, 2003), is highly recommended for its breathless tales of Bentleys (she was given one by her doting father on her 21st birthday, and a second model once she had ruined the clutch on the first: 'The Darracq had an early kind of pre-selector gearbox which I just could not get the hang of. The appropriate gear was selected, then you pumped the clutch down – or was it the other way round? Anyway, by the time I got the car back to the Ritz, I had burnt the clutch out'); high-society adventures; flying at Brooklands after six hours solo; her ATA years, in which she delivered 260 Spitfires; and going on, incredibly, to break the sound barrier in 1963. She was the first British woman to do so, at the age of 45. In a manner very similar to Pauline's own direct and clear-headed diplomacy, Diana gave the Minister of Defence twelve reasons why she should fly an RAF Lightning. 'I don't see why she shouldn't,' he concluded.

Diana was awarded the MBE in 1965, to complement her 1939–45 Star, the France and Germany Star, the Defence Medal and the War Medal, awarded for flying aircraft into Holland, Belgium, France and Germany. She features on the cover of *Sisters in Spitfires*, which includes the following sequence, 'Diana's Nine Lives', dedicated to her. The poem offers background detail to many of her flights that almost ended in disaster, but with characteristic ATA resilience and strength of mind was luckily averted. I found a pristine hardback copy of *Spreading My Wings* in Baggins Book Bazaar in Rochester, Kent in 2015, signed by Diana in curling blue ink: 'For Geoffrey, Thanks for the lovely drive, Best wishes always, Diana Barnato Walker.'

It is easy to imagine her being swept around the country lanes in an open-topped Bentley, trademark headscarf around neat, dark hair, chatting animatedly with some words perhaps lost to the wind. Her stories of ATA life reveal just how many opportunities Pauline Gower had opened up for women pilots, as well as their numerous narrow escapes and the courage needed to keep going throughout the war.

Diana's Nine Lives

The Powder Puff Moment
I tried a roll in the Spitfire, but somehow got stuck upside-
down at 5,000 feet and out flew that silver compact
from my pocket, showering the cockpit, the controls, the pilot …
The striking Flight Lieutenant striding to meet me stopped
short in his tracks – I was not the girl he was expecting, just a
powder-puff clown! He turned on heels and drove off …

The Bomb in the Basement

*By some strange coincidence, my father put his foot down that
night, telling me I was treating the place like a hotel. He was
quite right, but I'd never say so. We stayed in, the three of us
and later learnt that my club of so many happy memories had
been hit by a rogue bomb – down a vent, into the basement.
We shuddered as we thought of what might have been.*

Bullets Over Berkshire

*There were twelve of us packed liked sardines in the Anson
heading back to White Waltham. I was next to Jim Mollison in
the co-pilot's seat. We may have been a little heavy, but weren't
planning on an overnighter. We hadn't bargained on a Jerry
gunner aiming at us though! We hid in the overcast for as long as
we dared before all piling out to look for bullet holes …*

The Greenhouses and the Tractor

*Delivering my 13th Spitfire, I should have been ready for
something to happen … I was off to Essex and a murky mist
forced me to detour. I headed for a red dot of an aerodrome
so small I had to fly low over some greenhouses, causing a stir,
the crowd was delighted I'd seen the man on the tractor …
I bluffed my way out, with halo, tractor and greenhouses intact.*

Cushions to Clear a Windsock

*My first Hampden was unforgettable – it was a plane for a
long-legged pilot, not for little old me. For once the flight crew
were unhelpful – no cushions … If only they could have seen
me dicing with death! I wedged jacket, parachute and logbooks
behind me, but the G force whipped the throttle lever out of reach.
I missed the incoming windsock with inches to spare.*

Mustang Waltz in a Pixie-Hood

It was a lovely day, and I dipped the Mustang wings in time
with my own waltz, hair cascading from the red pixie-hood –
the only thing I'd found to replace my broken helmet.
I was suddenly boxed in by four Spitfires in formation
laughing Free Frenchmen keeping me on course to Kenley.
'Been out with the boys', I'd say, when Ops queried my delay.

Going Over the Top

It seemed the only option, taking a Spit from Eastleigh
to Cosford, flying over sunny Worcester. If I was spared
of course, as the next thing I knew I was in thick cloud.
I broke the rules, went up to 12,000 feet … saw a gap
and dived, nose down, fingers virtually crossed.
Vera Strodl understood – she'd been over the top too!

A Wing and a Prayer

Sun to cloud, it was one of those days … I was enjoying the
Spitfire IX, with the Cotswolds safely beneath me, when we
struck cloud … Max and Billy's recent lesson swam to mind,
if in doubt, bale out, but I was wearing a skirt and couldn't
sail down in a parachute, showing off hitched-up navy serge!
My landing was memorable, my knees just collapsed.

A Night in Silken Sheets

Flying a Mosquito, I ran into a heavy snowstorm, landing
gingerly at Chilbolton. I was offered a bed in an empty Nissen,
complete with the Colonel's very own silk sheets! Just the drip
on the roof to send me to sleep. I woke unable to move,
a corporal at my side. Roof collapsed, he'd come to my aid –
a guardian angel with a shovel and a cup of tea!

Alison Hill, *Sisters in Spitfires*

From her early days at Brooklands, when a disfigured and badly burnt pilot had thrown himself on her plane before her first solo flight, urging her not to fly, Diana was convinced she had a guardian angel keeping her mind focused, or at least on the flights where she was not being showered with her powder puff, dodging tractors, greenhouses and more. Diana flew her own light aircraft after the war, encouraging young women to join the Women's Junior Air Corps. She was also master of her local hunt for thirteen years and chairwoman of the ATA Association, keeping her contacts and passions alive, as her book reveals.

Flying over the clouds, without ground contact, was forbidden, but ATA pilots were often tempted, and did break the rules on occasion. Who was to know? And the Spitfire was *so* tempting to take dancing over clouds … If they lost sight of the ground, that glimpse of sunlight on cirrus was more than enough distraction. But it was dangerous without radios and not many did it for long. Some spoke of giving in to temptation. It was a memory that stood out, a chance to fly freely, solo, and unobserved. The Spitfires still got delivered safely in one piece.

The ATA was formally wound up in November 1945. There had been less need for delivery of planes during the final stretch of the war and it was clear that the organisation would soon become redundant. Many of the women feared they would too, in the traditionally male-dominated world of aviation, despite their technical skills and, thanks to Pauline, their ability to fly many different types of planes for ferrying duties. They were ahead of their time.

When interviewed decades later, Joy Lofthouse was candid in her summary: 'The war ended, and we all went back to being housewives. And nobody wanted to know what you did in the war. The men are asked but the ladies aren't asked as much.'

A Rapid Dispersal

We knew it was almost over; a few of us
posed to lay up the flag at White Waltham
November '45, many had already gone.

We smiled into the distance, still young
but perhaps wondering if the most exciting
part of our lives was behind us. We knew not.

Some of us were more than ready to hang up
our uniforms, take down our golden wings –
we knew we'd done our bit and more.

For others it was a wrench. We were simply
expected to pick up our lives, our jobs,
our kitchen sinks. But on that bitter-sweet

Winter's day, as Audrey Sale-Barker lowered
the flag, we knew we'd given our best years
to the skies and mostly seen it through.

Yet some part of us would emerge from stray
corners of chilly airfields; remembering
those we'd lost along the way.

Alison Hill, *Sisters in Spitfires*

The flag remains on display at White Waltham and is a fitting reminder of all that the ATA stood for in terms of war effort, strength and survival. Several of the women wrote their autobiographies (see Bibliography from page 249), which describe their post-war careers and provide valuable insights into their contribution, experience of the wartime years and, mostly, their spirit of adventure. And their resilience. Only seven of the women were flying ten years after the war ended.

ATA pilot Peggy Lucas was only able to find temporary jobs, such as as an instructor at Bembridge on the Isle of Wight one summer, and so returned to her first love: horses. She ran a riding school in Dorset and later taught in Austria, riding at the famous Spanish School in Vienna. While Dorothy Furey, one of the first American recruits, went on to breed racehorses and at the age of 77 took up scuba diving. Intrepid women!

Jackie Moggridge was desperate to find commercial employment, as were many others, but only a handful of the ATA women were lucky enough, or tenacious enough, to secure work. She wrote all her letters of application using just her initials – reminiscent of women authors today, including P.D. James and J.K. Rowling who have succeeded despite, or because of, not disclosing their gender. Once Jackie arrived for interview, the situation would quickly change. She describes her frustration at being grounded in her book *Spitfire Girl, My Life in the Sky*:

> I continued answering advertisements but every flicker of hope died by return post. It was a disheartening period. Now [writing in 1957] I am partially reconciled to the rebuffs of prejudice but in those earlier days I felt sick with humiliation and envy whenever an aircraft droned by in the sky.

A few weeks later, she had an invitation to an interview – the letter was addressed to Mr Moggridge! She was determined to break through the barriers. Jackie eventually flew Spitfires to Burma, broke the sound barrier and won her RAF wings.

Diana Barnato Walker enjoyed post-war aviation success, as outlined in her lively and informative biography, *Spreading My Wings*. She overcame prejudice in her equally spirited way and gained her coveted 'B' licence, coincidentally learning night-flying at Marshall's Aerodrome in Cambridge. This was Molly Rose's family business, so the ATA connections endured. Not long after Diana had got her licence, one of the First Eight, Gabrielle Patterson, asked her to fly with the Women's Junior Air Corps (WJAC), which involved flying the cadets at week-ends. She said that 'the aim was to make the girls into good citizens, as well as to promote this with an air-minded flavour'.

In 1962 Diana won the annual Jean Lennox Bird Trophy for her work with the WJAC and the presentation was made by top British aviator Lord Brabazon of Tara. Jean had been stationed at Hamble Ferry Pool and was the first woman to win her RAF wings, but sadly was killed in 1957 when a Miles Aerovan aircraft she was piloting crashed shortly after take-off from Ringway Airport. The following year, Diana successfully persuaded the Minister of Defence (Air), the Right Honorable Hugh Fraser MBE PC MP (an old friend) to let her fly a Lightning. The whole story is colourfully detailed in her memoir, but safe to say her plan of action worked. She arrived early on Monday morning at the Ministry of Defence, in smart uniform as opposed to being 'dressed up to the nines … with long trailing hair' at their weekend meeting. Like Pauline before her, she came fully prepared and won her case: 'Clutched in my clammy hand was a tiny card on which I had written 12 reasons why I wanted to fly the Lightning.' He agreed and Diana agreed in turn to RAF publicity; after all, it was not something with which she was unfamiliar. On 26 August 1963, after a lengthy photo shoot, she attempted what they had named the Women's Speed Record. She had had plenty of simulator training, during which she had some unusual health symptoms. The moment came, in her words:

> Oh, life was grand! The Mach-meter moved up, the instruments went haywire and the compressability [sic] 'cobbles' duly bumped, then went as we passed through the sound barrier, and the instruments came back to their normal readings again. Then suddenly, all was quiet – and I mean quiet. All our sound was left behind us.

The barrier firmly broken, Diana became a member of the Ten Ton Club (the 1,000 miles per hour fraternity) and was presented with a club tie. She had flown faster – at 1,262 mph – than any woman in the world at that time, beating Jacqueline Cochran of the US and Jacqueline Auriol of France.

Soon after the exhilarating flight, Diana found out she had cancer and spent several weeks in Middlesex Hospital. Against the odds that she later found had been placed on her recovery, she survived and flew for a few more years. Her summary is testament to the opportunities she had flying in the ATA; the times when her resilience and, perhaps, her guardian angel from her Brooklands first solo flight came to her rescue. She fully appreciated her chances: 'I have flown over 120 different types and marks of aeroplanes … I wouldn't have missed a single type, a single hour or any one of those flights. I have indeed been Spreading My Wings.'

Ann Welch enjoyed a fifty-year career in aviation, one of the luckier ones who was not relegated to the kitchen sink after the war. She flew over a hundred Spitfires and many 'friendly' Wellingtons with the ATA before leaving in 1942 to start a family with her RAF pilot husband who had been shot down twice. Ann had gained her pilot's licence in 1934, aged 17, and flown at Brooklands, like Diana. She had a passion for gliding and launched the Surrey Gliding Club in 1938. A pioneering spirit, she was devoted to training young pilots and cutting through bureaucracy. She also brought up three children and was manager of the British Team at World Gliding Championships from 1948 to 1968. Ann's skill and passion took her all over the world and she was awarded an MBE and OBE for services to gliding.

Mary Ellis was also lucky enough to enjoy a long and rewarding post-war career in aviation. She managed Sandown Airport on the Isle of Wight for twenty years, as Europe's first female commandant, and inspired many women to learn to fly at the Isle of Wight Aero Club, which she founded. Her achievements were recognised in later life. Although she was typically modest, she told me with a smile, 'I've had a marvellous life', which included much to do with wings, the sky, and the speed of her rallying days. A highly respected local figure, Mary was granted the freedom of the Isle of Wight in January 2018, as a 'national, international and Island heroine' and celebrated her 100th birthday with a Spitfire flight.

All of these women pushed boundaries, as they had done in wartime, and pushed against prejudice to achieve success in aviation. Pauline had inspired and led them throughout the war – she had paved the way with her own drive and determination that women should fly.

ATA RECOGNITION AND POST-WAR MEDALS

On 23 September 1950, Lord Beaverbrook, former Minister of Aircraft Production, unveiled a plaque in the crypt of St Paul's Cathedral, at a well-attended ceremony recorded for posterity by British Pathé. The ATA Association continues to lay an annual wreath in remembrance on each Armistice Day. The stone's inscription reads:

> To the memory of the one hundred and seventy-three men and
> women
> of the Air Transport Auxiliary representing many nations who gave
> their lives
> in the Allied cause during the World War of 1939 to 1945.

It concludes with a couplet from the poem 'Passage', written in 1919 by John Drinkwater (1882–1937): 'Remember then that also we, in a moon's course, are history.'

On 9 September 2008, sixty-three years after the ATA flag was lowered for the last time, Prime Minister Gordon Brown invited surviving ATA veterans – fifteen women and a hundred men – to a reception at Downing Street to receive a service medal in recognition of their contribution to the war effort. This was partly the result of a campaign by Nigel Griffiths MP to ensure that their service – and, in many cases, the ultimate sacrifice – to their country was not forgotten.

One 90-year-old veteran, Annette Hill, known as the 'Barracuda Queen' during her time in the ATA for her love of those wartime all-metal torpedo bombers designed by Fairey Aviation (when asked how she landed them without a great deal of training, she said with a twinkle 'it comes to those who wait'), was glad of the recognition. She was delighted to have the prime minister shake her hand, and to visit White Waltham Airfield for a reception beforehand as part of the event. 'We had a wonderful time because we were young girls and all the fellows chased after us. We did our job and while sometimes it was really hairy, I enjoyed my life.'

Joy Lofthouse, then 85, was equally enthusiastic, and told the *Wilts and Gloucestershire Standard*: 'It was the most wonderful day. Going inside Number Ten was a great thrill.' She was pictured outside with two medals, one for her and one for her elder sister Yvonne who lived in America at the time. 'It would be nice to bottle it,' she added. 'They laid on a wonderful day for us.'

The other women pilots present included Maureen Dunlop, Mary Ellis, Diane Home, Molly Rose and Freydis Sharland, alongside a hundred male pilots. It was a day of memories.

Gordon Brown said on the day:

> I am honoured to have this opportunity to give my thanks to the men and women of the ATA. Their dedication and efforts during the Second World War cannot be overestimated. They can be rightly proud of their contribution to defending this country during its darkest hours. It is a great privilege to meet so many of them today and to hear of the work they undertook and their sacrifice they made to ensure the delivery of aircraft for the front line.

While Aviation Minister Jim Fitzpatrick said: 'It is humbling to hear of the work undertaken by these brave men and women and it is right that we remember those who served and recognise their vital role in the war effort.'

In 2011 the Royal Aeronautical Society (RAeS) held a Spitfire Women seminar with four guests of honour: Molly Rose, Margaret Frost, Mary Ellis and Joy Lofthouse. They were given a standing ovation on entering the lecture theatre and their personal reminiscences were the highlight of the day. All of these women had been interviewed over the past decade or so about their wartime flying years and, although they remembered the Spitfire, above all, with huge admiration and fondness, they knew they were there to do an essential job. There was no hint of glorification in talking about the Spits, just a matter-of-fact acceptance that they ferried planes, of all types, and that was their part in the war. Many said they were just 'doing their bit', as was everyone else. They had their own memories of personal loss and tragedy, and there were no rose-tinted glasses in sight. The ATA pilots, men and women, had done just one of many jobs to support the war effort but, as Joy Lofthouse was keen to point out, 'they were young, everything was possible'. The flying was a thrill, mostly, and their youth kept them buoyant and relatively fearless. 'Let's face it,' she said, 'all women did something in the war.' But they were fully aware that their job, dangerous as it could be, was far more exciting than most other wartime work.

In the summer of 2015, I was fortunate to meet veteran bomber pilot Ralph Ford, a year before he died aged 95. He was more than happy to talk about the (unknown) woman who had delivered his first Spitfire, but his eyes filled as he recalled the bombing raids, the long dark nights of the war. It was hard to fully comprehend the risks he had taken every day, the deep memories of his friends who had not survived. He had lost many. And he was too modest for any formal acknowledgement; he did not want his name on a poem. The tweed jacket over his daytime pyjamas spoke of his inherent pride and a determination to set aside age and frailty for our meeting. Ralph's next-door neighbour, Graham Singleton, had listened to his wartime memories over many years and painted a Spitfire mural on his garden wall in recognition of a man who had more than done 'his bit' for the war effort, for the freedom of others. Ralph's well-attended funeral service was testament to his strength of character and his rich community life after the war. My poem for Ralph, 'One Fine Day', has been read in front of a Spitfire at the RAF Museum and a Wellington at Brooklands Museum – the title is taken from a phrase he used often in our conversation. He had seen the poem in draft form, given it his approval, and we had swapped *Spitfire Society* magazines over a cup of tea.

One Fine Day

I'd been told my first Spit was waiting at the airfield.
It was a day we all looked forward to, amid the sorties
the bombs, the long days and the darkest of nights.

So one fine day I went to collect it, watched as it taxied
towards me, sun gilding its wings, catching it just so.

Here I was, my first Spit and out stepped the pilot
but would you believe – just a slip of girl!

There I was, put firmly in my place, but glad she'd
ferried it my way, glad to slip into her seat, to climb
and dive like a bird set free, on that vivid, virgin flight.

8

MARRIAGE, BIRTH AND LIVES CUT SHORT

A cold and foggy night in January 1944 brought Pauline and her future husband together. She was staying with her close friend Kitty Farrer and her husband Oliver on their farm near St Albans, having been ordered by a specialist to take three weeks' complete rest to help recover from a particularly bad spell of depression. Pauline had just returned from a long trip to South Africa, followed by travels to Cairo, Palestine and Iran, and a friend in Cairo thought she looked well. But the doctor clearly thought otherwise, so the farm and friendship were both very welcome at that time and proved to be a turning point in her life.

Wing Commander Bill Fahie was an old friend of Kitty's and had been driving to see his sister Norah in Aldenham, Hertfordshire. The weather took a turn for the worse, with visibility next to nothing, and he stopped by the farm on the chance of a bed for the night. Bill was introduced to Pauline in the dining room and was 'absolutely enthralled' – he could not take his eyes off her for the rest of the evening. We can only presume that Pauline was equally smitten! She had been courted by many men, but found him 'different to the others' and clearly gave him more of a chance.

Born on 27 April 1918, the youngest child and only son of a Dublin family, Bill Fahie became a high-flying academic and talented mathematician. He was very close to his two sisters, Norah Pauline and Ita Mary. Bill excelled at his studies and published an article 'Galileo and Mathematical Demonstration' as a student; the abstract set out to correct the misquotation of the work of his uncle, the late Mr J.J. Fahie, on the famous astronomer. Perhaps Bill's academic interests appealed to Pauline's own fascination with the sky; it may well have been an early talking point. They also shared a keen sense of humour. He graduated with a first-class honours degree in 1938 and a year later was awarded a master of science from University College Dublin. Commissioned straight into the Royal Air Force as flying officer, Fahie served throughout the war, some of the time in France. At the time of the farm encounter, he had just returned from overseas – postings in Malta and Africa – where he had served as an RAF radar expert. Eight years Pauline's junior, he certainly made an impact.

After their first meeting, Pauline and Bill spent as much time together as they could, given the nature of their wartime work and the imminent invasion of Europe. *A Harvest of Memories* gives an insight into their courtship, as intrigue grew in Pauline's office as to who her regular caller 'Bill, Darling' was. They did not have long to wait.

Kitty Farrer, Pauline's great friend from White Waltham days, was to play another part in their blossoming relationship. By Easter 1945, with ferrying not quite as busy as it had been, Pauline took another much-needed break on her friend's farm. She and Bill had arranged to meet there on Easter Sunday. Kitty and her husband made themselves scarce, perhaps with an inkling that something was in the air, and went off to play tennis with Peter Mursell, ATA director of recruitment, and his wife, Dil. Kitty clearly had a happy premonition. By the time they arrived back for lunch, Bill had proposed to Pauline and the newly engaged couple were apparently reading the Sunday papers with just a hint of a grin. Kitty opened a bottle reserved for such an occasion – Sunday lunch turned into a happy celebration.

Robert Gower hosted an engagement party at his London house at 6 Stanhope Gate in Mayfair. The papers were full of the news; this was the engagement that mattered. Pauline's father had himself remarried earlier that year, to Vera Daniels, the widow of a prominent doctor. He and Vera had a shared interest in animal welfare and, as his secretary, she had worked closely with him for several years. Their wedding coincided with the last of his scrapbooks. Robert had been on his own for nine years and this was a new chapter, without the need for newspaper cuttings.

A SUMMER WEDDING

Pauline Gower and Bill Fahie were married on 2 June 1945 at the Church of the Immaculate Heart of Mary, known as the Brompton Oratory, in Kensington, London. The ceremony was officiated by Father Mark Taylor and Pauline was given away by her father. The couple's best man was their good friend ATA Director Senior Commander the Honorable Ben Bathurst, and the ATA pilots formed a guard of honour on the steps outside. Pauline wore a belted pink dress, with a spray of pink flowers and a blue feathered hat. Her shoes were particularly stylish. The formal photograph of the couple leaving the packed church, through the guard of honour, portrays a proud husband and wife who have made it through the war and are ready for their new life ahead. The ATA women look equally proud of their senior commander; it was a photo for posterity, for Sir Robert's scrapbook. Glasses were raised in a rousing toast at the reception afterwards, which was again held at 6 Stanhope Gate. The happy couple then left for a short honeymoon in Surrey before resuming work duties.

Pauline was presented with a silver salver as a wedding present from her ATA pilots, signed by over ninety of the women, although it appears that Lois Butler signed twice! Diana Barnato Walker was later given a similar one, also inscribed. There is something poignant about such silverware outlasting their owners, the same names gathered on the same trays, to be polished by unseen hands who could only guess at the women behind the signatures.

Pauline Gower (she did not change her name) and Bill Fahie began married life at their new house in Chelsea, which they had to renovate, a slow process given the shortage of materials in bomb-damaged London. When the ATA wound down and pilot Audrey Sale-Barker lowered the flag for the last time, on 30 November 1945, Pauline took the opportunity to resign. The RAF discharged Bill in January 1946 and Pauline resigned as a director of BOAC the same month. They were finally free to take time off and relax, and enjoyed a holiday in St Moritz, Switzerland. Pauline was pictured on skis, smiling in her sunglasses, without a uniform or plane in sight. Sadly, she suffered a miscarriage while they were away, which cast a shadow over the trip. She was unwell for some time afterwards, with a lingering cough. Pauline's lungs had been affected by bouts of pneumonia, and she was prone to chest infections.

Back in London, and with Pauline's encouragement, Bill got a new job as a scientist with the British Iron and Steel Research Association. She kept busy with speaking engagements and writing stories and articles. There was a house to finish renovating, too. She became pregnant again in June and was delighted.

Six months into her pregnancy, Pauline had to come to terms with a great loss. Dorothy Spicer was killed in a plane crash on 23 December 1946, along with her husband Richard Pearse. He had been appointed air attaché to Argentina, partly due to his fluency in Spanish, and they were travelling to Buenos Aires. The couple had left their young daughter, Patricia, in the care of relatives and planned that she would join them once they had settled. Their plane, an Avro York of the Flota Aerea Mercante Argentina airline, was diverted due to bad weather and crashed into a mountainside on approach to Rio, in thick fog, killing all twenty-one passengers onboard. Her death was much mourned in aviation circles.

Pauline was distraught at the sudden loss of Dorothy, after their adventurous years together, and did all she could to help look after Patricia, who was also her goddaughter. The friends' final meeting had been in September, when Dorothy had gone to visit Pauline to discuss the forthcoming trip and her intended move to South America. It is easy to imagine them drinking tea, chatting excitedly about Pauline's pregnancy and discussing possible baby names. Looking ahead to a new chapter with a shared laughter borne of an easy friendship.

Pauline paid homage to Dorothy in the January issue of *The Aeroplane*:

> During our years of close and happy partnership, I came to appreciate Dorothy not only for her skill as an engineer, but also for her many other attributes, and to know her for what she was, essentially feminine, charming and unassuming, with that rare sense of humour and infectious gaiety which endeared her to so many.

The long summers spent flying from town to town, the records they broke as pilot and engineer, and the sheer hard work and determination had led to a remarkable partnership. Pauline concluded:

> She was one of the true pioneers of civil aviation in this country, and her unfailing sense of fun, complete lack of conceit, her ability and kindliness, will always be remembered by everyone with whom she came in touch. Those of us who knew her well have lost the type of friend who can never be replaced.

DOROTHY SPICER AWARD

As the first woman in the world to gain all four Air Ministry licences in aircraft engineering, it was fitting that the Royal Aircraft Establishment set up the Dorothy Spicer Memorial Award to commemorate her achievements for future generations. The award ceased in the 1980s.

Her daughter, Patricia, who settled near Johannesburg in her early 20s, told me: 'Sadly I missed so much. I hardly knew her.' She has a distant memory of being taken to 'a lovely flat in London' aged around 4 or 5, to visit Pauline, but not much more. She was only 6 when her parents died, and her mother's elder brother Athol and his wife Margot took her under their wing. She lived for some time near Farnham in Surrey, where she was born, and remembers wartime raids on Farnham Common. Patricia was keen to stress that she had 'ploughed her own furrow' and had not overly dwelt on the past and her mother's career, although was naturally proud of her achievements. We talked about her mother's record-breaking certificates and her esteemed reputation in aviation circles. Patricia had inherited a striking portrait of Dorothy, painted by Edward Irvine Halliday in 1934, which still hangs in her house in South Africa, but she hopes it will eventually come back to England. A loop of time, coming full circle.

Edward Halliday (1902–84) attended the Liverpool College of Art and continued his studies at Académie Colarossi, the Royal College of Art and the British School at Rome. He served in the RAF in Bomber Command during the war. In 1948 he was commissioned to paint Princess Elizabeth, the first of several royal portraits, including one of the young Queen Elizabeth and Prince Philip. Other famous sitters included Winston Churchill, Edmund Hillary and Air Commodore Sir Frank Whittle, who invented the early turbojet engine. Halliday preferred to paint military figures, as uniforms held more interest to paint than suits, and Dorothy's flying overalls, cap and goggles would have held his attention. The resulting portrait is certainly arresting.

I went to visit Charlotte Halliday HNEAC RWS, an award-winning artist who specialises in intricate townscapes and drawings, to see black and white copies of her father's painting. She invited me to her London home and studio in St John's Wood, near where her father had lived and worked. Charlotte's parents had been good friends with Dorothy and her husband. She recalls her mother collecting her from school, aged around 11 or 12, and them coming out of the railway station and seeing a newspaper placard headline about the fatal plane crash. It was an awful shock to her parents to 'learn the sad news about Dorothy and Dickie'. There were some pencil notes on the back of one of the photographs, which Charlotte kindly gave me permission to scan and include in this book: '1934 Pioneer Air Woman, Miss Dorothy Spicer (Mrs Dorothy Pearse).' Charlotte had dug out her father's notebooks to discover more about the commission and told me that he had painted the queen twice when she was a young woman. She thought Dorothy's portrait would have been sent to the Royal Academy, as was most of his work. Her rooms and hallway were a rich blend of hers and Edward's work.

In 1938, Dorothy had also been photographed by Bassano Ltd, in two sittings, one in cap and goggles, the other in necklace and knitwear, and they are part of the National Portrait Gallery collection. Pauline too had a series of six photographs taken by Bassano in November 1937, and another in 1945, which graces the cover of *A Harvest of Memories*. She was also the subject of a lithograph series in 1941 by Ethel Léontine Gabain (1883–1950), which can be seen in the Imperial War Museum's collection.

Patricia was proud of her mother's achievements in aviation. She did not know which traits she had inherited, but her own successful motor racing and equestrian career clearly reflected Dorothy's spirit and determination. Pat Sonnenschein, as she became, raced between 1963 and 1969, competing in the Kyalami 9 Hours in a Mini, in 1964 and 1965, finishing sixth and fifteenth respectively. In 1969, she drove with Christine Beckers in an Alfa Romeo 1750 Berlina, coming eighteenth overall. Patricia's 'chief claim to fame', however, was winning the Index of Performance award in 1964, with her racing partner George Armstrong. They were third on the index the following year. Once Patricia knew we shared an interest in horse riding, she admitted her other talent: 'Indeed I did ride for 30 years, winding up judging dressage at the highest level in this country. I competed at eventing, dressage and as much show jumping as was necessary for eventing. I also taught schooling and dressage, so I was very involved!'

It seems that a love of planes, cars and horses united Pauline, Dorothy, Amy and Patricia, and many more of the women pilots – thinking again about the light that danced in Mary Ellis's eyes at 100, as she watched an Allard speed by us at White Waltham. Her passion for flying had led to a passion for fast cars, and Mary had rallied her own Allard on the Isle of Wight, winning several cups and fuelling her desire for speed.

Pauline had to come to terms with the loss of her friend and would have turned her attention to the new life ahead, anticipation of parenthood. She had learnt from experiences in the ATA not to dwell on death, but to get through tough times with resolution and resilience.

Norah Fahie recalled that Pauline was hugely excited about expecting twins and told all her friends it would be 'two with one boiling':

> She was delighted to be having a child and when the doctor revealed that there would be two, she was so excited that she told the taximan who drove her home, and thereafter led the quest for double equipment, very difficult with post-war shortages. She was convinced that you would be boys and chose only the names that you bear.

In fact, they had all spent ages deliberating. Final choices were Paul, after Pauline, and perhaps with a nod to Robert Gower, who had hoped for a boy and chosen the feminine 'Pauline' for his second daughter. The other choice was Michael, a 'good solid name'. Middles names, as is often the case, had proved trickier.

The winter of 1946 was extremely harsh and ongoing electricity cuts did not help their preparations. Pauline wrote to Bill's mother, a week before the birth, and said 'we are quite expecting that they will have to arrive by candlelight and oil stove'.

A home birth had been planned, following her friend Joan Bathurst's positive experiences, although Pauline's pregnancy was not straightforward. She was confined to bed for the last six weeks, which, for someone so active, may have been difficult. Since her earlier miscarriage, she would have done what was best under the circumstances. That unique, hollow emptiness would have surely been alleviated to some extent by the thrill of expecting twins, and she would have followed her doctor's orders to help ensure their safe arrival. And avoid additional stress on her weakened heart.

Yet nothing is entirely within our control, and the delivery of twins can still cause unforeseen problems, even with all the current medical knowledge and expertise to hand. Pauline's lungs had never fully recovered from the serious mastoid operation at school, aged 17, and the extra strain on her body had clearly taken its toll. The years spent flying at high altitudes in unpressurised aircraft had also affected her health. However, her natural good cheer and optimism, and the imminent arrival of two babies, would have helped her through those weeks. And the comfort and company of friends, family and her sister-in-law, Norah.

But hope and good cheer could not conquer all this time. Pauline's labour was induced, on the advice of specialist Dr Shaw, and she was attended by her friend Joan Bathurst and the community midwife, Sister Sylvester. The twins were born safely, albeit with forceps for Paul and a breech delivery for Michael, and all seemed well. But there was not much spare oxygen, and perhaps not enough medical assistance to hand at just the right time. The midwife had checked regularly on Pauline, while tending to the new-born twins, and the room where the new mother lay sleeping was warm. An atmosphere, no doubt, of the singular weariness of childbirth and aftermath, when babies are birthed, personalities formed on entrance into this world. A time of rest and relief. Tragically, Pauline Gower – woman of so many firsts, so many amazing achievements, for herself, for women, for aviation – was not destined to enjoy this personal first. She died a few hours after their birth, from heart failure, without fully knowing what fine boys she had produced. But her children, and future grandchildren, would remember and celebrate her achievements throughout their lives.

Rosemary Rees, one of the First Eight women pilots of the ATA, said that a mutual friend of hers and Pauline's, Joan Bledisloe, recalled that:

> Pauline was in her house and all tidied up after the birth of her twins when all of a sudden she got a terrible haemorrhage and said 'Oh, I'm going to die!' and she did. The Doctor did what he could but that was not much – if she had been in a hospital something might have been done, but she and Joan Bled, and I believe a lot of other women, think it is more fun to have their babies at home.

Rosemary's characteristic matter of fact tone did not reduce the tragedy, but may have raised questions about Pauline's choice of place to give birth – from society's point of view, if not Pauline's. Not one to conform readily, and having a natural optimism and resilience, she may have hoped that she would sail through childbirth as she had all her other challenges. But if Pauline had been firm in her belief that all would be well, then that should have carried her through. She was always her own woman.

Pauline's sudden death at 36 was a shock to everyone, and her husband was naturally devastated. To have been looking forward to a family of four, and then to lose Pauline so swiftly and without warning, was heart-breaking. Friends and family were equally affected, but Norah Fahie was a tower of strength for her brother in the immediate aftermath of Pauline's death. Arrangements had to be made, babies tended, people notified. There was a general air of disbelief, a heavy sadness falling like a blanket of cloud over a darkening sky.

Robert Gower had been devoted to his daughter and was never quite the same after her death. The twins were cared for initially by Norah and other family members. Their father spoke about Pauline for a while, but then withdrew, and fell silent on the subject. Norah encouraged him to keep talking about her, to keep including her in their memories, but to no avail.

The Associated Press made a brief announcement that would have sent shock waves to all those reading, at the suddenness of her death, prey to the age-old risk of childbirth, which naturally increased with twins. One wonders, as a woman who wrote poems and appreciated the white space around words, if she would have minded her name and role being split across the column, but perhaps she would have appreciated the neat summary – airwoman, leader, mother, wife and daughter. No words wasted, yet some things left unsaid:

Pauline Gower Dies
Giving Birth to Twins
London, Mar. 3.–Pauline Gower, British airwoman and commandant of the women's section of
the Air Transport Auxiliary during

the war, died last night after giving
birth to twin sons. The babies were
reported 'doing well'.

Miss Gower, who retained her
maiden name, was the wife of Wing
Comdr. William Fahie and the
daughter of Sir Robert Vaughan
Gower, former member of Parliament.

The Times reported the next day that 'her courage, skill, and ability, her
quiet charm and her ready smile endeared her to a very large circle of
friends and acquaintances'.

Sister Mary Coke, fellow pupil at Beechwood, recalls the tremor of
sadness felt by all those around Pauline, on hearing the news: 'Hers was
such a vibrant personality, so full of life and fun, and she is truly one of
those who left the world a poorer place at her death.'

Pauline's faith had not wavered throughout her life and had helped
her through dark times, including the sudden, shocking death of her
mother and her own periods of depression. Cemented during her convent school years, especially after her operation, it was a solid comfort
to her down the years. Her kindness was remembered by all who knew
her, and her clarity of vision shines through her photographs. Pauline
wrote a prayer for a friend in need, in 1940, which hung in the chapel
at Beechwood for many years. It was also in the entrance hall for a time
and is now carefully preserved in the school archive.

> *Lord you see me when I'm sleeping,*
> *when I'm waking, working, weeping –*
> *You know my thoughts, my mind you read –*
> *You see my weakness and my need –*
> *Then why should I, assailed by fears,*
> *Give way to grief, despair or tears –*

I know that you are by my side,
to love and guard me and to guide –
And knowing this, I won't complain,
or dread the thought of bearing pain –
My hands in yours this race I'll run,
and may, O Lord, thy will be done.

Pauline would have heard that last line many a time at mass, from her school days onwards, and the final couplet is particularly poignant given her untimely death. Maybe she felt that none of us ever know just how long the race will be. She would have been glad to know that generations of Beechwood pupils took refuge in her prayer; a former famous pupil whose own light shone bright and true and fair. There was a real sense of peace in the school chapel, when I visited, and just the faint echo of an orange or two escaping from the bloomers of two runaway schoolgirls, suppressed giggles from fellow pupils and, perhaps, an understanding nod from a nun or two. She had been a prize pupil, and even runaway oranges could be overlooked.

There were many tributes to Pauline Gower and letters poured into the family home. People also remembered her decades later, delighted to hear about Michael's book in her memory.

Sir Peter Masefield told Michael Fahie in 1993 that he had:

the happiest and most cordial memories of your mother from pre-War days and during her commanding of the Women's Section of the Air Transport Auxiliary, right through her life. Everyone in British aviation was so pleased when Pauline happily married just after the War, but, of course desolated in her sad loss when she died when you and your twin brother were born.

While Alex Henshaw, looking back some sixty years, had clear recollections: 'I used to see her with Dorothy Spicer at Hunstanton in the Summer of 1933 as I lived at Wisbech. They were giving flights over the sea in a Miles Hawk. I remember her as a warm delightful person who had both character and dignity.'

Joan Wheatley, Yolande's sister, had known Pauline very well at school and they kept in touch after they had both left Beechwood. She went to her engagement party and stayed on afterwards at 6 Stanhope Gate. Joan also attended her wedding. Her friend's death came as a great shock as she had not been aware of any underlying heart trouble. She remembered Pauline many years later; in a letter dated July 1993 she told Michael Fahie: 'Pauline worked so hard and lived life to the full. She was an extremely kind person and would always help people in any way she could.' Joan apologised for her bad typing but assured Michael that her handwriting would have been much worse. She also revealed that Pauline knew she had not long to live and had said, using a familiar RAF term, 'My number's up'. She had asked to hold her babies in her arms.

Such a gathering of threads and memories decades later must have evoked many mixed emotions, but perhaps a greater connection for both her sons.

Norah Fahie also told Michael, in a letter dated on his birthday in 1993, that his mother had arranged the baptism beforehand, to take place at the local church of the Most Holy Redeemer. She had chosen their 'good straightforward' Christian names, while their middle names, Francis and Joseph, had been chosen by an old friend of Pauline, Princess Marie Louise, who wished to be godmother. The names were after the former emperor of Austria and king of Hungary, Franz Josef, a friend of hers. It was a bitterly cold spring, following an equally harsh winter, and the twins were allowed special permission to be baptised at home. Princess Marie Louise was too old and frail to attend, but had sent her equally old and frail lady-in-waiting, who, as a Protestant, had to stand behind Norah at the ceremony. The princess had presented the family with 'exquisite' jade rosary beads, which have, over time, gone missing.

In her next letter, a month later, it seems Norah had been mulling over the baptism and recalled more details. She was keen to let Michael know that following Pauline's death the ceremony naturally took place quietly and, as the original intended godparents were not informed in time, proxies took their place. She had not been invited to any birthday parties, as one of those proxies, hence some details had got lost, along with the missing beads. There was a sense from her letters that Norah was trying her best to draw threads together for the twins, to provide as much background as she could to colour in their early years.

Memories are jogged by events; details can be recalled long afterwards. While researching his mother's life, Michael Fahie visited some of those who had been close to Pauline, before and during the war. Two further letters will add a fitting touch here. Firstly, from Joan, a fellow pupil at Beechwood, who remembered Pauline's distinctive singing voice. And the fact that the nuns were impressed with the choir girl who 'can even hit top C'. Joan had enjoyed Michael's visit, which had helped recall some good memories. She closed her letter with these lines:

I had an odd feeling (a feeling one does when those one knew well died very suddenly) to write to your mother and say – 'I was so very pleased to meet your son and to hear about his family. A delightful family of seven. I saw their photographs, they all look so bright and intelligent, you must be very proud of them' – but I can only say to you …

Sir Peter Mursell was equally pleased to meet Michael in England and had copies made of some photographs to send him. He recalled something important, his memory perhaps stirred by meeting Pauline's son. He said:

After you had gone I remembered the third line of the couplet your Mother had told us, making it a triplet. It went:
'Two little pillows trimmed with lace,
Two little faces, face to face.
Everything else in its proper place.'
I thought it delightful at the time, in fact quite dashing 46 years ago, and still do.

There is a passage in *Women with Wings* that is particularly poignant. In chapter 10, Pauline becomes reflective, putting her own part in aviation in historical context, looking ahead while looking back at the same time. There is a similar passage in her 1935 article in AERO (quoted here in Chapter 4). She imagines herself as an old lady looking back on her early days at Stag Lane, as those *were* the days. The aerodrome, which had already been sold for houses at the time of writing her book, will always 'recall my early days in the workshops, my first meeting with Dorothy, and, more vividly than all, a certain winter day when, with Amy Johnson and others who have since distinguished themselves as pilots, we snowballed one another in our "dinner hour"'. This was caught on camera, the fun and camaraderie clear to see. These are the lines that really resonate: 'In twenty or thirty years' time, I can picture myself being looked upon in very much the same light as one now regards the retired captain of a windjammer, and Dorothy and I may be invited to aeronautical dinners as curiosities.'

She imagines that when they are both old ladies and 'it's fun to dash to Australia for the weekend in Comets' they will be seen 'taking the air on a warm afternoon in an antiquated biplane such as we fly today'. Her writer's imagination could not have foreseen the wartime years ahead or the way in which her life would change. The heady air circus days would be replaced with the responsibilities and rigour of the ATA: selecting women, leading women, looking after them on all fronts. Pauline and Dorothy sadly did not get to dash around in Comets, but their legacy lives on.

In her seminal article in *The Woman Engineer*, Claudia Parsons said:

It was grimly tragic that these partners who risked, endured and enjoyed so much together should die within a year of each other … they filled the brief interval between attaining majority and leaving life with a record of hard work, pioneering experience and fine achievement that was as gallant as it was short-lived.

Claudia was a woman who chose her words carefully and questioned her own use of 'gallant'. Not because it did not apply – their 'aim was never more than to pursue a private ambition and do it well'. But because she thought that 'the word "gallant" would have been held by them in derision'. The raised eyebrows, the hidden laughter; she knew them well.

Pauline's poetry helps keep her spirit alive, revealing her natural good cheer and sense of fun. Published in *A Harvest of Memories* and in *Fifty Ways to Fly* (2017), a few copies of her *Piffling Poems for Pilots* can still be found. In 1994 Michael Fahie republished his mother's original two collections. She may have been proud to know that they have since been read in schools, and to audiences in museums, libraries, galleries and airfields, in order to help raise awareness of what she and Dorothy achieved as pioneering pilot and engineer. A true partnership of the air.

The Happy Airman

The birds are singing; the sun is on high.
I must be winging my way through the sky.
Away in the blue, so carefree and gay,
Too good to be true, this glorious day.

Far from all sordid, the evil the bad;
Leaving the morbid, the troubled, the sad.
Sorrows behind me, away from me hurled.
Care cannot find me on top of the world.

As I typed that poem from Pauline Gower's collection *Piffling Poems for Pilots*, autumn light playing across my desk, I recalled the small plane circling over the sprawling Kent and Sussex graveyard on that sunny May afternoon in Tunbridge Wells. It is a peaceful spot, the Gower family grave, and the inscriptions speak of several lives forever entwined. I think Pauline may have forgiven that flight of fancy and would have shown more interest in flying the plane overhead. Onwards, upwards – dancing over clouds.

9

LEGACY – THE BRITISH WOMEN PILOTS' ASSOCIATION

HONOURING THOSE WHO FLEW AHEAD

Pilot Sue Rose learnt to fly at the age of 62 and has always fully appreciated the significance of the Spitfire Women, particularly their leader. She is still flying in her 80s and regularly nips across the Channel for lunch with other pilots. I was keen to hear more about her flying inspiration:

Every time I take to the air in a single engine PA 28 (Warrior) and head over the Thames Estuary en route for the south coast or for France, aided by modern navigation systems and ever-helpful air traffic controllers, I am in awe of the remarkable achievements of Pauline Gower's magnificent women in their Second World War flying machines.

Three years after I gained my private pilot's licence in 2004 Giles

Whittell published his excellent book, *Spitfire Women of World War II*, finally giving overdue recognition to the formidable achievements of the women pilots of the Air Transport Auxiliary, led by Pauline Gower. They have been my inspiration ever since and, in my quest to discover more about them, I have since paid a few 'flying visits' to their base at White Waltham, where the ATA is remembered in an evocative collection of photos and memorabilia.

In fact, since Whittell's book was published, the activities of the ATA women have been the subject of television documentaries, biographies and Alison Hill's own eloquent book of poems, *Sisters in Spitfires*. Pauline Gower was herself a poet and I am sure would have appreciated Alison's perceptive poems. So, a good match for this biography.

Often flying in appalling weather conditions, with no radio contact and only the most rudimentary flight manuals, ATA pilots took on the formidable challenge of piloting many different and unfamiliar types of aircraft 'hot off the presses' from the manufacturers to deliver them to the RAF bases ready for the men to fly into action. Not infrequently they were met on arrival with male incredulity and suspicion. As the chaps sought 'the pilot' of the newly landed Wellington Bomber flown in by the redoubtable Mary Ellis she responded crisply: 'I am the pilot.' It took five men to fly a Wellington bomber in combat but just one female pilot to deliver it!

Together with female pilot colleague, Amy Chau, flying Alison to Sandown in the Isle of Wight to meet Mary Ellis, shortly before she died in July 2018, was a particularly significant and poignant experience. Mary ran Sandown Airfield for twenty years, with her husband Donald, and she continued to live in a house strategically positioned overlooking the airfield. Mary went on flying professionally for many years after the war, unlike many of her colleagues. In her later years she was taken on a Spitfire flight in Sussex for a TV documentary and, to her delight, took over the controls, subsequently describing herself as 'The oldest Spitfire pilot in the world'.

The contribution of Pauline and her pioneering female 'crew' to the formation of the US counterpart, the Women Air Service Pilots, is acknowledged in Katherine Landdeck's recently published book, *The Women with Silver Wings*. But like their American counterparts, the ATA women were scandalously consigned to the kitchen when the war ended. They would have been horrified to discover, given the enormous expansion of civil aviation and equality, that 77 years later only about 6 per cent of today's airline pilots are women.

A legacy of the ATA women has, however, been the establishment of the British Women Pilots' Association (BWPA) now actively campaigning to increase female representation on the flight deck. The BWPA has been working closely and successfully with easyJet to increase the training opportunities for women pilots. In addition, BWPA offers several scholarships to aspiring women pilots to help pay for their training. When she published her anthology of flight poetry, *Fifty Ways to Fly,* Alison donated the proceeds in support of the BWPA scholarships.

I have had a lifelong love affair with aeroplanes. My father worked on the Frank Whittle team developing the first jet engines during the Second World War. I have always enjoyed air travel and aeroplane spotting. At the age of 62 I had my first trial lesson at Stapleford Flight Centre in Essex. For me, like Pauline, it was love at first sight, so with the support of my family and the encouragement of a wonderfully patient young instructor, I started flying lessons. I did not find it easy to master new and completely different skills, but it has proved to be well worth the effort. I have made so many new friends among the flying fraternity, enjoyed unforgettable experiences and flown to over 100 different airfields in seven different countries worldwide.

I now have the luxury of being able to choose to fly when the Met Office indicates that the weather will be favourable. Before flying a different type of aeroplane, I have the benefit of 'differences training' with an instructor. Whenever I take off, I have the support of modern avionics, a twenty-first-century GPS SkyDemon navigational and planning app, and a network of air traffic controllers helping me negotiate the crowded skies in the south-east of England.

I can well understand what attracted Pauline Gower and her pilots to flying and their eagerness to play their part in the war effort, putting their already honed piloting skills to the service of the nation. And there was the sheer love of flying. Once bitten by the aviation bug it becomes totally addictive.

So, I salute them for their pioneering work on behalf of women in aviation and the equality of women, and for the inspiration they have provided to so many of us women pilots. We owe it to them to redress the gender imbalance and increase the percentage of women commercial pilots.

THE BRITISH WOMEN PILOTS' ASSOCIATION

In 1955, ten years after the war ended, ATA pilot Freydis Sharland founded the Women Pilots' Association based at White Waltham, Berkshire – now with the addition of 'British' and commonly known as the BWPA. She was their first chairwoman, and typically modest about her Spitfire flights during the war – 'just four years of a longer flying service' as she told BWPA archivist Beverley Harrison, who became fascinated to find out more. After the ATA wound up, Freydis was active in the Women's Junior Air Corps (WJAC) and the Girls Venture Corps, worked as a freelance commercial pilot and won, but never collected, her RAF Wings. In 2008 she was one of the veterans to receive an ATA service medal from then Prime Minister Gordon Brown. Freydis died in 2014, aged 93, after a full and active life in the skies, encouraging others to follow their own ambitions, as she had done from a young age.

The association she founded exists to inspire and support women in all areas of aviation and all types of flying, including fixed wing, rotary, gliding, microlights and ballooning. It runs annual scholarships and awards, outreach activities and regional membership networking events. The association is flourishing and welcomes new members who share a common passion. You can join online at www.bwpa.co.uk.

So many of the ATA women were reluctant to stop flying, sell their planes if they had them, and slow down, even into their 70s and 80s.

They would have to settle for a life on the ground, predictable home lives, jobs if they were lucky. As Joy Lofthouse said: 'The war ended and we all went back to being housewives.'

Readjusting was difficult for some after flying so many types of planes in their youth; could a wet walk with the dog on a grey Sunday afternoon take on the same cloud-bound excitement? Some turned to fast cars, horse riding and scuba diving to fulfil the need for adventure! They would have been proud of the ongoing success of the BWPA, which encourages girls and women to fly, and which supports new generations to become engineers and pilots.

The BWPA's three core aims are: (1) to promote the training and employment of women in aviation, and the promotion of practical schemes to assist women to gain air licences, including raising awareness of opportunities for females of all ages; (2) to act as advisers to women on training required and openings available in aviation; (3) to promote and encourage collaboration between members of the association, and to enable women in aviation to meet and exchange knowledge of mutual interest and to communicate views from the association.

BWPA chair, Sharon Nicholson, has been involved in the aviation industry since 1976. She started her career as a flight school administrator and an AFISO (NATS), then became a flight instructor and examiner. As an ATPL and former line training captain, she now provides regulatory oversight for the UK Civil Aviation Authority, while continuing to enjoy weekly instructing. Sharon is a BWPA STEM ambassador and actively encourages girls to consider flying as a career choice.

On World Pilots' Day on 26 April 2021, Sharon gave a Zoom presentation about her long career, and there were similarities with Pauline's own personal challenges, four decades earlier. She displayed the same grit and determination as Pauline in her desire to learn to fly against the odds. 'If they could, I could' she said of her two older brothers and did anything she could to pay for her flying lessons, like many who joined the ATA, including Pauline. Sharon worked at Stapleford Flying Club in the 1970s and got paid partly in flights. Reminiscent of Mary de Bunsen, who also took some of her salary in flying hours, when she worked at Heston in the 1930s – the golden age of private flying. Like Mary, Sharon also had to overcome eyesight difficulties but discovered that she did not need to read the last line in the sight test … there is always a way to overcome obstacles. Mary did a similar thing in her day, flew without incident throughout the war and her logbooks detailed 1,280 hours on sixty different types of aircraft.

Sharon went on to become a successful commercial pilot, a jet pilot and a training captain – enjoying a long and varied career in aviation. Some things shone out of her talk, apart from her clear enjoyment of flying and training pilots of the future, which she found completely fulfilling. A unique bond between trainer and trainee, a trust that must work both ways to ensure safety and success. Sharon tells them: 'If you get it wrong, forget it, just get on with it and find a way to cope. If you don't make a bad landing, you can't improve.' She is of course teaching them resilience, a lifelong skill which the ATA women had to learn along the way, particularly faced with planes they had not encountered before. Or new routes every day. Or the dangers of the ever-changing English weather. The captive Zoom audience of BWPA pilots and trainees was enthralled by Sharon's tales of long-haul flights and adventure, reminiscent of the earlier aviation pioneers. 'Flying in Hawaii is all about the rainbows,' she told us. 'If there is no rain, there are no rainbows.' A perfect idea for a (piffling) poem or two, had Pauline been in the audience.

At the BWPA's Diamond Jubilee in May 2015, a busy weekend of presentations and talks, with many members flying in from around the country, I had the opportunity to share some poems from *Sisters in Spitfires* – although reading aviation poems (in draft) to an audience of a hundred or so pilots at White Waltham was somewhat daunting! Gusts of wind whipped around the marquee, with the sound of the ropes hitting metal, in the lull between poems.

Honor Salmon's Pale Blue Shirt

Hung in Diana's wardrobe for nearly fifty years,
brushing against her sway of silk dresses –

poignant memories of a pilot who helped
a novice before floundering on high ground,
caught in the English weather, almost home.

The pale blue wool was soft to the touch, much
softer than ATA issue, and fitted Diana perfectly.
Her family had wanted her things to be shared.

She burst into tears the only time she tried it on,
alone in her digs. Honor's blue-grey eyes twinkled
back from the mirror – it was too much to bear.

She remembered with pride the young First Officer
who befriended her, taking it down now and then
shaking out the clouds, before slipping it back

between shot-silk blues. Honor's presence lingering
her kindly words drifting down the decades.

First Officer Honor Isabel Salmon, granddaughter of Sir Isaac Pitman of shorthand fame, died on 19 April 1943 aged 30. Diana Barnato Walker never forgot her.

WOMEN IN AVIATION

Only 5 per cent of pilots are women and there is some way to go to achieve higher numbers and more opportunities at commercial level. Here are some of the current initiatives that support, encourage and raise the profile of women pilots.

The Aviatrix Project was launched on 1 November 2015, in partnership with the BWPA, and has to date supported over 500 educational institutions and STEM organisations in raising awareness of aviation as an exciting and accessible career choice. Its strapline is, quite simply, 'Inspiring women and girls to fly'.

Founder and director Kanchana Gamage gained her private pilot's licence in 2015 and set up the Aviatrix Project the same year to inspire others to take to the skies. She has had a lifelong passion for aviation and wanted to ensure that her experience as an educator and a pilot could be combined to provide opportunities for others. Commercial pilot and instructor Julie Westhorp, a former BWPA chair, is a fellow director, alongside Joanne Gibson who specialises in careers guidance and inspiring young people. During 2020, and in response to the many challenges of Covid-19, the Aviatrix Project assisted the Nuffield Foundation to support talented but less-advantaged year 12 students to complete online placements and research projects in STEM subjects through the Nuffield Future Researchers programme. Full details can be found at www.theaviatrixproject.com.

The charity Project Wingman was founded in March 2020 in direct response to the pandemic. BWPA member Captain Emma Henderson MBE, a retired easyJet pilot, wanted to explore how grounded aircrew could support NHS staff during the current health crisis. A call was put out to the airline community with the idea of taking crew into NHS hospitals to look after NHS staff during their breaks in dedicated lounges and so Project Wingman was born. An incredible 6,500 airline crew responded, from across every UK airline. They offer their time, knowledge and skills to serve and support NHS staff, providing wellbeing and mental health support.

Emma was amazed by the positive response to the 'tea and empathy' project; she has received hundreds of emails and messages thanking Project Wingman for the care it provides. She has been equally pleased to hear personal stories where people have been profoundly affected by the service and the company. More details are to be found at www.projectwingman.co.uk.

'THE SKY IN MY SOUL'

Captain Henderson, interviewed for the BWPA membership magazine, *Take Off*, explained why she flies:

> Although I didn't grow up in an aviation family, I was always fascinated by things that fly. Watching birds is something I love to do, and trips to science museums always see me drawn to the flying displays. I think I was born with the sky in my soul … what drives me is what drives anyone who flies – we somehow belong in the air and it just feels natural to those of us who do it.
>
> One of the things I love most about being a pilot is the opportunity to encourage others into it. I have spent a lot of time mentoring young pilots, as well as giving presentations in schools as part of STEM initiatives to help bust the image of pilots only being male. I have met people who have asked for photos so they can show their daughters that they can be pilots too. Inspiring the next generation, regardless of gender, is one of the biggest joys for me.

One of the BWPA annual awards is the Faith Bennett Navigation Cup, awarded to a British Woman Pilot for a navigation exercise undertaken during the current year of special merit or that stretches the experience of the pilot to the limits, reaching goals beyond the pilot's expectations. This was won in 2020 by Amy Whitewick with her 'aerial artwork'.

Amy learnt to fly microlights in 2018, then bought a Cessna 150 in which she completed her private pilot's licence a year later. She first flew with Sue Rose in 2012 as a teenager and was so enthralled she wrote a poem, 'From a Bird's Eye View', which was published in *Take Off*. Inspired to prove that aviation can be as creative as any other endeavour, Amy decided to fly a route to recreate Picasso's 1961 'Dove of Peace' as a GPS image. This was a challenging experience, given the changing coastal winds, difficult traffic and moderate turbulence on the day – made even harder by Covid-19 restrictions preventing a fellow pilot accompanying Amy as a lookout. Resilience and determination won the day.

THE CHAIRWOMAN'S CHALLENGE

The BWPA awards several scholarships and trophies each year and the Chairwoman's Challenge trophy is given to the pilot who has used their aircraft in the most imaginative and interesting way. The flight should be no longer than 120 minutes, with only one interim landing. In 2020, Amy Chau, co-pilot with Sue Rose in our flight from Stapleford to Sandown on the Isle of Wight in May 2018 to visit ATA pilot Mary Ellis, won the challenge. Her successful entry was a message of support and thanks to the NHS during the pandemic.

Amy planned a route of a heart and two diamonds as a GPS image, which would take in many of the blue waters of her chosen area, to reflect the challenge theme of 'Blue Sapphire'. On 23 June she set off from Fowlmere Airfield in her Cessna 152 G-BXVB. Her interim stop was at Main Hall Farm Airfield, landing as planned on a wide grass runway – Amy 'felt like a VIP walking over a massive green carpet!'

After taking off again she made two tight turns to create the diamonds in her route, with views over more lakes and rivers, but with a few head spins from all the turns. Her final stop was at Little Gransden Airfield where she bumped (not literally) into a pilot with whom she had attended ground school. On the way back to her home airfield at Stapleford, Amy completed her heart and two diamonds outline. She was pleased to have won the challenge that year:

> I was very lucky to have had the opportunity to fly solo in the quiet sky during these unusual times. We often take our freedom for granted and appreciate when it is lost. We owe a lot to the frontline staff who have been working tirelessly through this challenging time.

In 2021, Amy reached a milestone age and filled it with flying milestones. One was to have flown to 100 airfields, so I invited her to summarise her aviation highlights in 100 words:

I started flight training back in 2003. It was hard with one teenage daughter and a full-time hectic job. There was time when I almost gave up. I joined BWPA and met lots of inspiring female pilots and good friends who helped me get through the lows. The best thing I have done as a confidence booster. I attempted five Chairwoman Challenges over the years and they were all fun to fly and required imagination and planning. 2020–21 pandemic time happened to be a memorable time for flying – winning the challenge, flying most aircraft types and one hundred airfields.

And in numbers …

60 years on earth and first encounter of pandemic restrictions.
65th BWPA anniversary in 2020 and a privilege to solo fly the Chairwoman Challenge over green vegetation as a heartfelt thanks to NHS for their tireless contributions. Winning the challenge was beyond my expectation.
16 new airfields added since covid lift and hit 100 target for celebration.
5 aircraft types flown within 26 days, with no time for familiarisation, was a record.
1 warbird Harvard added to the list for loop and roll was true exhilaration.
250k on 2 wheels after 3 injuries to remember 2 lost friends will offer a chance for reflection.

I can only think that the ATA women pilots would have applauded Amy's courage and resilience, in their similarly modest manner. Women pushing boundaries, meeting challenges, overcoming the odds. Their legacy lives on.

Amy Chau. (Author)

10

BOOK LAUNCH
CIRCLES – HARVESTING
MEMORIES

Published in 1995, forty-eight years after Pauline's death, *A Harvest of Memories: The Life of Pauline Gower MBE* was the result of much dedicated and detailed research by her son Michael; a gathering of threads, a following up of leads, finding those who knew her from across the world and across the decades. He kept every letter and had them bound into volumes, reminiscent of his grandfather's and his mother's carefully preserved scrapbooks. He sent me copies from Australia, during lockdown in 2020, and I was honoured to revisit his research journey some twenty-five years later. It was a fascinating insight into his personal quest and into all those from aviation circles and beyond who responded with such enthusiasm about the mother he and his brother never knew. The book had an eager audience.

Michael's research sparked people's memories in a fruitful way and at a time when letter-writing was a key form of communication – many had interesting letterheads and annotations – a disappearing art form in the era of emails and digital communication. There were real-time delays too, as letters disappeared under a pile of Christmas cards, in one case, or were answered in between other engagements. There were many shared connections across aviation circles, and it was intriguing to see who knew whom, and who remembered which event, person, plane. A painstaking search for memories.

One correspondent threaded through the carefully bound letters provided a warm, familiar voice with each reading. I can only imagine Michael would have opened Norah Fahie's letters with anticipation, as every Dublin-marked envelope included a tantalising snippet of information; a memory or thought to be chased to its conclusion, moving the story on, but leaving a thirst for the next instalment.

There's something of the layers of a historical novel unravelling in Norah's letters. She usually opened them with a gentle observation or two about the weather, thus keeping each in a seasonal context with a reminder of the changeable skies that played such a key part in Pauline's flying years. Fine detail, careful brushstrokes that built a rich picture of the woman at the heart of her son's research: 'You all look warm and tanned [of Michael and his family, framed in Australian sunshine] – here we are pale and limp after a long dreary winter which is having its final kick this week – temperature -30 and snow showers …'

Norah was writing from Dublin in 1993, a relentless winter of endless rain and sleet. The weather becomes a background character to her correspondence, much as it did during the ATA years. With pilots constantly on the look-out for an ominous change in the clouds, shivering up to Lossiemouth in open-cockpit Tiger Moths, or waiting around the mess for a break in the rain on washout days. Weather that could and did cause fatal accidents.

Norah firmly believed that Pauline deserved a tribute and was distressed that her career was 'lost in silence'. She was more than glad to help with the book's research and was very impressed with what Michael had achieved. I imagine it drew them closer.

This new biography is published twenty-seven years after the launch of *A Harvest of Memories*. It was no ordinary book launch, and this is an ideal opportunity to remember the weekend that Michael Fahie and his publisher Graham Simons of GMS Enterprises organised so carefully. A chance also to hear from some of the people at the event, now of historical interest, as all the ATA pilots present at the launch have since found their own 'blue skies'.

Michael's book title did not come easily at first. Norah Fahie was a 'test pilot' and said she was not sure if she would pick up *Her Spirit Soars* (too religious?) or *The Passion of Flight* ('psych analysis of elopement?') in a bookshop. She looked through Pauline's poems for inspiration. She considered the line *Winging Her Way* but knew that the publisher thought wings had been overdone and was too close perhaps to Pauline's own memoir. She wondered if readers would understand the significance of *Cabotage*, a game Pauline made up and which might reflect the arc of her life – 'airborne over obstacles to destination'.

Norah pondered the title over Christmas, a time she kept firmly for family visits and festive ritual. In her next letter to Michael, dated 26 January 1995, she had clearly let 'her imaginary forces work (Henry V)' and suggested a list of five titles. In February, she wrote that she was 'touched and honoured' that Michael had chosen her middle title on the list and went on to consider how it might be woven throughout the chapter headings. She was also planning on the best way to attend the launch, lecturing on folk medicine to a local community association and had been invited to join a team representing the British Legion at the RAF 'Quiz' – she hoped that she would not let the family name down. Norah's life seemed as varied as Pauline's had always been – following her interests and alert to all new opportunities to connect with others. Both had a keen interest in people.

Aviation bookseller Brian Cocks was at the launch and told me that he had given Diana Barnato Walker a lift in his vintage Bentley to see some of the weekend's activity. Daughter of one of the famous Bentley Boys, she was more than thrilled. Brian has been based in Peterborough for many years and, although he has now sold his business, he would find moving a little difficult as he has just over 10,000 books left, plus a 'small motoring library' and, of course, his Bentley. Brian has helped many a researcher on their way to publication with his personal sourcing of just the right book at the right time, and his name is well-known in aviation circles. A lifetime dedicated to the written, flying word.

Brian still has first-edition books by ATA women and a much-treasured copy of *Reminders to Pilots and Flight Engineers* that he took to Hunstanton and had signed by all the pilots who were there. He sold a copy of Pauline's 'super little booklet' *Piffling Poems for Pilots*, but later regretted the sale and replaced it with a second copy that stayed firmly in his collection. Brian also sourced and sold four copies to me on my research trail in 2014: one was presented to Mary Ellis, two to the pilots who flew me over to the Isle of Wight to visit her, and the fourth remains firmly in my ATA collection. There is another interesting link. Brian acquired *More Piffling Poems* from the library of Dr Buchanan Barbour, who was chief medical officer of the ATA. He is mentioned in a poem from *Sisters in Spitfires*, below, with a reminder of the fine details of war-time spirit. Brian also had the doctor's signed copy of Pauline's *Women with Wings*, addressed to 'Doc with love'.

Chits for Chocolate

We collected our chits each morning
from a polished wooden shelf – the thrill
of a new plane would often keep us going.
It was decided we need a little more for safe
energy levels, so when we returned our chits
we got a 2oz bar of Cadbury's Dairy Milk.
(This was thanks to Dr Buchanan Barbour,
who persuaded the Ministry that us girls needed
chocolate – has it not always been the case?)
One pilot, it may have been Jackie, used hers to
send love letters, she'd wrap them in a note
and drop them from her Spitfire –
the finder was to keep the chocolate in return
for delivering the letter. It was such small things
that kept us going sometimes, it really was.

Alison Hill, *Sisters in Spitfires*

Checking out of his hotel, after the close of the busy weekend's events, Brian found himself standing behind two of the 'ATA girls' and (when they had gone) asked the receptionist if she realised that 'they' had been Spitfire pilots. Their modesty had not left them, and they would not have mentioned their wartime role, so at least Brian was there to share their stories. Many more have been shared in the intervening years, so this 1995 launch was perhaps the spark for more books and a raising of awareness, with many more stories in between the lines and video clips. ATA films too have been made, novels written and more works are in progress – but these first-hand accounts, both oral and written, are priceless.

Michael and his publisher planned the weekend in detail and were careful to cater for all their 300 international guests, many of whom flew in to celebrate Pauline's life and achievements. Sir Peter Masefield had been invited to open the proceedings, but had written in May to say that he was fully committed that week at Brooklands. The museum had been delighted to welcome Dorothy Spicer's daughter, Patricia, around that time, and I asked her if she recalled the visit. She remembers being shown around by Sir Peter, who was a huge fan of her mother Dorothy, with plenty of accompanying stories.

Morag Barton, Brooklands' director at that time, was very glad to have been invited to the launch and immediately offered to help promote the book through the museum's *Spirit* magazine which was circulated to all friends and members. In 1977 Morag had curated an exhibition for nearby Weybridge Museum, 'Wings over Brooklands', with support from the local British Aerospace, the Vintage Aircraft Flying Association and the Brooklands Society. The exhibition proved a success, highlighting its unique place in aviation and motorsport history, and Morag went on to campaign for a museum dedicated to the history of Brooklands. Ten years later she became museum director.

Aviation circles overlap in the sky and across the decades, and Brooklands remains a hub of connections as it was before the war. The museum keeps the spirit of Brooklands very much alive and, when I read Pauline's poems in 2017 in the Bluebird Room on a warm summer's day, 1940s jazz danced through the open window and it was easy to imagine sociable scenes from decades past. Brooklands holds regular motorsport and aviation events, and it was an honour to read next to a Wellington, being restored by a volunteer, as I recounted some of the many flights represented in *Sisters in Spitfires*. Time marches on and planes need regular maintenance, as Dorothy Spicer knew only too well.

The 'Happy Hunstanton' weekend of 9–10 September 1995 was no ordinary book launch, reflecting as it did the remarkable woman at the heart of the story. A Tiger Moth flypast was planned, to 'flour-bomb' a catamaran at sea, in the same way that Pauline used to announce her arrival and readiness to take up joy-riders. She had been based there during 'two glorious summers' of 1934–35 and made 3,000 flights, bringing plenty of tourists into the area. She was good for business! The book launch Tiger Moth flight was cleared by the Civil Aviation Authority and timed to coincide with high tide so that the boat could get close to shore.

So how did Pauline do it? She recounts with amusement the process of one of their favourite 'advertising dodges', complete with willing participants:

> We arranged with the proprietor of a speed-boat that he should allow our passengers to 'bomb' his passengers with small bags of flour. The passengers in the boat took their tickets with a full knowledge of what was to happen to them … I would fly out over the sea with my passengers and swoop down over the speed-boat, which went all out, swerving around in the water trying to avoid me. My passengers would then try to get a 'bull's-eye' with their bombs as we pass a few feet over our objective.

Her skill and accuracy ensured her passenger's safety and drew ever-increasing crowds to the circus each day. It was a fine and fitting tribute for Michael Fahie to recreate the fun of her flour-bombing escapades during the launch weekend in Hunstanton. The letters of thanks from all those attending, which Norah suggested should be made into a collection, were testament to both Pauline and her remarkable life story.

The Gower family grave in Tunbridge Wells. (Author)

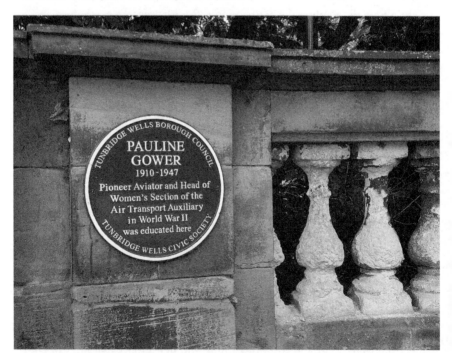

Pauline's red plaque on the gates at Beechwood School. (Author)

APPENDIX I

THE ATA WOMEN PILOTS AND ENGINEERS

After the First Eight trailblazing pilots were recruited in January 1940, the ATA grew rapidly and, as more planes were needed as the war progressed and after the Battle of Britain, more ferry pilots were recruited to meet demand. Pilots were accepted on an *ab initio* basis from 1943, trained from scratch, and then handed any number of planes to deliver each day, moving through the ranks and flying as many types as were needed. Hours were long, days were long, service was rigorous. This may be a list of names, and ranks, and dates of joining, but behind every name was a woman willing to fly for her part in the war effort, just as there were countless men willing to do their duty throughout the war. All should be remembered.

WOMEN FERRY PILOTS AND FLIGHT ENGINEERS

Agazarian, Monique J., 3rd Officer, joined 18 Oct. 1943
Alexander, Susan M.A., 3rd Officer, joined 8 May 1944
Allen, Joan M.,1st Officer, joined 15 Jul. 1942
Allen, Mrs Naomi, 1st Officer, joined 24 Feb. 1942
Allen, Myrtle R., 2nd Officer, joined 12 Aug. 1942 (USA)
Anderson, Mrs O.P.L., 1st Officer, joined 10 Jun. 1942 (USA)
Arkless, Irene, 1st Officer, killed 3 Jan. 1943
Arthur, J.H., 3rd Officer, joined 8 May 1944
Baines, R.P., 3rd Officer, joined 28 Dec. 1943
Ballard, Ruth E., 1st Officer, joined 25 Jun. 1940
Bannister, Mrs E.R., 3rd Officer, joined 12 Jul. 1943
Barnato Walker, Mrs Diana, 1st Officer, joined 2 Dec. 1941
Beaumont, Edith, 3rd Officer, joined 20 Sep. 1943
Bennett, Mrs Faith, 1st Officer, joined 8 Jul. 1941

Bennett, Philippa, Flight Captain, joined 26 Jun. 1940
Beverley, Mrs Patricia, 1st Officer, joined 29 Jul. 1942
Bird, Jean, 1st Officer, joined 1 Aug. 1941
Black, Betty E., 1st Officer, joined 15 Apr. 1942 (New Zealand)
Blackwell, Mrs P. Ann, 1st Officer, joined 24 Feb. 1942
Bonnett, Mrs R.L., 3rd Officer, joined 21 Feb. 1944
Bragg, Mrs Dorothy R., 1st Officer, joined 10 Feb. 1942 (USA)
Bragg, Mrs Felicity, Captain, joined 1 May 1941
Broad, Jennie, 1st Officer, joined 30 Jul. 1940
Butler, Mrs Lois, 1st Officer, joined 15 Feb. 1940
Chapin, Emily, 2nd Officer, joined 18 Aug. 1942 (USA)
Chapman, Susan P., 3rd Officer, joined 21 Feb. 1944
Cholmondeley, Victoria, 1st Officer, joined 10 Mar. 1941 (Australia)
Clayton, Mrs E.V. 'Sammy', 2nd Officer, joined 1 Mar. 1941
Cochran-Odlum, Mrs J., Hon. Flight Captain, joined 24 Jan. 1942 (USA)
Cripps, Mrs B. P., 3rd Officer, joined 14 Jun. 1943 (South Africa)
Crossley, Fidelia, 2nd Officer, joined 16 Dec. 1940
Cunnington, Joan, 3rd Officer, joined 1 Jun. 1943
Curtis, Lettice, 1st Officer, joined 6 Jul. 1940
Daab, Mrs Anna, 1st Officer, joined 6 Jan. 1941 (Poland)
Davison, Mrs Joy, 2nd Officer, killed 8 Jul. 1940
De Bunsen, Mary, 1st Officer, joined 1 Aug. 1941
De Neve, Mrs Aimee, 3rd Officer, joined 8 May 1944
Douglas, Mrs Anne C., 1st Officer, joined 1 Dec. 1940
Duhalde, Margot, 1st Officer, joined 1 Sep. 1941 (Chile)
Dunlop, Maureen A.C., 1st Officer, joined 15 Apr. 1942 (Argentina)
Dutton, The Hon. Mrs Joan, 1st Officer, joined 1 Mar. 1941
Ebbage, Mrs Margaret, Flight Captain, joined 1 Jan. 1940
Edwards, Mrs Sylvia I., 2nd Officer, joined 9 Aug. 1943
Eveleigh, Mrs Y.M., 3rd Officer, joined 21 Feb. 1944
Everard-Steenkamp, Mrs Rosamund, 2nd Officer, killed 19 Mar. 1946 (South Africa)
Fair, Mrs Winifred, Flight Captain, joined 1 Jan. 1940
Fairweather, The Hon. Mrs Margaret, Flight Captain, killed 4 Aug. 1944
Falkner, The Hon. Mrs Lucy, Flight Captain, joined 1 Apr. 1941
Farnell, Mrs Diane, 2nd Officer, joined 16 Sep. 1940
Farquhar, Marjory J., 3rd Officer, joined 22 Jan. 1944
Farr, Virginia, 1st Officer, joined 10 Feb. 1942 (USA)
Faunethorpe, Diana, 3rd Officer, joined 21 Feb. 1944
Ferguson, Joy, 2nd Officer, joined 1 May 1943
Ford, Mrs Mary E., 1st Officer, joined 10 Jun. 1942 (USA)
Ford, Suzanne H., 1st Officer, joined 14 Apr. 1942 (USA)
Forward, Mrs Mona, 1st Officer, joined 1 Jan. 1940

Frost, Margaret, 3rd Officer, joined 25 Nov. 1942

Garrett, Mrs Sheila, 3rd Officer, joined 3 Mar. 1944

Garst, Virginia, 3rd Officer, joined 14 Apr. 1942 (USA)

Gething, Mrs Margaret (Mardi), 1st Officer, joined 12 Aug. 1942 (Australia)

Glass, Mabel, 1st Officer, joined 8 Jul. 1940

Gollan, Mrs Pamela, 1st Officer, joined 15Aug. 1941

Goodwin, Una, Cadet, joined 10 Jun. 1942 (USA)

Gore, Margot, Commander, joined 25 Jun. 1940

Gough, Joyce, 3rd Officer, joined 28 Dec. 1943

Gower, Pauline, Senior Commander, joined 1 Dec. 1939

Guthrie, Mary, 3rd Officer, joined 18 Oct. 1943

Hansen-Lester, Mrs D.E., 2nd Officer, joined 23 Sep. 1942

Harrington, Janice, Flight Engineer, killed 2 Mar. 1944

Harrison, Mrs Helen M., 1st Officer, joined 1 May 1942 (Canada)

Hayman, Mrs Beatrice, 1st Officer, joined 16 Dec. 1941

Hennings, Sophie, E.V.A., 3rd Officer, joined 29 Nov. 1943

Heppell, Rhoda, 3rd Officer, joined 16 Dec. 1941

Hill, Bridget, G.M.L., 3rd Officer, killed 15 Mar. 1942

Hirsch, Mrs K.M.S., 3rd Officer, joined 8 May 1944

Horsburgh, Mrs Francis, 3rd Officer, joined 21 Feb. 1944 (Canada)

Howden, June C., 3rd Officer, joined 6 Dec. 1943 (New Zealand)

Hudson, Evelyn, 1st Officer, joined 10 Jun. 1942 (USA)

Hughes, Joan, Flight Captain, joined 1 Jan. 1940

Hunter, Mrs Mary, 1st Officer, joined 1 Mar. 1941

Hunter, Trevor, 1st Officer, joined 20 Nov. 1941 (New Zealand)

Illsley, Mrs K.D., 1st Officer, joined 1 Sep. 1941

Irwin, Mrs Zita, 1st Officer, joined 15 Aug. 1941

Jenner, Zoe, 3rd Officer, joined 6 Sep. 1943

Johnson, Amy (Mrs Mollison), 1st Officer, killed 5 Jan. 1941

Keith-Jopp, Betty, 3rd Officer, joined 8 May 1944

Kerly, Ruth, 3rd Officer, joined 23 Aug. 1943

Lang, Mrs Dora, 1st Officer, killed 2 Mar. 1944

Lankshear, Barbara L., 3rd Officer, joined 21 Dec. 1944

Large, Gloria, Cadet, joined 5 Jul. 1942 (Canada)

Leaf, Freydis, 1st Officer, joined 17 Feb. 1943

Leathart, Constance R., Flight Captain, joined 14 Aug. 1940

Lennox, Mrs Margaret, 1st Officer, joined 10 Jun. 1942 (USA)

Lester, Mrs K.M., 3rd Officer, joined 14 Jun. 1943

Lovell-Pank, Mrs J. A., 3rd Officer, joined 15 Nov. 1943

MacDonald, Mrs Yvonne, 3rd Officer, joined 6 Sep. 1943

MacDougall, Elizabeth A., 2nd Officer, joined 16 Sep. 1942

Mackenzie, Mrs Audrey, 1st Officer, joined 26 Jun. 1940

Macleod, Mrs Rosemary T., 3rd Officer, joined 7 Jun. 1943

Mahon, Mrs Annette E., 3rd Officer, joined 8 May 1944

Marshall, Joan, 3rd Officer, killed 19 Jun. 1942

May, The Hon. Elizabeth, Flight Captain, joined 1 Mar. 1941

Metcalfe, Mrs Ursula, 1st Officer, joined 23 Jun. 1940

Miller, Nancy, 1st Officer, joined 9 Jul. 1942 (USA)

Milstead, Violet, 1st Officer, joined 5 Apr. 1943 (USA)

Moggridge, Mrs Delores T. (Jackie), 1st Officer, joined 31 Jul. 1940 (South Africa)

Moore, The Hon. Mrs Ruth, 1st Officer, joined 15 Apr. 1941

Morgan, Audrey, 3rd Officer, joined 6 Sep. 1943

Mullineaux, Joan E.F., 3rd Officer, joined 1 May 1943

Murray, Leslie, 3rd Officer, killed 20 Apr. 1945

Nayler, Joan, E. 1st Officer, joined 16 Dec. 1941

Nicholson, Mary W., 2nd Officer, killed 22 May 1943 (USA)

Obermer, Ruth, Cadet, joined 11 Oct. 1943 (USA)

Orr, Mrs Marion, 2nd Officer, joined 5 Apr. 1943 (Canada)

Paddon, Zita, 2nd Officer, joined 27 Aug. 1943

Parker, Patricia M.B., 3rd Officer/Flight Engineer, joined 30 Apr. 1941

Patterson, Mrs Gabrielle, 1st Officer, joined 1 Jan. 1940

Peterson, Stella J., 3rd Officer, joined 5 Jul. 1943

Pierce, Mrs Phyllis O., Flight Engineer, joined 26 Oct. 1943

Pierce, Winnie R., 1st Officer, joined 10 Feb. 1942 (USA)

Piłsudska, Jadwiga, 2nd Officer, joined 15 Jul. 1942 (Poland)

Plant, Jane, 1st Officer, joined 31 Mar. 1943 (USA)

Power, Cecile E.R., 2nd Officer, joined 26 Jul. 1943

Powys, Mary E.A., 3rd Officer, joined 1 Jun. 1943

Provis, Patricia M., 3rd Officer, joined 21 Feb. 1944

Raines, Hazel, 2nd Officer, joined 14 Apr. 1942 (USA)

Ramsay, Diana, 1st Officer, joined 16 Dec. 1941

Ratcliffe, Mrs Margaret, 3rd Officer, joined 10 Sep. 1943

Rees, Rosemary, Captain, joined 1 Jan. 1940

Rhonie, A.H., 3rd Officer, joined 30 Nov. 1943 (USA)

Richey, Helen, 1st Officer, joined 25 Mar. 1942 (USA)

Rose, Mrs Mollie, 1st Officer, joined 16 Sep. 1942

Rowland, Mrs Marigold, 2nd Officer, joined 1 May 1943

Rumball, Mrs Daphne A., 3rd Officer, joined 25 May 1943

Russell, Margaret E., 2nd Officer, joined 25 Sep. 1943 (Canada)

Russell, Ruth M.H., 3rd Officer, joined 21 Feb. 1944

Sale-Barker, Audrey D., 1st Officer, joined 26 Jun. 1940

Salmon, Mrs Honour I.P., 1st Officer, killed 19 Apr. 1943

Sandoz Leveaux, Mrs R.B., 2nd Officer, joined 12 Aug. 1942 (USA)

Sayer, Betty E., Cadet, killed 15 Mar. 1942

Schuurman, Louise E.M., 1st Officer, joined 10 Feb. 1942 (Holland)
Sharpe, Ethel E., 3rd Officer, joined 1 Nov. 1943
Sharpe, Roy M., 1st Officer, joined 3 Sep. 1941
Sheil, Maureen E., 3rd Officer, joined 20 Sep. 1943
Slade, Eleanor 'Susan', Flight Captain, killed 13 Jul. 1944
Smith, Diana P.M., 1st Officer, joined 7 Oct. 1942
Stearns, Mrs Edith, 1st Officer, joined 10 Jun. 1942 (USA)
Stevenson, Grace, 1st Officer, joined 14 Apr. 1942 (USA)
Stokes, Winifred, 3rd Officer, joined 21 Feb. 1944
Strodl, Vera E., 1st Officer, joined 2 Dec. 1941 (Denmark)
Tharp, Mrs Joyce A., 3rd Officer, joined 21 Feb. 1944
Thomas, Mrs Barbara, 3rd Officer/Flight Engineer, joined 19 Apr. 1943
Tulk-Hart, Pamela, 3rd Officer, joined 25 Aug. 1942
Van Doozer, Catherine, 2nd Officer, joined 9 Jun. 1942 (USA)
Van Zanten, Ida L.V., joined 18 May 1943 (Holland)
Volkersz, Mrs Veronica, Flight Captain, joined 1 Mar. 1941
Wadsworth, Eleanor D., 3rd Officer, joined 1 Jun. 1943
Walker, Anne, 1st Officer, joined 17 Jul. 1942
Whittall, Taniya, 2nd Officer, killed 8 Apr. 1944
Wilberforce, Mrs Marion K., Commander, joined 1 Jan. 1940
Wilkins, Mary (Ellis), 1st Officer, joined 1 Oct. 1941
Willis, Mrs Benedetta, 1st Officer, joined 1 Sep. 1941
Wilson, Mrs Irene M.E., 2nd Officer, joined 1 Jun. 1943
Winstone, Jane, 2nd Officer, killed 10 Feb. 1944 (New Zealand)
Witherby, Mrs Joan D., 2nd Officer, joined 17 Jun. 1942
Wojtulanis, Stefania, 1st Officer, joined 1 Jan. 1941 (Poland)
Wood, Ann W., 1st Officer, joined 29 Apr. 1942 (USA)
Wynne-Eyton, Mrs Helen, 1st Officer, joined 1 Nov. 1940

Source: Lettice Curtis, *The Forgotten Pilots* (first pub. 1971) and online sources. Joining dates are not available for pilots killed.

INTERVIEWS PAST AND PRESENT

CANDIDA ADKINS, DAUGHTER OF JACKIE MOGGRIDGE

Pauline Gower was Jackie's mentor when she first arrived at Hatfield aged 18, ready to do her bit; putting her at her ease and looking out for her, as a fresh young pilot who had travelled alone from Pretoria, South Africa. Jackie ferried almost 1,500 aircraft and later became the first female airline captain in Britain to carry passengers on regular commercial flights. Her younger daughter, Candida Adkins, has kept her aviation achievements firmly in the public eye through regular talks, events and a website, *Spitfire Girl*.

What did your mother remember most about her CO, and how did she feel supported?

My mother always said Pauline was her guardian angel in the ATA as Jackie was not only the youngest in 1940 when she joined as the fifteenth female pilot at No.15 Ferry Pool Hamble, but also the most innocent, having been raised by her very religious Catholic grand-mother. She knew nothing of love, men or sex, so Pauline took Jackie under her wing, taught her the facts of life and my mother worshiped her for it. After all, Pauline was Jackie's heroine – my mother had asked her to autograph the front of her ATA logbook and in the front of her WRAF(VR) logbook I found a press cutting of Pauline with the First Eight ATA girls and my mother had written: 'These are the girls I most admire.' My mother's prize possession was a signed photograph of Pauline who had written 'To Jackie, with best wishes. Pauline Gower.'

Pauline enabled women to fly with the ATA and achieved many firsts, including equal pay for equal work. To what extent did her tireless campaigning and strong leadership effect your mother's own flying career and her commercial success after the war?

My mother was in awe of Pauline from the moment she met her. Pauline had achieved so much herself, quietly proving her girls were equal and capable to fly the same planes as their male counterparts. Having gently cajoled the grey-haired men in command of the ATA into taking women in the first place, Pauline continued to campaign and achieved equal pay for her girls. Unheard of in 1943. Ahead of her time, Pauline's tireless campaigning and quiet strength greatly influenced my mother's post-war flying career, for once war was over and the ATA closed abruptly and most of the girls went back to being housewives, my mother took the Wings course in the RAF(VR) and was the second out of only five women at the time to gain her full RAF Wings. She graduated just before women were stopped from taking the Wings course as it was deemed unsuitable to train women in the RAF.

Jackie also campaigned to be the first woman to fly through the sound barrier, wanting this first to be one for Britain. The powers that be continually refused to release her the jet she needed in time, so she was beaten to this accolade by [American] Jackie Cochran. However, with Pauline's determination at the back of her mind Jackie went on to fly over thirty Israeli Spitfires to Burma in the 1950s, with three male pilots, and went on to be awarded the King's Commendation for Valuable Services in the Air. She was also awarded the Queen's Commendation Medal, in response to which Pauline wrote a letter of congratulations, which Jackie treasured all her life.

Pauline had wanted total equality; however girls in the ATA were not allowed to be promoted above pilot officer. My mother had been mentioned for promotion to flying officer in despatches; this was then cancelled when they found out she was a woman. With this unfair prejudice in mind, Jackie went on to use her commercial pilot's licence after the war to strive for flying jobs. After hundreds of rejections, despite her huge number of flying hours on eighty-three types of plane, she eventually realised her dream job working for Channel Airways, where she became the first British woman airline captain to fly passengers on scheduled flights. Jackie was given the accolade of being the first woman to be awarded the Jean Lennox Bird Trophy by the BWPA 'For furthering the cause of women in aviation'. She knew that Pauline would have been proud of her as she accepted the trophy saying: 'Although I am proud to receive this, I long for the day when it will not be unusual for a woman to become an Airline Captain.' Jackie strived to continue Pauline's legacy.

Sadly, Pauline died young, giving birth to her twins, something my mother often mentioned with tears in her eyes. I found, neatly pressed between her flying books, the press cutting of the obituary for Pauline, just a small couple of column inches for a woman who had achieved so much in the advancement of women in aviation and who had paved the way for women pilots everywhere to take on flying, equal in jobs and pay with the men, unheard of before the war – before Pauline.

INTERVIEWS PAST AND PRESENT

How do you think Jackie would like Pauline to be remembered by future generations?
As a true pioneer who furthered the cause of women in aviation. It was Pauline's belief in the utter equality for her girls that kept my mother pushing the boundaries, battling the prejudice for the rest of my mother's long flying career, in honour of her commanding officer, her heroine and mentor Pauline Gower. Such was her influence on her girls in the ATA.

What do you think was her legacy to aviation?
She was the World War II unsung hero who campaigned for and won equality into aviation in the ATA. In the words of the ATA motto 'Anything to Anywhere'. I think Pauline would have added 'Anything to Anywhere by Anyone'.

Remembering Jackie

*Jackie danced with the wind – she flew by the seat
of her skirt, raised on a cushion, head in the clouds.
She loved to watch the sun appear, craved peace
and solitude, the sheer delight of soaring free.
Jackie showed her daughters petals unfurling, dew
glistening on grass, rain-splash on yellow roses.
They billowed under duvets, learning how to fly.
She wrote poems by streetlight, caught in the glow
embraced her family, lived for fun and flight,
Jackie relaxed into handstands at Hamble, or turned
her morning somersaults, dark eyes shining.
She pushed boundaries with a tilt of her chin, longed
to break the sound barrier, flew Spitfires to Burma.
Captain Jackie was proud of her post-war wings –
paving the way for women with a blazing Spitfire trail.*

Alison Hill, *Sisters in Spitfires*

In 2021, Senior Aircraftwoman Megan Gammon was the proud recipient of the inaugural Jackie Moggridge Spitfire Award, instigated by Jackie's daughters, which will be presented annually to the 'Best female aircrew or engineer who has demonstrated outstanding potential'. A General Technician Mechanical based at RAF Odiham, Megan was awarded the trophy for demonstrating outstanding determination, skill, enthusiasm and teamwork during her specialist professional training. The ceremony took place on 23 September 2021 at RAF College Cranwell and the award was presented by Her Royal Highness, The Princess Royal. The ATA women would have been honoured – their stalwart leader in particular – to know that their legacy lives on.

ELLIE CARTER, TRAILBLAZING YOUNG PILOT

Ellie Carter's Twitter profile reads: 'Missed school to solo on my 14th birthday. Warbird pilot. Breitling trophy winner. Chair of YES. Stuntgirl/Presenter/boxer Aerobatics, Astronautics/aero student.' At the time of writing, Ellie's pinned tweet spoke volumes: 'Playing in the clouds yesterday. A loop, stall turn, half reverse Cuban and an aileron roll. Loving flying the aerobatics. Dreams are for chasing.' At which point, Pauline and Dorothy may well have invited her to join Air Trips Ltd!

Ellie regularly posts about her amazing stunts and flights, using a modern-day GoPro camera to share her experiences in the clouds. Light years on from paper maps tucked into flying boots and keeping a weather eye out for railway lines or clumps of trees – and avoiding landing on cows. I was fascinated to find out more.

Can you tell me about your drive and desire to fly, and what set you on your flightpath?
From as long as I can remember I have always wanted to fly and was fascinated by the concept of it, so much so that I used to make flying machines and parachutes for the dolls that my gran bought me that I never played with and threw them out of the window.

As I don't come from a flying background I never knew how to make that progression from being fascinated with flying to actually getting near an aircraft, but being fascinated with the Maths and Physics of flight I wrote a letter to the crews of the U2 spy plane. After realising that I really was a young girl fascinated with flight, they took me to RAF Fairford to meet them and the aircraft, they then took me to Beale AFB and they arranged my first flight.

The connections that followed started me flying, leading to soloing gliders on my 14th birthday, soloing powered aircraft at 16 and collecting my pilot's licence on my 17th birthday.

I have too many exciting flights to mention, from flying to Belgium in the cub, to landing on the D-Day training beaches – landing on sand is a little different to grass or concrete and is something that most pilots don't get to do. My first solo flights and my first aerobatic flights were also memorable. Flying the procedural sim [simulator] at Beale AFB, although not a flight, was really awesome. I have also had an engine failure. Challenging flights into small strips and islands are also fun.

How do you think the early pioneers paved the way for women pilots?
They are at the top of the fountain of change. Each generation has their difficulties in being perceived as equal and that gathers pace all the way down to hopefully merge into a pool of equality at the bottom. Those pioneers climbed to the top and started that fountain, making everything possible. Ambition that we all benefit from today.

What challenges have you come across along the way?
Oh, many. Just being seen as a pilot is a challenge in itself when you are often discriminated against for being young and a female. The age discrimination is something that probably both sexes don't understand.

I remember being told at 10 that I would never be a pilot. My dad then wrote two books about amazing girls in 1918 to teach me that I could.

Today we still face those challenges. I can remember as a 14-year-old watching a gliding aerobatic instructor teaching a boy about the physics of flight and then when it was my turn being told, 'I won't explain it to you as you won't understand.' I was a top (gifted) Physics student so the only thing I can surmise is that it was said because I was a girl; my journey has been full of stories like that. I wasn't even allowed back to my aircraft at one airfield because they didn't believe I had flown it in [memories of Mary Wilkins Ellis and 'I *am* the pilot'].

At school there were also difficulties. Being different risks ridicule or bullying, which can deter a lot of girls from pursuing careers like aviation. For many it is easier to fit in than to stand out.

Another challenge is the obvious financial one. Aviation is a tough enough place as it is and it takes a huge amount of work to afford it, let alone achieve it.

How have you overcome these challenges?
I think in many cases it is learning to live with it rather than overcome. As a girl you have to work twice as hard because you have all that other stuff to deal with as well as the flying. Being young adds another huge layer of complications, attitudes and assumptions and there are always those who will never accept you, who constantly try to put you down and judge you. You just get your head down and get on with it as there is little support.

As for the financial side of things, it's just a case of really hard work. At times I was at college, studying and working and managing a twenty-hour day and that's where the inspiration of the likes of Bessie Coleman [an early African American aviator] and Pauline Gower come into their own, as they did the same.

What would you say to young girls wanting to fly?

If it's your dream, then chase it. It is an amazing journey – a tough one at times, but an amazing journey. It's your opportunity to emulate the pioneers of the past and become one for the future, and just seeing the world from up there is just such a privilege that most don't ever get to see. Don't let the hard times put you off, use them to propel you further.

Do you see yourself as an ambassador?

I think every girl that thrives in a male-dominated environment is an ambassador in a way. I do all I can to work hard for others and have taken over twenty girls for their first flights, one of whom recently did her qualifying cross-country. If that makes me an ambassador, I am happy to carry the label.

Ten Little Aeroplanes

Ten little aeroplanes taking off in line:
One did a somersault; then there were nine.
Nine little aeroplanes going for a flight:
One got left behind; then there were 'aight'
Eight little aeroplanes so near to heaven:
One flew into clouds; then there were seven.
Seven little aeroplanes going through their tricks:
One did the wrong one; then there were six.
Six little aeroplanes in a nose-dive:
One hit a tree-top; then there were five.
Five little aeroplanes, watch how they soar:
One lost its airspeed; then there were four.
Four little aeroplanes wonderful to see:
One got wing-flutter; then there were three.
Three little aeroplanes flying in the blue:
One stalled on a turn; then there were two.
Two little aeroplanes playing in the sun:
One got a heat stroke; then there was one.
One little aeroplane looping for fun:
Pilot pulled the wings off; then there were none.

Pauline Gower, *Piffling Poems for Pilots* and *Fifty Ways to Fly*

ACKNOWLEDGEMENTS

I am grateful to all those who helped shape this book, and who kindly shared their time, knowledge, insights and memories.

ATA pilots Molly Rose, Mary Ellis and Joy Lofthouse all spoke highly of Pauline Gower, and I was glad of the chance to talk to them about their wartime leader.

Anne Grant, who runs the Solent Aviatrix website, gave much time and research support, with introductions to Dorothy Spicer's daughter, Patricia Sonnenschein in South Africa, and to Nick Thomas in the US, son of parachutist and pilot Naomi Heron-Maxwell. Both Patricia and Nick were helpful in checking details, giving permission to use quotes and to include the portrait of Dorothy Spicer, courtesy of Charlotte Halliday.

Candida Adkins, daughter of ATA pilot Jackie Moggridge, offered anecdotes and a signed photo of Pauline, given to her mother. Daughters of Monique Agazarian and Joy Lofthouse also added rich detail, and Graham Rose elaborated on his parents, Molly and Bernard Rose. While my mother Patricia shared her own valuable wartime memories.

Biographer Melody Foreman offered insights from her many conversations with Mary Ellis and much encouragement along the way.

Thank you to Spartan-owner Rod Hall-Jones for his contribution to Chapter 2, to Jane Priston for sharing her detailed knowledge of Amy Johnson and to John Webster, secretary of the ATA Association, for all his help.

Susan Rogers at Tunbridge Wells District Libraries enabled a second visit to Robert Gower's collection of fifty scrapbooks, a rich primary source, and provided much research assistance. Nick Waite, then head-teacher of Beechwood Sacred Heart School in Tunbridge Wells, and teacher and former pupil Candy Prodrick, gave guided tours with a real flavour of Beechwood life past and present.

Archivist Gary Haines provided timely access to the RAF Museum London's archive and a spark for a new project. Bomber Command researcher Di Ablewhite lent me a rare copy of *Women with Wings*, while her daughter Rosie Ablewhite kindly provided the cover illustration of Pauline, to add a vintage touch.

Photographs came from a range of sources, as credited, with particular thanks to the Centre for Maidenhead Heritage & ATA Museum.

Thank you to Dawn Bauling and Ronnie Goodyer of Indigo Dreams for letting poems from *Sisters in Spitfires* take off again here.

Sue Rose, whose appreciation of the early pioneers forms a fitting introduction to Chapter 9, believes that Pauline was always 'the unsung heroine' of the ATA. Thanks again to Sue, and co-pilot Amy Chau, for the flight to Sandown in 2018, to visit Mary Ellis and hear her first-hand memories of Pauline Gower.

I am grateful to other contributors, Candida Adkins and Ellie Carter, and to Maggie Appleton MBE for endorsing Pauline's enduring legacy in her Foreword.

I would like to thank Michael Fahie for all his help and encouragement, for sharing of source material, and for allowing me to include his mother's poetry from *Piffling Poems for Pilots* and *More Piffling Poems for Pilots*.

Many thanks, as ever, to David, Alexander and Oscar for reading early drafts, and for all their support – and many cups of tea – along the runway!

And finally, thank you to editors Amy Rigg and Rebecca Newton, and to Graham Robson at The History Press for all their dedicated work on this book and for enabling it to fly.

BIBLIOGRAPHY

There have been a range of books published over the past few decades that focus on the ATA, some with chapters about the role of the women pilots, some by the pilots themselves – lively, spirited first-hand accounts of their lives before, during and after the war. Copies of many of these books are now few and far between, including Pauline Gower's own *Women with Wings*. The following titles offer a range of impressions and first-hand accounts of those wartime years, with several devoted to the plane many of them favoured – the Spitfire.

Babington Smith, C., *Amy Johnson* (Collins, 1967).

Bakowski, J., *Calm Amidst the Waves, A History of Beechwood Sacred Heart School, Tunbridge Wells 1915–2004* (Gresham Books Ltd, 2004).

Barnato Walker, D., *Spreading My Wings* (Patrick Stephens Ltd, 1994; Grub Street, 2003).

Bishop, P., *Air Force Blue, The RAF in World War Two* (Williams Collins, 2017).

Bunsen, M. de, *Mount Up with Wings* (Hutchinson & Co Ltd, 1960).

Boase, W., *The Sky's the Limit, Women Pioneers in Aviation* (Osprey Publishing Limited, 1979).

Brown, M., *Spitfire Summer, The Story of the Battle of Britain* (Welbeck, 2020).

Cadogan, M., *Women with Wings, Female Flyers in Fact and Fiction* (Academy Chicago Publishers, 1993).

Cros, R. du, *ATA Girl, Memoirs of a Wartime Ferry Pilot* (Frederick Muller Ltd, 1983).

Curtis, L., *The Forgotten Pilots, A Story of the Air Transport Auxiliary 1939–45* (Nelson and Saunders Ltd, 1971).

Curtis, L., *Lettice Curtis, Her Autobiography* (Red Kite, 2014; first pub. 2004).

Fahie, M., *A Harvest of Memories: The Life of Pauline Gower MBE* (GM Enterprises, 1995).

Foreman, M., *A Spitfire Girl, Mary Ellis as Told to Melody Foreman* (Frontline Books, 2016).

Gillies, M., *Amy Johnson, Queen of the Air* (Phoenix, 2003).

Gower, P., *Piffling Poems for Pilots* (ed. Michael Fahie) (Heritage Printers, fourth impression, May 1994; first pub. John Hamilton Ltd, March 1934).

Gower, P., 'The Flying Farrants', *Chatterbox* (Dean & Son Ltd).

Gower, P., *Women with Wings* (John Long Ltd, 1938).

Hill, A. (ed.), *Fifty Ways to Fly* (Rhythm & Muse, 2017).

Hill, A., *Sisters in Spitfires* (Indigo Dreams Publishing, 2015).

Howman & Cetintas with Clarke, G., *Secret Spitfires, Britain's Hidden Civilian Army* (The History Press, 2020).

Hyams, J., *The Female Few, Spitfire Heroines of the Air Transport Auxiliary* (The History Press, 2012).

Hyams, J., *Spitfire Stories* (Michael O'Mara Books Limited, 2017).

Johns, Captain W.E., *Spitfire Parade* (Geoffrey Cumberlege, Oxford University Press, 1941).

Johns, Captain W.E., *Worrals Flies Again* (IndieBooks Ltd, 2013; first pub. Hodder and Stoughton, 1942).

King, A., *Golden Wings, The Story of Some of the Women Ferry Pilots of the Air Transport Auxiliary* (White Lion, 1975; first pub. C. Arthur Pearson Ltd, 1956).

Landdeck, K.S., *The Women with Silver Wings: The Untold Story of the Women Airforce Service Pilots of World War II* (Ballantine Books, 2020).

Lomax, J., *Women of the Air* (John Murray, 1986).

BIBLIOGRAPHY

Miller Livingston Stratford, N., *Contact! Britain! An American Woman Ferry Pilot's Life During WWII* (CreateSpace, 2010).

Moggridge, J., *Spitfire Girl, My Life in the Sky* (Head of Zeus, 2014; first pub. in UK as *Woman Pilot*, Michael Joseph Ltd, 1957).

Nichol, J., *Spitfire* (Simon & Schuster, 2018).

Robson, M., *The Spitfire Pocket Manual* (Conway, 2010).

Smith, S., *Magnificent Women and Flying Machines* (The History Press, 2021).

Welch, A., *Happy to Fly, An Autobiography* (John Murray, 1983).

White, A., *Frost in May* (Virago, 1978; first pub. 1933).

Whittell, G., *Spitfire Women of World War II* (HarperPress, 2007).

Wynn, S., *Air Transport Auxiliary at War: 80th Anniversary of its Formation* (Pen & Sword Military, 2021).

SOURCES OF ATA INFORMATION

The following websites and archives provide valuable sources of further information. White Waltham, now home to the West London Aero Club and base for the BWPA, keeps the ATA flag on display. The Maidenhead Heritage Centre, containing a wealth of archive material, is housed just a couple of miles from the historic airfield. The informative Solent Aviatrix website is regularly updated by editor Anne Grant and is worth following. The ATA Association, which welcomes new members, publishes newsletters and holds memorial events, including the wreath-laying ceremony in St Paul's Cathedral, London.

A Fleeting Peace: www.afleetingpeace.org
Air Transport Auxiliary Association: www.airtransportaux.org.uk
British Newspaper Archive: www.britishnewspaperarchive.co.uk
British Women Pilots' Association: www.bwpa.co.uk
Brooklands Museum: www.brooklandsmuseum.com

Imperial War Museum: www.iwm.org.uk
Maidenhead Heritage Centre: www.maidenheadheritage.org.uk
RAF Museum London: www.rafmuseum.org.uk/london
RAF Museum Midlands: www.rafmuseum.org.uk/midlands
Royal Aeronautical Society: www.aerosociety.com
Solent Aviatrix: www.solentaviatrix.wordpress.com
Spitfire Society: www.spitfiresociety.org
Women's Engineering Society: www.wes.org.uk

INDEX

INDEX